Religion in the Soviet Republics

Religion in the Soviet Republics

*A Guide to Christianity, Judaism, Islam,
Buddhism, and Other Religions*

Igor Troyanovsky

editor

HarperSanFrancisco
A Division of HarperCollinsPublishers

Unless otherwise noted, all Scripture quotations contained herein
are from the King James Version of the Bible.

RELIGION IN THE SOVIET REPUBLICS: *A Guide to Christianity, Judaism,
Islam, Buddhism, and Other Religions*. Translation copyright © 1991
by the Copyright Agency of the USSR. All rights reserved. Printed
in the United States of America. No part of this book may be
used or reproduced in any manner whatsoever without written
permission except in the case of brief quotations embodied in critical
articles and reviews. For information address HarperCollins
Publishers, 10 East 53rd Street, New York, NY 10022.
FIRST EDITION

Library of Congress Cataloging-in-Publication Data

Religion in the Soviet Republics : a guide to Christianity,
    Judaism, Islam, Buddhism, and other religions /
    Igor Troyanovsky, editor.—1st ed.
        p. cm.
    Translation from the Russian.
    Includes index.
    ISBN 0-06-250875-X
    1. Soviet Union—Religion—1917– I. Troyanovsky, Igor
Aleksandrovich.
BL980.S65R34 1991
291'.0947'09049—dc20   90-55791
                                                        CIP

91 92 93 94 95 RRD(H) 5 4 3 2 1

Religion in the
Soviet Republics

In our country religious views play a particularly harmful and reactionary role. They interfere with Soviet democracy, with the process of involving all working people in running their country. They prevent the individual from relying on his own strength and potential and feeling fully responsible for the destinies of communism. During elections to the Supreme and local soviets of working people's deputies in various regions and areas, for example, some religious people abstained from voting and spoiled the ballot papers. This can only be explained by the fact that a person brainwashed by religion fails to recognize his duties and his role in a country wherein the working people themselves are the masters. Such a person keeps thinking that he can do this or that only if God is willing, that man proposes and God disposes. Meanwhile, in our country everything depends on the will of the people, who not only propose but also dispose.

A believer usually thinks that his religious convictions are his private matter and nobody else's business since they do not interfere with other individuals. In fact, this is not so. As we have seen, a religious person is only an inferior builder of communism, who lacks the enthusiasm and the internal conviction without which successful communist construction is unthinkable. He remains in the grip of various vestiges of the past, and his mind and will are split so that he is inclined to doubt the ultimate success of his cause and would rather turn to God and pray.

What is more, anti-Soviet quarters working against communism try to take advantage of religious vestiges. It would be very much to the advantage of the enemies of communism if religion in the USSR does not die but prospers, if children are stupefied with religious poison, if religion is entrenched in daily life, rituals, and customs. All this interferes with the building of a new life and facilitates the hostile activities of anti-Soviet quarters. It is common knowledge that under the cover of religion many priests, rabbis, mullahs, and preachers of religious sects have been engaged in espionage and subversion as agents of foreign intelligence services. In some cases honest Soviet people, who were believers and belonged to religious organizations, were used against their will by such scoundrels in cassocks.

Every religious person in our country must face in all seriousness the questions: Should you believe in god, who, as has been demonstrated by science, does not exist? Does your religion promote the cause of the workers and collective farmers? Is it not the time to do away once and for all with the poison of religion, which has caused people so much pain and suffering over the centuries? There can be only one answer to these questions: now that the toiling masses have learned to rely on their own strength in building a new and wonderful life, it is high time to do away with religion once and for all.

—F. Oleshchuk
from "Table Calendar, 1941" published in Moscow

We need spiritual values, we need a revolution of the mind. This is the only way toward a new culture and new politics that can meet the challenge of our time. We have changed our attitude toward some matters such as religion. Now, we not only proceed from the assumption that no one should interfere in matters of the individual's conscience; we also say that the moral values that religion generated and embodied for centuries can help in the work of renewal in our country, too.

—Mikhail Gorbachev
quoted in *Time* magazine

Contents

Introduction   *xi*

HISTORICAL DOCUMENTS ON RELIGION IN THE SOVIET STATE

Letter by Lenin   *3*

Letter by Trotsky with Notes by Lenin: May 15, 1922   *12*

LEGISLATION ON RELIGION

The New Laws: An Introduction   *19*

Law of the Union of Soviet Socialist Republics on Freedom of Conscience and Religious Organizations   *23*

Law of the Russian Soviet Federative Socialist Republic on Freedom of Worship   *31*

Ministry of the Internal Affairs of the USSR: Guidelines for Correctional Labor Facilities   *38*

RELIGION IN POLITICS AND CULTURE

Clergy in Soviet Parliament   *43*

Religion and Charity in Soviet Society   *54*

Religious Programs on Radio and Television   *60*

RELIGIOUS GROUPS IN TODAY'S SOVIET REPUBLICS

The Russian Orthodox Church   *65*

Declaration of the Holy Synod of the Russian Orthodox Church, 3 April 1990   *66*

Will the Lord Help Us? An Interview with Patriarch Alexis II of Moscow and All Russia   *72*

The Church and Perestroika, by Metropolitan Kirill of Smolensk and Kaliningrad   82

Rehabilitation of Stalinist Reprisal Victims   90

Father Pavel Florensky, Back from Obscurity, by Archpriest Alexander Kozha   99

Revival of Traditions at Russian Monasteries, by Archpriest Alexander Kozha   103

The Armenian Apostolic Church   109

Supreme Patriarch and Catholicos of All Armenians Vasken I and the Armenian Apostolic Church   110

The Georgian Autocephalous Orthodox Church   115

In the Shadow of the Grapevine Cross   116

The Greek Catholic Church   123

The Greek Catholic Church Is Given Legal Status   124

The Roman Catholic Church   133

Cardinal Vincentas Sladkevicius Supports Lithuanian Independence   134

Protestant Christians   139

Charter of the All-Union League of Evangelical Christian Baptists   140

Protestant Movements   151

Perestroika and the Baptists, by Denton Lotz   154

Bright Prospects for Seventh-Day Adventists, by Mikhail P. Kulakov   158

Islam   165

Muslim Revival   166

Islam and Other Religions   171

Buddhism   177

Rebirth of Buddhism   178

The Jewish Community   185

Judaic Religious Life   186

Officially Sanctioned Yeshiva in Moscow, by Rabbi Gedaliah A. Rabinowtz   191

Directory of Religious Organizations   193

Index   206

Introduction

This book gives a panorama of religious life in the Soviet republics at this difficult but exciting time. Public attention has turned in recent years to universal human values, and many religious organizations are experiencing spiritual rebirth.

Expert analyses and authentic documents in this book portray the Soviet religious situation in its dynamism and provide insight into both its positive and negative aspects. While the religious situation will most certainly continue to change in coming months and years, this book records several history-making events and trends and offers insight to the future.

Perestroika in church-state relations reached its peak when the Soviet and Russian parliaments passed new acts to guarantee freedom of conscience and unhampered work of ecclesiastical institutions. A complete translation of these acts is included in this book, though their implementation is uncertain in light of ongoing political change.

Even though the Soviet and world public met these acts with enthusiasm, a thoughtful reader will notice certain oblique wordings and contradictions in these laws concerning minor issues. As to practical matters, they offer a pretty muddle. Take the registration of new religious communities. As the Union law has it, religious groups shall apply to the local council, irrespective of its level, while some republican legislations demand registration with regional or republican legal bodies. Every parliament is trying to prove the priority of its own acts, and believers are likely to suffer in this red tape warfare.

Still, the new laws mark a more positive Soviet stance toward religion today than in the past. The October 1917 Revolution proclaimed freedom of religious activities, but too many Bolsheviks were wary of priests as political rivals. Lenin's and Trotsky's secret letters appear in this book to reveal their true goals and the methods of struggle they secretly used. The letters show the roots of later outrages when, in the early Soviet years, thousands of religious activists fell victim to lawless, arbitrary actions.

A small item from the 1941 calendar shows the stance of the then Soviet leadership to religion. At that time, all major religious centers were suppressed, as the ruling ideology demanded. Thousands of churches and all monasteries stood abandoned. All theological schools were closed down. All hierarchs were in jail but for several whose loyalty the regime never put to doubt—but even those lucky few were exiled or, at least, repeatedly summoned for interrogations.

The Nazi aggression against the Soviet Union made Joseph Stalin change his attitude to the church, which by then had been branded as bitter enemy of the working people and spiritual poisoner. A few days after the war started, surviving hierarchs and priests spoke on the radio to inspire their flock to battle. Propaganda set in motion feverish activities. Russian Orthodox delegations were sent abroad one after another to win the Allied public opinion. A large volume was published in 1942, with a speed amazing for wartime, to denounce "Nazi propaganda allegations concerning persecution of believers in the Soviet Union" on behalf of the Moscow patriarchate.

Worried by religious revival in the enemy-occupied areas, Stalin allowed many churches to reopen in the Soviet rear. In 1943, he met Metropolitans Sergius and Nicholas to allow the Russian Orthodox Church to gather for a local council, renew its press and book publication, establish a theological institute, and reconsecrate churches and monasteries.

The clergy and hierarchy received considerable privileges. Now they were welcome to government receptions and were awarded orders and medals "for service to the motherland."

As the Soviet army advanced to liberate area after area, the churches and monasteries revived under enemy occupation were not closed down, but many priests were prosecuted for alleged collaboration with Nazis. During the Second World War, Stalin established two high offices to keep religion in check—the Council for the Affairs of the Russian Orthodox Church and the Council for Religious Affairs—which merged into one Council for Religious Affairs under the USSR Council of Ministers in Khrushchev's time.

The early 1960s sent atheism into a new attack. Nikita Khrushchev's motto, "This generation of Soviet people will live to see communism," implied that faith must be fought as legal opposition to the dominant ideology. Secular officials clutched at every pretext to close churches, monasteries, and theological schools. The number of religious institutions was soon halved.

However, no criminal proceedings were opened against religious activists at that time. The 1970s and early 1980s were harsher, with several dozen dissidents jailed, and atheistic propaganda was promoted to the rank of official policy. Every region received its Scientific Atheism Club. Some were sacrilegiously housed in former churches, as was the case in Leningrad. All colleges and universities were obliged to teach so-called scientific atheism. Students had to pass the required examinations, including students who openly professed their faith. Even Arabs, in whose countries Islam was the official religion, were not exempt.

Shortly before *perestroika*, the Soviet secular authorities started normalizing their relations with the church. They were driven by pressure from the world public, the necessity for closer links with the West, and the desire to stop the ruinous arms race.

No churches were closed down in the early 1980s, and some new ones appeared—mainly Protestant. Russian Orthodox Christians, too, felt some improvements. In 1984, for instance, the Orthodox Church received back the giant St. Daniel's Monastery in Moscow to start its administrative center, house the new patriarchal residence, and build a hotel and a conference hall.

The long-awaited process gained momentum after Mikhail Gorbachev came to office. Change took place on an amazing scale. The number of churches, monasteries, and theological schools grew three times in a mere five years. The output of religious literature skyrocketed, and all barriers were removed from its importation. Clergy appeared on all elective bodies, up to the Soviet Parliament. The year 1989 introduced religious radio and TV programs. Rarely does a social undertaking proceed without the church taking part.

The church is the main vehicle of Soviet charity. Evangelical pastors and Russian Orthodox priests no longer meet obstacles in visiting jails and convict camps. The church looks after orphanages, hospitals, and homes for old and disabled people.

This does not mean that church life is approaching the ideal. Godless church bureaucrats are loath to surrender their power. The highest hierarchies of all religions and confessions include too many men who made their careers in the so-called stagnation years and now oppose new invigorating trends. Many religious leaders who came to the fore in the 60s and 70s with the backing of the authorities have been compelled to cede their positions. For example, at the demand of believers and the clergy, Mufti Shamsutdin Babakhan left his post in Tashkent, as did a number of Muslim leaders in the Caucasus. There have also been changes in leadership in the Russian Orthodox Church, in communities of Baptists, and in other religious organizations.

Conflict between and within various ethnic and religious groups has also surfaced. The Moscow Patriarchate of the Russian Orthodox Church, for example, has lost both membership and church property to the Greek Catholic Church and The Ukrainian Autocephalous Orthodox Church. A number of communities and clergymen in Russia also refuse to be subordinated to the Patriarch of Moscow and All Russia, preferring to go over to the jurisdiction of the Russian Orthodox Church abroad. This is what prominent theologian Archpriest Lev Lebedev has done.

There are also other problems. There is a shortage of clergy in nearly all faiths, and a shortage of money to restore dilapidated monasteries and houses of prayer. Not all households can buy edifying books. Shortages of Bibles for children, catechisms, other religious literature, and audio and video cassettes are acute.

Still, the change is irrevocable, however thorny its road. And this book will convince you of that.

In the directory at the back of this book, important addresses, telephone and fax numbers, names, and other reference materials concerning many Soviet religious organizations appear in print for the first time, so you may establish contacts in the Soviet republics and learn more about the life of your brothers and sisters in faith.

Quite recently, secrecy and misinformation reigned in the Soviet Union. Now, another barrier—to information—is coming down.

HarperSanFrancisco has performed an act of piety by spending so much time, money, and effort in preparing this unique edition. Its idea arose when Mr. Clayton Carlson, senior vice-president and publisher of the firm, visited the Soviet Union, saw its religious life, and met Alexis II, Patriarch of All Russia; Vasken I, Patriarch-Catholicos of All Armenians; and other prominent hierarchs. Mr. Carlson was active in the preliminary effort, when every topic and illustration was hotly debated. The industrious and efficient Ms. Kandace Hawkinson, special project editor, stood at the cradle of the book. The venture was slow and tiresome, but her erudition and persistence overcame all obstacles.

Events are moving swiftly in Soviet society, and the edition was put off time and again due to new developments. The August 1991 coup attempt and ensuing events, for example, called the nature of the Union between Soviet republics to question. Alexis II, in an epistle issued to all members of the Russian Orthodox Church, referred to the failed coup as "the real end" to the regime begun in 1917. It remains to be seen how relationships between Soviet republics are redefined. In any case, since the pace of change has not lessened, the publishers said, "Enough is enough," and appointed a deadline for completion of the manuscript in September 1991.

We are praying to the Lord that this noble project be a success as we undertake the Russian edition. Later we shall publish another English one if our readers so wish.

Igor Troyanovsky

Historical Documents
on Religion
in the Soviet State

Letter by Lenin

Letter to V. M. Molotov, for members of the Politburo of the Central Committee of the Russian Communist Party (the Bolsheviks).[1]

19 March 1922

Strictly confidential

It is requested that no copies should be made under any circumstances and that each member of the Politburo (including comrade Kalinin[2]) should make his notes on the document itself.[3]

Lenin

To comrade Molotov for members of the Politburo

Regarding the events in Shuya,[4] an issue that has already been submitted for discussion in the Politburo, it seems to me that we must make a firm decision without delay in connection with the general plan of the struggle in this sphere. Since I doubt that I will be able to attend personally the meeting of the Politburo on 20 March,[5] I will therefore put forward my ideas in writing.

The events in Shuya should be related to the communication that ROSTA[6] sent to the newspapers to be published a short time ago, that is, the communication about the opposition to the decree on the seizure of church valuables,[7] which was being prepared by members of the Black Hundred[8] in Petersburg. By comparing this with what the newspapers are reporting about the attitude of the clergy to the decree on the seizure of church valuables and then with what we know about Patriarch Tikhon's secret appeal,[9] it will become absolutely clear that the Black Hundred clergy, headed by its leader, is pursuing a carefully thought out plan to engage us in a decisive battle right now. It is obvious that this plan was discussed and adopted with sufficient firmness at secret meetings of the most influential group of the Black Hundred clergy. The events in Shuya represent only one manifestation and application of this general plan.

I believe that in this respect our enemy has committed a major strategic mistake by trying to get us involved in a decisive struggle at a time when this struggle is particularly hopeless and particularly disadvantageous for him. On the contrary, this is not only a very favorable moment for us, but generally the only moment when we have 99 chances out of 100 to succeed completely in defeating the enemy and ensuring the necessary positions for us for many decades to come. It is now and only now, when in the territories afflicted by famine people are eaten for food and hundreds if not thousands of corpses are lying in the roads, we can (and therefore we must) carry out the seizure of church valuables with wildest and most merciless energy and not stop short of suppressing any opposition. It is now and only now that the vast majority of the peasant masses will either support us or, anyway, will not be capable of supporting decisively the handful of the Black Hundred clergy and the reactionary city people who can and want to resort to the policy of violent opposition to the Soviet decree. It is absolutely necessary for us to carry out the seizure of church valuables in the most decisive and speediest manner, which will make it possible for us to create a fund totaling several hundred million gold rubles (let us think about the giant treasures of some monasteries and lauras). Without such a fund any state work generally, any economic development in particular, and any attempt to defend our position in the Genoa Conference specifically are unthinkable. We must take possession of a fund totaling several hundred million gold rubles (and possibly several billion rubles) now at any cost. And we can successfully do it only now. All the indications are that we will not be able to do this later, since no other factor, apart from desperate starvation, can ensure for us this kind of sentiment on the part of broad masses of the peasantry. No other factor would either ensure the support of these masses for us or at least ensure the neutralization of these masses in the sense that victory in the struggle for the seizure of valuables will unconditionally and totally be on our side.

One clever writer on questions of state said correctly that if it is necessary to resort to harsh measures in order to implement a given political objective, then it is necessary to implement these measures in the most energetic manner and in the shortest period of time, because the popular masses will not tolerate a long application of harsh measures. In particular, this thought is supported by the possibility that after Genoa the international situation in which Russia will find herself will or can be such that harsh measures against the reactionary clergy will be politically nonrational and perhaps even too dangerous. At present, the victory over the reactionary clergy is totally assured us. Also, the major part of our foreign enemies among the Russian emigres abroad, i.e., Social Revolutionaries and Milyukovites,[10] will find it difficult to wage a struggle against us if, right at this moment and in connection with the famine, we suppress the reactionary clergy with maximum speed and mercilessness.

Therefore, I come to the inevitable conclusion that we should engage the Black Hundred clergy now in the most decisive and merciless struggle and suppress their opposition with such harshness that they would not forget it for several decades. I envision the campaign to implement this plan in the following way:

Only comrade Kalinin should officially suggest any practical measures, while comrade Trotsky should not put forward anything either in the press or elsewhere—never and under no circumstances.

The telegram regarding the temporary suspension of the seizure, which has already been sent out on behalf of the Politburo, should not be canceled.[11] It is to our advantage, because it will make the enemy think that we vacillate and that it has succeeded in scaring us. (The enemy will, of course, find out very soon about this secret telegram, especially because it is a secret one.)

It is necessary to send to Shuya one of the most energetic, intelligent, and skillful organizers from VTSIK[12] or other representatives of the central government agencies (better one than several),[13] who should be given oral instructions through a member of the Politburo. These instructions should be as follows: when in Shuya he should arrest as many members of the local clergy, local reactionary city people, and local bourgeoisie as he can, not less than several dozen of them, on charges of being suspected in either direct or indirect involvement in the violent opposition to the decree of the VTSIK on the seizure of church valuables. As soon as this work is completed, he should travel to Moscow and present in person a report to the full meeting of the Politburo or to two members of the Politburo authorized to receive it. On the basis of that report the Politburo will issue, also orally, a detailed directive to the judicial agencies so that the trial of the Shuya rebels opposed to the assistance to the famine-stricken population be carried out with maximum speed and concluded by an execution by firing squad of a very large number of the most influential and dangerous members of the Black Hundred in the city of Shuya[14] and, if possible, not only in that city, but also in Moscow and several other spiritual centers.[15]

I believe that it is expedient for us not to touch Patriarch Tikhon himself, although he undoubtedly stands at the head of this mutiny of slave owners. A secret directive should be given to the State Political Department concerning him, so that all the connections of this leader be observed and revealed with the utmost accuracy and in the greatest possible detail at this very moment. Dzerzhinsky[16] and Unshlikht should be ordered to present reports about this personally at the weekly meetings of the Politburo.

At the Party Congress a secret meeting of all, or nearly all, delegates should be held regarding this question, together with the most important members of the GPU, NKU,[17] and the Revolutionary Tribunal.[18] At that meeting a secret decision of the Congress should be taken to the effect that the seizure of valuables, particularly in the richest lauras, monasteries, and churches should be carried out with a merciless decisiveness, stopping at nothing and in the shortest period of time. The more reactionary clergy and reactionary bourgeoisie we are able to execute by firing squad regarding this matter, the better. It is right at this time that we should teach a lesson to these members of the public, so that for several decades to come they should not dare think about any opposition.

To supervise the speediest and most successful implementation of these measures we must appoint a special commission at the Congress, i.e., at the secret meeting of the Congress with the obligatory participation of comrade Trotsky and comrade Kalinin without any publication about this commission in order to ensure that all operations are subordinated to it and carried out not on behalf of the commission but in a general party manner. The most responsible and best workers should be appointed to carry out these measures in the richest lauras, monasteries, and churches.

Lenin

19 March 1922

I ask comrade Molotov to try and send this letter to the members of the Politburo one by one today (without making any copies) and to ask them to return it to the secretary right after reading it with a short note stating whether each member of the Politburo is in agreement with this basic formulation or whether the letter meets with any disagreement.

Lenin

19 March 1922

Received by telephone by M. Volodicheva

NOTES

1. Published in the April 1990 issue of *Izvestia TSEKA KAPEESES,* an official publication of the Communist Party of the USSR. Both this letter by Lenin and the letter that follows by Trotsky were previously withheld from the public. Lenin's letter is found in the Central

Party Archives of the Institute of Marxism-Leninism, f. 2, op. 1, d. 22947; typescript.

2. N. I. Kalinin (1875–1946), member of the Communist party from 1888. Chairman of VTSIK [All-Russia Executive Committee of the Soviets of the Workers, Peasants, Cossacks, and Red Army Deputies—Ed.] from March 1919, member of the Central Committee of the party from the Eighth Congress of the Russian Communist Party (the Bolsheviks), alternate member of the Politburo of the Central Committee.

3. The document carries only one note by V. M. Molotov: "I agree. However, I suggest that the campaign should be extended, not to all gubernias [a territorial-administrative unit in Russia before and after the revolution—Trans.] and cities, but to only those where many valuables really exist, appropriately concentrating the effort and the attention of the party. 19 March V. Molotov."

4. The *Izvestia VTSIK* newspaper, in issue no. 70 of 28 March 1922 published the government communication of 27 March 1922, "On the Events in the City of Shuya in Connection with the Seizure of Church Valuables," adopted by the VTSIK Presidium. The communication described the events in great detail and assessed the situation. In particular, it reported that on 3 March 1922 in accordance with the decree of VTSIK of 23 February 1922, "On the Procedure Regarding the Seizure of Church Valuables Used by Groups of Believers," and the instruction of VTSIK and the People's Commissariat of Justice of the same date regarding the decree (*Izvestia VTSIK*, nos. 46 and 47 of 26 and 28 February 1922), a special commission was set up by the Shuya Regional Executive Council. On 13 March 1922, having seized the valuables from three small churches, the commission presented itself at the cathedral but was met by a crowd of excited believers and postponed the work until 15 March. On 14 March the commission seized the valuables from a synagogue without opposition. On 15 March a large crowd gathered in Sobornaya Square. When the mounted militia (six riders on horseback) arrived on the scene, they were met by threats, stones, and sticks. The big bell in the belfry began to ring. Then a half-company of the 146th Infantry Regiment and two trucks with machine guns arrived on the scene. Shots were fired from the crowd, which tried to surround the soldiers. The commander of the platoon gave orders to Red Army soldiers to fire over the heads of the crowd. However, this did not help, and the second volley was fired into the crowd, which then dispersed. Four people were killed and ten wounded. By the end of the day, traders, teachers, etc., who had been seen in the square were arrested. In the evening of the same day, representatives of the congregation handed in 3.5 poods [A pood equals just over 36 pounds.—Trans.] of silver from the cathedral's valuables to the Regional Executive Council. On 23 March the Regional Commission and representatives of the congregation proceeded to seize the cathedral's valuables in the presence of the members of the VTSIK Commission. Over ten poods of silver were handed over to the Department of Finance, and precious stones, pearl-inlaid icon mounts, and other valuables were deposited into the state repository of valuables. All seized valuables were registered by the Central Commission for the Assistance of Famine-Stricken People.

5. The meeting of the Politburo of the Central Committee of the Russian Communist Party (the Bolsheviks), held on 20 March 1922 adopted a decision to suggest to the Presidium of VTSIK that a commission should be sent to the city of Shuya composed of P. G. Smidovich (chairman), N. I. Muralov, and I. I. Kutuzov. On 21 March the commission arrived and on 23 March completed its work and came to the following conclusion: "(1) It has been decided

that the actions of the Regional Commission in seizing church valuables are correct and in keeping with the instructions of the center. (2) It has been decided that the actions of the local authorities are generally correct but not sufficiently energetic or orderly both in the preparation of the work to seize valuables and in the maintenance of public order. (3) It has been suggested that the commission on the seizure of valuables immediately complete this work. (4) It has been suggested that the *gubernia* and *uyezd* [a territorial-administrative unit smaller than the *gubierna*—Trans.] authorities should take measures to investigate in great detail the violations of public order in connection with the seizure of valuables, identify the people guilty of resisting the authorities and attacks on Red Army soldiers and militia men, and that the whole matter should be passed on to the Revolutionary Tribunal for final investigation and exemplary punishment."

The meeting of the Politburo of the Central Committee of the Russian Communist Party (the Bolsheviks), held on 20 March and attended by L. B. Kamenev, I. V. Stalin, L. D. Trotsky, and V. M. Molotov discussed the draft directive on the seizure of church valuables put forward by Trotsky. The following draft was adopted with some amendments:

1. In the center and in gubernias secret decision-making commissions on the seizure of valuables of the type of the Sapronov-Unshlikht commission in Moscow should be set up. All these commissions should necessarily include either the secretary of the Gubernia Commission or the head of the Department of Agitation and Propaganda.

Note: In major *gubernias* the earliest date of the seizure should be named, while in minor *gubernias* it is necessary to name the latest date. This should be done after the information about the seizures in Petrograd and other central *gubernias* has spread all around Russia.

2. The Central Commission should consist of its chairman comrade Kalinin, comrades Yakovlev and Sapronov (after the departure of comrade Sapronov, comrade Beloborodov should join the commission as his deputy, who should become acquainted with the situation not later than Wednesday, 23 March), comrade Unshlikht, Krasikov (Galkin's deputy), Vinokurov, and Bazilevich. The commission has set up a working party which meets daily (Yakovlev, Sapronov, Unshlikht, and Galkin). Comrade Trotsky attends the meetings of the commission once a week.

3. In the central cities of *gubernias* the commission also includes the commissar of the division or brigade, or the head of the Political Department.

4. Alongside these secret preparatory commissions there are official commissions or boards under the Committees for the Assistance to the Famine-Stricken People, which conduct the formal transfer of valuables, negotiations with groups of believers, etc. Strict measures should be taken so that the ethnic composition of these official commissions should not be a pretext for chauvinistic agitation.

5. In every *gubernia* a nonofficial week of agitation and preliminary organization for the seizure of valuables should be decided on (naturally enough, without any announcement actually being made). To this end the best agitators, military ones included, should be selected. The agitation's character should be totally devoid of any references to the struggle with religion and the church and be totally aimed at assisting the famine-stricken population.

6. At the same time a schism should be provoked in the clergy. A decisive initiative should be taken in this respect,

and those priests who come out openly in favor of the seizure should be taken under state protection.

7. Naturally enough, our agitation and the agitation of loyal priests should under no circumstances merge, but in our agitation we should refer to the fact that a significant part of the clergy has engaged in open struggle against the criminal and covetous attitude to valuables on the part of inhuman and greedy "princes of the church."

8. Right throughout the campaign, particularly during the week, ensure that all information is available about everything that is taking place in different groups of the clergy, believers, etc.

9. If bourgeois merchant elements, former clerks, etc., are identified as organizers of resistance, their ringleaders should be arrested. If the need arises, particularly if the reactionary Black Hundred agitation goes too far, organize demonstrations with the participation of armed garrison troops carrying banners reading, "Church Valuables to Save the Lives of Famine-Stricken People," etc.

10. If possible, prominent priests should be left in peace until the end of the campaign. However, they should be secretly but officially (by making them sign an affidavit at the Gubernia Political Department) warned that if they take any unauthorized actions, they will be the first to answer for them.

11. Organizational work should be carried out alongside agitation: prepare appropriate personnel in order to keep the records and carry out the seizure and ensure that this work is completed in the shortest possible time. The seizure of valuables should begin at the church headed by a loyal priest. If there is no such church, then begin at the most important cathedral, and everything should be meticulously prepared (Communists should position themselves in all nearby streets, preventing people from assembling; a reliable military unit, CHON [unit of special troops—Ed.] is best, should be positioned close by, etc.).

12. Where possible representatives of famine-stricken people should speak in churches, at meetings, and in the barracks, calling for the seizure of valuables at the earliest date.

13. To keep the records of the valuables seized from the church, representatives of the loyal clergy should be allowed to take part in the work of commissions for the assistance of famine-stricken people in both gubernias and the central agencies. It should be publicly announced that the population will have every chance to ensure that no church assets are put to any use other than for the assistance to the starving population.

14. If groups of believers offer to buy valuables back, declare that each question should be dealt with individually in the Central Committee of Pomgol [Commission for the Assistance to the Starving Population under VTSIK (with N. I. Kalinin as chairman)—Trans.] without stopping the work to seize valuables under any circumstances. Experience in the provinces has shown that such negotiations are conducted without any serious intent to buy back and only cause indeterminacy and demoralization.

15. In Moscow the work should proceed in accordance with the established order, so that the seizure of valuables should start not later than 21 March.

16. I believe that for Petrograd a similar deadline should be set, subject to comrade Zinovyev's agreement. However, under no circumstances should the campaign be pushed too far or force resorted to until politically and organizationally the whole operation is totally prepared.

17. As for *gubernias,* relying on this instruction and noting the deadline set in Moscow, *gubernia* commissions under the supervisions of the Central Commission should set their own deadlines and, on the one hand, ensure meticulous preparations and, on the other, delay this matter for not a single day, so that the first campaigns are in the major gubernias (Central Party Archives, f. 17, op. 3, d. 283, pp. 6–7).
The Politburo adopted a decision to send these directives to all gubernia commissions.

6. ROSTA is the Russian Telegraph Agency.
—Ed.

7. This communication by ROSTA has not been found. Judging by subsequent developments in Petrograd, it described the preparations of the clergy headed by Metropolitan Veniamin for resistance to the commissions on the seizure of church valuables. As a result demonstrations took place near the Kazansky cathedral, the Vladimirsky cathedral in the Petrogradsky district, the Pokrovskaya church in Borovaya Street, etc., the Church of God's Mother in Sorrow, etc. Some members of the commissions and citizens who tried to calm the crowd were beaten up and several people were injured.

8. The Black Hundred was the name of a counterrevolutionary organization that chose the objective of overthrowing Soviet power. —Trans.

9. Patriarch Tikhon (V. I. Belavin) (1875–1925) was ordained in 1891 and in 1917 was made Metropolitan of Moscow. On 5 (18) November 1917 he was elected Patriarch of All Russia by the First All-Russia Local Council. In 1922 Tikhon was tried and put under house arrest in the Donskoy monastery. In May 1923, at the Second All-Russia Local Council convened by the *obnovlentsy* [renovators, who called for a loyal attitude to Soviet power—

Trans.], he was stripped of the rank of patriarch, but Tikhon and his supporters refused to recognize the decision as legal. On 16 June 1923, in his letter to the Supreme Court, Tikhon admitted that he was guilty and asked for pardon. (See the text of his letter in *Russian Orthodoxy: Landmarks of History* [Moscow, 1989], pp. 624–25. In Russian.) By a decision of the Central Executive council of the USSR of 21 March 1924 the Tikhon case was closed.

10. P. N. Milyukov (1859–1943) was a member of the Provisional Government.—Trans.

11. This is a reference to the telegram sent out in accordance with the decision of the Politburo of the Central Committee of the Communist Party (the Bolsheviks) of 16 March 1922: "Having asked the opinion of comrades who were involved in the seizure of valuables from churches, the Politburo has come to the conclusion that as far as the organization of the seizure of church valuables is concerned, preparations have not been completed and it is necessary to postpone the seizure in at least some areas" (Central Party Archives, f. 17, op. 3, d. 282, p. 2).

12. VTSIK: All-Russia Executive Committee of the Soviets of the Workers, Peasants, Cossacks, and Red Army Deputies.—Ed.

13. See note 5.

14. At the trial after the events in Shuya it was established that the demonstration was prepared and led by priests Rozhdestvensky, Svetozarov, Lavrov, and Smelchakov, deacon Paramonov, merchants Pokhlyebkin and Afanasyev, former landlord Kokovnikov, and Social Revolutionary Yazykov, etc.

15. In Moscow the organizers of the antigovernment demonstrations were tried by a revolutionary tribunal that on 8 May 1922 sentenced eleven people (priests, deans, and lay people) to death, four people to five years' imprisonment, thirteen to three years, ten to one year; fourteen people were released. (See

Pravda, no. 101, 9 May 1922.) On the same day, L. B. Kamenev suggested that the Politburo discuss canceling the tribunal's sentence, but the Politburo of the Central Committee of the Communist Party (the Bolsheviks) did not agree with him. Those sentenced to death lodged a protest with the Appeals Department of the Supreme Tribunal asking for the sentence to be commuted. (See *Pravda,* no. 119, 31 May 1922.) On 8 May 1922 the protest of those sentenced to death was discussed at the meeting of the VTSIK Presidium and the following resolution was adopted: "Regarding the convicted priests Khristofor Nadezhdin, Vassili Sokolov, Makariy Telegin, Serguei Tikhomirov, and Aleksandr Zaozyersky, the appeal is turned down and the sentence of the Revolutionary Tribunal remains in force. With respect to the other six people sentenced to death the sentence of the Revolutionary Tribunal was replaced by that of five years' imprisonment."

On 11 May 1922 L. B. Kamenev again raised the question of pardoning the convicts at the meeting of the Politburo of the Central Committee of the Russian Communist Party (the Bolsheviks). The following suggestion by L. D. Trotsky was adopted: "(a) The execution of the sentence should be suspended; (b) Comrade Trotsky should be instructed to make investigations and by the evening of 12 May of this year submit a written report to the Politburo" (Central Party Archives, f. 17, op. 3, d. 292, p. 4). On 14 May 1922 L. D. Trotsky submitted his report, which contained no facts justifying a decision to commute the sentence passed on the five convicts (the same persons as mentioned in the resolution of the Presidium of VTSIK; see above). The decision to commute the sentence passed on the other six convicts was explained "exclusively by considerations of the possibility to answer the appeal of the progressive clergy with a minimum of damage to the essence of the sentence, which is just with respect to all eleven people" (Central Party Archives, f. 17, op. 3, d. 293, p. 12). On 18 May 1922 the Politburo of the Central Committee of the Russian Communist Party (the Bolsheviks) agreed with this report.

16. F. E. Dzerzhinsky (1877–1926) was a member of the party from 1895. From 1917 he was chairman of the All-Russia Extraordinary Commission and from February 1922 was chairman of the Central Political Department under the People's Commissariat for Internal Affairs. At the same time he was People's Commissar for Internal Affairs, chairman of the Central Commission for Obligatory Work, People's Commissar for Transportation, and was a member of the Polish Bureau of the Central Committee of the Russian Communist Party (the Bolsheviks) and the Provisional Revolutionary Committee of Poland. After the Fourth Congress of the Russian Social-Democratic Workers' party he was a member of its Central Committee, and from 1921 he was also a member of the Organizational Bureau of the Central Committee of the Russian Communist Party (the Bolsheviks).

17. GPU: the State Political Department under the People's Commissariat for Internal Affairs. NKU: People's Commissariat of Justice.—Ed.

18. On 25 May 1922 the Central Committee of the Russian Communist Party (the Bolsheviks) approved the agenda for the Eleventh Party Congress. The item suggested by V. I. Lenin was not included. In the Congress documents there is no information about the meeting. The Eleventh Congress of the party was held in Moscow from 27 March to 2 April 1922.

Letter by Trotsky
with Notes by Lenin

L. D. Trotsky to the Members of the Politburo of the Central Committee of the Russian Communist Party (Bolshevik Party).[1]

15 May 1922

Top Secret

To all members of the Politburo of the Communist party, cc. to the editorial boards of *Pravda*, *Izvestia*, and comrade Lenin

Regarding the appeal of the loyal group of clergy, headed by Bishop Antonin,[2] *Pravda* published a short article,[3] while *Izvestia* has not published anything. I fear that the press will not give due attention to this document, which, however, will have major consequences in the sense that it will provoke a total split between the democratic part of the church supporting *smenovekhovstvo*[4] and monarchist counterrevolutionary elements. Today, naturally enough, we are totally and exclusively interested in supporting the church group identifying with *smenovekhovstvo* in its opposition to the monarchist group without, of course, abandoning our principle of the separation of church from state, and moreover, our philosophical-materialist approach to religion. Today, however, the main *political* task is to make sure that the clergy identifying with *smenovekhovstvo* is not terrorized by the old church hierarchy. The separation of church from state, which we have carried out once and for all, does not mean that the state is unconcerned about the negative developments in the church, as a material-social organization and not as a community of believers. The top echelons of the church have at their disposal the most diverse threats to scare the loyal elements. The policy of extreme church terrorism has lost none of its vigor up to now. The opposition, that is, the loyal and progressive elements of the clergy, did not expect that the state would support them as citizens and as representatives of groups of believers in the face of the encroachments and measures of material repression from the top echelons of the church. They did not expect this in part because of the fallacious and formally understood principle of the separation of church from state and in part because they saw that the state was extremely tolerant toward the counterrevolutionary top echelons of the church.

Today, one of the tasks of the press as far as this question is concerned is raising the loyal clergy's morale and giving them confidence that within the framework of their undisputed rights the state will not tolerate any attacks on them, although, naturally enough, the state does not want to get involved in the regulation of purely religious disputes and relations.

In any case it is necessary:

1. to give priority to Antonin's appeal, as a symptom of historic significance;

2. to publish in the press as much information as possible about the movement in the church and to take all measures to publicize, emphasize, and comment on voices speaking from the position of *smenovekhovstvo;*

3. without concealing our materialistic attitude toward religion not to bring it to the fore *in the immediate future,* that is, in the assessment of the current struggle, so as not to push the two sides closer to each other, but on the contrary to make it possible for the struggle to unfold in the most dramatic and decisive form;

4. to conduct criticism of the clergy identifying with *smenovekhovstvo* and the laity associated with it, not from the materialist-atheistic point of view, but from a qualified religious-democratic point of view: you are too frightened by princes, you do not draw all conclusions from the domination of the monarchists in the church, you do not appreciate the guilt of the established church toward the people and the revolution, etc., etc.;

5. however, even now to publish historical-materialist articles about the Orthodox Church in order to clarify the most important aspects of its development as an organization based on class identity (explaining why there was no bourgeois reformation in the Russian Orthodox Church, how the incipient bourgeois reformation in the church is interconnected with the proletarian revolution, the state, etc., etc.;

6. for Glavpolitprosvet[5] to make all-around preparations, so that all questions concerning not only the church but also religion should be formulated very clearly and in the most popular and accessible form in leaflets and oral speeches in the immediate future, when the struggle inside the church attracts the attention of the broadest popular masses and prepares the ground for the seeds of atheism and materialism.

L. Trotsky

14 May 1922

P.S. I repeat again that the editorial board of *Pravda* and *Izvestia* do not realize sufficiently the tremendous historical significance of the developments in the church and surrounding it. It is only by exerting the greatest pressure that we succeed in getting an article on this question published. Then everything gets back in the same old rut. *The puny Genoa rubbish takes up whole pages,*[6] while the most profound spiritual revolution in the Russian people (or more precisely, the preparation for this most profound revolution) is assigned to the back pages of the newspapers.

L. Trotsky

15 May

true! one thousand times true! Down with rubbish!

Lenin

NOTES

1. This letter is found in the Central Party Archives of the Institute of Marxism-Leninism, f. 2, op. 1, d. 27072. As with the preceding letter by Lenin, this letter was withheld from the public until published in the April 1990 issue of *Izvestia TSEKA KAPEESES*, an official publication of the Communist Party of the USSR. The end notes by V. I. Lenin are an autograph. Additionally, a note also dated 15 May 1922 at the top of this letter says "See: p. 2: to Steklov and Bukharin" and "return." A later note says "It has already been sent to us. N. Bukharin." Y. M. Steklov (1873–1941) took part in the Social-Democratic movement from 1893 onward. After the October revolution he was editor of *Izvestia VTSIK*. N. Bukharin was also a prominent Bolshevik and Communist Party member.

2. Antonin (A. A. Granovsky) (1860–1927), a bishop, one of the most active participants in the *obnovlenie* ("renovation") movement in the Russian Orthodox Church ("The Living Church"). From 13 April 1922 he was a member of the Central Committee for Assistance to the Famine-Stricken Population Regarding the Sale of Church Valuables. From May 1922 Antonin was a member of the Supreme Church Department. From June 1923 he was at the head of the independent church, "The Union for the Revival of the Church," which largely concentrated on the social aspects of the Christian teaching and virtually ignored the transformations in the sphere of dogmatics, the lifestyle of the church and rituals.

The renovation movement of the Russian Orthodox Church ("The Living Church") came out against the leadership of the Russian Orthodox Church headed by Patriarch Tikhon, and it proclaimed the principle of loyalty to the Soviet government.

3. In its issue no. 106 of 14 May 1922 *Pravda* published the appeal "To the Believing Sons of the Russian Orthodox Church," which was signed by Bishop Antonin, priests S. Kalinovsky, I. Borissov, and V. Bykov of Moscow; V. Krasnitsky and E. Belkov, archpriest A. Vedensky and psalm singer S. Stadnik of Petrograd; archpriests Russanov and Ledovsky of Saratov. The appeal condemned the activities of those hierarchs and

pastors who were guilty of organizing resistance to the government in its effort to give assistance to famine-stricken population and in its other works for the benefit of workers. The priests asked for permission "to convene a local council to judge those guilty of the ruin in the church and to resolve the question of the administration of the church and the establishment of normal relations between the church and the Soviet government." The appeal was followed by a short article published by the newspaper's editorial board entitled "Church Democracy against Church Feudalism." The articles called on believers to read the appeal.

4. *Smenovekhovstvo* was a sociopolitical movement in the Russian bourgeois intelligentsia during the 1920s.—Trans.

5. Glavpolitprosvet was the Central Political and Educational Committee of the Republic under the People's Commissariat for Education of the Russian Federation in the 1920s and the 1930s.—Trans.

6. The Genoa international conference was held from 10 April to 19 May, 1922. More than thirty countries participated, including the USSR.

Legislation on Religion

The New Laws: An Introduction

The Law on Freedom of Conscience and Religious Organizations, passed by the USSR Parliament, and the Law on Freedom of Worship—an effort of Russia's Parliament—appeared in print on 9 October and 10 November, 1990, respectively. The new acts were natural manifestations of the emergent democracy.

Both legal acts mean to give believers a worthy place in Soviet society and allow them to perform their duties to the community unimpeded; establish organizations and unite for worship; teach religion to children and bring them up in conformity with the religious convictions of parents or guardians; profess and preach religion; and, last but not least, have "certain duties replaced by others on the grounds of their convictions" in legally stipulated cases (primarily involving military service).

For the first time in the Soviet years, religious communities received the status of juridical persons, and their basic rights were legally confirmed—the right of charity and mission work, and of owning buildings and other property. The status of religious organization employees is now equal to that of persons employed by state-owned enterprises and offices, and public organizations.

The secular authorities no longer treat religious organizations and individual believers as opponents, but think of them as allies tackling tasks of concern to the entire country. The previous Soviet legislation determined only the status of religious societies. Now it concerns all structural units of religious organizations without exception, including monasteries, schools, charitable societies, and missions.

Nevertheless, the new laws abound in contradictions and it is uncertain how they will be implemented, particularly in light of the changing relationship between the Union and various republics. Federation and State Legislation should rival Union Legislation only in the extent of personal freedoms they provide and rights they guarantee. If they compete in restrictions and repression, thwarting public hopes for rights and freedoms, some laws are doomed to be violated.

The Union law should specify that republican legal norms shall not be less democratic than this law—but it does not. No less regrettably, the law of the Russian Federation does not specify its status with regard to the Union law and Soviet international obligations in human rights and freedoms. Its preamble, for instance, says that freedom of confession "shall be an inalienable right of citizens of the Russian Federation, guaranteed by its Constitution and international obligations." But then, the Federation has not yet signed any international understanding concerning believers' rights, while the pact on human rights, to which Russia's MPs referred more than once in their public addresses, was signed by the Union, rather than the Federation, as was the case with many other pacts and conventions.

Article 5, Item 5 of the USSR Law on Freedom of Conscience and Religious Organizations guarantees the right of religious organizations to take part in community affairs, giving legitimacy to what actually occurs in Soviet life. By contrast, the Law of the Russian Federation (Article 8, Item 3) fails to recognize such extensive rights of religious organizations, pointing out only that "religious communities may take part in social and cultural affairs," though they are, in fact, active in many other spheres of community life, politics, in particular.

A freely formed religious community may cease to exist without any impact from without—either through spontaneous disintegration or by self-dissolution (theoretically possible, though there have been no such instances to this day). The Union and Russian Federation acts envisage both cases plus a third: a religious organization disbanded by decision of the body that registered it "should it violate the present Law." Such decisions may be appealed in court.

In case of any violation of the law specified by the present norm, legal action shall be taken against the culprits. Why, then, will the entire religious community suffer for someone's illegal conduct?

The Union and Russian Federation laws give a somewhat different treatment to the right to teach and study religion. The Union law grants the right of religious education to both children and adults. Its Article 6, Item 3 reads: "Religious organizations whose statutes have been officially registered have the right to establish, in conformity with these statutes, groups and classes to teach religion to persons under and over age, and conduct teaching in other forms on the premises they own or lease."

Russia's law avoids such explicit formulas. Its Article 9, Item 2 says: "Religion may be taught . . . optionally in all pre-school establishments and schools by representatives of religious communities with officially registered statutes."

Comparison of the two reveals different standpoints on another matter. The Union law allows religious organizations to independently provide premises for religious classes—a logical stance, considering our overcrowded schools. Russia's law, on the contrary, gives secular educationists the baffling task of looking for a place for optional religious studies. Independent schools under religious organizations do not in the least violate the secular purport of state schooling. Nevertheless, the Russian Federation law does not allow them to set up such schools. So we have two mutually contradictory norms concerning this matter.

Both laws interpret certain norms in an entirely new way with respect to income taxation of religious organizations' production. Article 19, Item 2 of the Union law says: "Production profits and other incomes of religious organizations shall be taxed according to the existing legislation, at the rates and in the procedure for public organizations engaged in production." Religious communities were tax-exempt before this law entered into force though some religious enterprises, such as wafer bakeries of the Russian Orthodox Church and matzo bakeries of many Jewish communities were highly profitable.

Interestingly, the new Union law exempts altar bread and matzo profits from taxation, though bakeries might well be qualified as public organization enterprises. Russia's law is harsher here, again. Says Article 30, Item 2: "With the exception of charitable, cultural and educational expenditures, profits from production based on religious community property shall be taxed in conformity with the legislation of the Russian Federation and in the procedure stipulated for enterprises owned by public organizations."

For the first time in Soviet legislation, the state pledges to guarantee religious organizations' property rights (Article 18, Item 6 of the Union law). This was for a long time the dream of many believers. Still, it is absent in the Russian Federation law.

Again in contrast to the Union legislation, the Russian Federation law does not recognize religious organizations' right to serve liturgies at hospitals, senior homes, and prisons—a practice long existent and publicized by the media.

Article 21, Item 3 of the Union law says: "The command of military units shall not impede soldiers from taking part in public worship and performing religious rites when out of duties." Here, the Russian Federation law allows more freedom, saying: "Citizens have the right to perform religious rites in military units of all branches and services"—meaning that public worship may take place in barracks and cantonments.

As I see it, the republican legislation should always follow this pattern, offering more freedom than the Union.

The Union law makes no specifications on religious feasts whereas Russia's law has its Article 14, "State Bodies and Religious Feasts," which reads: "On request from large religious communities, government bodies of the Russian Federation may declare major religious feasts as public holidays"—a right that private entrepreneurs and state-owned enterprise managers legally enjoyed in the early Soviet years, unless production interests demanded otherwise. Local authorities also had this right.

The Union and Russian Federation legislations take different stances on the registration of religious organizations' statutes, to breed a wealth of complications. Article 7, Item 1 of the Union law defines religious organizations as "religious communities, boards, centers, monasteries, fraternities, missions and missionary societies, theological schools, and associations of religious organizations" such as the Russian Orthodox and Armenian Apostolic churches, and the All-Union Council of Evangelical Christian Baptists.

The republican law treats the matter differently and uses the term "association" instead of "organization." Its Article 17 refers to "voluntary associations of adult citizens" and specifies that they may be established "for public worship, witness by word of mouth and through the mass media, missionary activities, charity, religious education, feats of ascesis in monasteries, hermitages, etc., pilgrimages and other activities." Further on, the article says that "religious associations may unite in regional and central associations with managerial bodies and other structures." The Russian Federation law does not list all the kinds of religious associations/organizations, though it explains the term explicitly enough.

There are two basic differences between the Union and republican laws. The first becomes evident if we compare the lists of religious organizations in the former and associations in the latter. Where the republican law specifies, for instance, eparchies as objects of legal control, the Union law has eparchial boards.

The second difference concerns the definition of the government body that shall register the statutes of religious organizations. The Union law names executive committees of district and town councils, irrespective of the territories in which these organizations are active. In Moscow, for instance, district executives shall register not only local parochial statutes but the Statute of the Moscow Patriarchate, while their functionaries will be hardly competent enough to judge whether it is in keeping with the Union legislation. The Russian Federation law, on the other hand, specifies different levels of government bodies to register religious associations' statutes. These issues shall be in the jurisdiction of the republican Ministry of Justice and its local bodies, rather than local authorities—a premise that raises the lowest competent bodies to a regional level, as executive committees of town and district councils have no departments of justice. Still, this norm will be hard to implement with the preceding practice, which demanded town and district executives' participation in registering religious organizations.

The republican law has another contradictory point. Autonomous republics in the Russian Federation have the right to issue laws of their own, including legislation to regulate church-state relations. Still, the final passage of Article 19 says: "All religious associations in the Russian Federation . . . shall act in conformity with its legislation." Does this mean that the Federation legislators do not care about autonomies' laws?

There is yet another obstacle to the smooth implementation of the laws under review. Russia's law passes supervision and expert analyses to a republican parliamentary committee, while the Union law leaves these functions in the competence of executive bodies, to be more precise, a state organ for religious affairs.

The latest acts are the first Soviet attempt to reflect in legislation the wealth of secular authorities' relations with religious organizations and individual believers. Hence their understandable imperfection.

Law of the Union of Soviet Socialist Republics on Freedom of Conscience and Religious Organizations

SECTION I.
GENERAL PROVISIONS

Article 1. The Objectives of this Law

This law shall guarantee the rights of citizens to determination and expression of attitudes to religion and to religious convictions, to confession of a faith and performance of religious rites without let or hindrance; it shall also guarantee social justice and equality and uphold the rights and interests of citizens irrespective of attitude to religion and regulate relations connected with the activities of religious organizations.

Article 2. Legislation on Freedom of Conscience and Religious Organizations

Legislation on freedom of conscience and religious organizations shall consist of this law, which shall enshrine the principal guarantees of freedom of conscience in accordance with the Constitution of the USSR, and also of laws issued by the USSR, union, and autonomous republics in accordance with this law.

Article 3. The Right to Freedom of Conscience

In accordance with the right to freedom of conscience, each and every citizen shall determine his or her attitude to religion, be entitled to individually or jointly with others confess any faith or confess no faith and to express and proclaim convictions connected with his or her attitude to religion.

Parents, or persons replacing parents, shall upon mutual agreement be entitled to raise their children in accordance with their own attitude to religion.

Coercion of any kind shall be prohibited in respect to determination by a citizen of his or her attitude to religion, to confession of or refusal to confess a faith, to participation or nonparticipation in religious services, rites, or ceremonies, and to religious instruction.

The exercise of the freedom to confess a faith or proclaim convictions shall be subject solely to those restrictions that are necessary in the interests of maintaining public safety and order, protecting life, health, and morality, and also upholding the rights and freedoms of other citizens; are enshrined in law; and comply with international obligations of the USSR.

Article 4. Equality Irrespective of Attitude to Religion

Citizens of the USSR shall be equal before the law in all spheres of civic, political, economic, social, and cultural life, irrespective of attitude to religion. Indication in official documents of a citizen's attitude to religion shall be prohibited, unless a citizen should desire such indication.

23

Any form, be it direct or indirect, of restriction of rights or institution of privileges arising from and connected with citizens' attitudes to religion shall result in liability as established by law, as shall vilification and incitement of enmity and prejudice against citizens on such grounds.

No person shall be released from obligations established by law due to religious convictions. Substitution of one obligation with another due to such convictions shall be permissible only as provided for by legislation of the USSR.

Article 5. Separation of Church (Religious Organizations) from State

All religions and denominations shall be equal before the law. The institution of any form of privileges or restrictions for one religion or denomination in comparison to others shall be prohibited.

The state shall not impose upon religious organizations the performance of any functions of state and shall not intervene in the activities of religious organizations unless they should be in contravention of the law. The state shall finance neither the activities of religious organizations nor the propagation of atheism.

Restrictions on the conduct of research, including that financed by the state, on the dissemination of research results and on the inclusion thereof into secondary education programs on grounds of compatibility with or contradiction of the tenets of any religion or of atheism shall be prohibited.

Religious organizations shall not perform functions of the state.

Religious organizations shall be entitled to take part in public life, and also to utilize the mass media, as equals of public organizations and associations.

Religious organizations shall not take part in the activities of political parties nor render them financial support. Members of the clergy of religious organizations shall be entitled to take part in political life as equals of all other citizens.

Religious organizations shall be obliged to comply with the requirements of existing legislation and of law and order.

The state shall promote mutual tolerance and respect between those citizens confessing a faith and those not, between religious organizations of differing denominations, and also between adherents thereof.

Article 6. Separation of School from Church (Religious Organizations)

The state system of education in the USSR shall be separated from the church and be of a secular nature. Access to various kinds and levels of education shall be enjoyed by citizens irrespective of their attitude to religion.

Citizens may receive tuition in religious faith and religious education in the language of their choice individually or jointly with others.

Religious organizations, the statutes (regulations) of which have been registered in the proper procedure, shall be entitled, in compliance with such statutes, to establish religious educational institutions and study groups for children and adults and also to engage in other forms of tuition, using for these purposes premises belonging to them or supplied for their use.

SECTION II.
RELIGIOUS ORGANIZATIONS IN THE USSR

Article 7. Religious Organizations

Religious organizations in the USSR shall be religious societies, boards and centers, monasteries, brotherhoods, missionary societies (missions), spiritual educational establishments, and also associations of religious organizations. Religious associations shall be represented by their centers (boards).

Religious organizations in the USSR shall be formed for the purpose of satisfying the religious needs of citizens to confess and proclaim a faith, shall function in accordance with their organizational structure, and shall select, appoint, and replace their personnel in accordance with their statutes (regulations).

Article 8. Religious Societies

A religious society shall be formed by citizens for the purposes of joint confession of a faith and satisfaction of other religious needs and shall function on a voluntary basis.

Notification of state authorities of the formation of a religious society shall not be obligatory.

Article 9. Religious Boards, Centers, and Associations

Religious boards, centers, and associations shall function on the basis of their statutes (regulations), insofar as they shall not contravene existing legislation.

Religious organizations in the USSR possessing headquarters abroad may be guided in their activities by the statutes (regulations) of such headquarters insofar as they shall not contravene Soviet legislation.

Those regulations between the state and religious boards, centers, and associations, foreign included, that are not regulated by law shall be regulated by agreements achieved by such religious organizations and state authorities.

Article 10. Monasteries, Brotherhoods, Missions

Religious boards and centers shall be entitled, in accordance with their registered statutes (regulations), to found monasteries, religious brotherhoods, and missionary organizations (missions), which shall function on the basis of their own statutes, registered in the procedure stipulated by law.

Monasteries and religious brotherhoods may also be founded in the procedure stipulated by this law for religious societies, with registration of their statutes (regulations).

Article 11. Theological Educational Establishments

Religious boards and centers shall be entitled, in accordance with their registered statutes (regulations), to found theological educational establishments for the training of members of their clergy and persons in other religious professions required by them. Such establishments shall function on the basis of their statutes (regulations), registered in the procedure stipulated by law.

Full-time students at higher and secondary theological educational establishments shall, in the procedure stipulated for students of state educational establishments, enjoy rights and concessions with respect to postponement of military service, taxation, and inclusion of the duration of study into their work records.

Article 12. Statutes of Religious Organizations

Statutes (regulations) of religious organizations defining their legal capacity in accordance with the civil law shall be registered in the procedure stipulated by law. Such statutes shall state location and denomination; place in the organizational structure of a religious association; nature of assets; rights to establish enterprises and mass media outlets, found other religious organizations, found educational establishments; other entitlements; the procedure for settlement of property and other issues upon termination; and also other information connected with specific aspects of the activities of the given religious organization.

Statutes (regulations) or other documents governing religious teaching and miscellaneous internal aspects of a religious organization shall not be subject to registration with state authorities. The state shall note and respect the internal regulations of religious organizations on condition that such regulations are submitted to the appropriate state authorities and that they shall not contravene existing legislation.

Article 13. Religious Organizations As Juridical Persons

Religious organizations shall be recognized as juridical persons from the moment of the registration of their statutes (regulations).

Religious organizations shall, as juridical persons, enjoy the relevant rights and bear the relevant liabilities in accordance with legislation and their own statutes (regulations).

Article 14. Registration of the Statutes of Religious Organizations

In order for a religious society to receive the legal capacity of a juridical person, not less than ten founding persons (aged eighteen and over) shall submit an application with the statutes (regulations) attached to the executive committee of the district (city) Soviet of People's Deputies within whose territory the proposed location of such society falls. Should a society belong to a religious organization, this shall be stated in the statutes and endorsed by the appropriate religious board or center. The executive committee shall process the application and pass the appropriate decision within one month.

Should endorsement as stipulated in the first part of this article be lacking, the executive committee of the local Soviet of People's Deputies shall be entitled to request additional materials and to receive qualified advice; in such circumstances, applications shall be processed within three months.

Religious associations, and also centers, boards, monasteries, brotherhoods, missions, and theological educational establishments founded by religious organizations, shall submit for registration statutes (regulations) endorsed by such organizations to the executive

committee of the district (city) Soviet of People's Deputies of location. Registration shall be effected by the executive committee within one month.

A different procedure for the registration of statutes (regulations) of religious organizations may be stipulated by legislation of union and autonomous republics.

Article 15. Refusal to Register the Statutes of a Religious Organization

Refusal to register the statutes (regulations) of a religious society or organization shall be communicated to the applicants in written form, stating the grounds for refusal. Such refusal, and also failure to effect registration within the time limit stipulated by this law, may be contested in a court of law pursuant to the established procedure for appeals against unlawful acts by government bodies and officials infringing on citizens' rights.

Article 16. Closure of a Religious Organization

The activities of a religious organization may be terminated solely upon its liquidation in accordance with its own regulations or upon violation of the provisions of this law or other laws of the USSR, union, and autonomous republics.

A decision to terminate the activities of a religious organization may be taken by the authority that registered its statutes (regulations); such decision may be contested in a court of law pursuant to the procedure stipulated by civil procedural legislation.

SECTION III.
ASSETS OF RELIGIOUS ORGANIZATIONS

Article 17. Use of Assets Owned by the State, Public Organizations, or Individuals

Religious organizations shall be entitled to use for their own needs premises and assets made available to them on a contractual basis by state and public organizations and individuals.

Local Soviets of People's Deputies and state bodies may transfer houses of worship and other assets of a religious nature in state ownership to the ownership of, or for use free of charge by, religious organizations.

Religious organizations shall enjoy priority right with respect to the transfer of houses of worship and adjoining grounds.

A decision on the transfer to a religious organization of a house of worship and religious assets should be passed within not more than one month of receipt of the appropriate petition and communicated to the petitioners in written form.

The transfer to, and use by, religious organizations of buildings and items that are historical and cultural landmarks shall be effected in accordance with existing legislation.

Religious organizations shall own and use land in the procedure stipulated by existing legislation.

Article 18. Property of Religious Organizations

Religious organizations may own buildings; items of a religious nature; installations of production, social, or charitable designation; financial means; and other assets required by them to provide for their activities.

Religious organizations shall be entitled to ownership of assets acquired or created by them by way of their own resources, donated by individuals and organizations, or transferred by the state, and also of assets acquired by them in other lawful ways.

Religious organizations may also own assets situated abroad.

Religious organizations shall be entitled to appeal for, and receive, voluntary donations of monies and other assets.

Donations of monies and other assets to, and also other incomes of, religious organizations shall be exempt from taxation.

The rights of religious organizations to ownership shall be upheld by law.

Article 19. Production and Commercial Activities of Religious Organizations

Religious organizations shall be entitled, pursuant to legislation and their statutes (regulations), to found publishing, printing, production, restoration and construction, agricultural, and other enterprises, and also charitable establishments (shelters, boarding schools, hospitals, and others) possessing the status of juridical person.

Profits derived from production activities and other incomes of enterprises of religious organizations shall be subject to taxation pursuant to the law and in the procedure and to the extent stipulated for enterprises of public organizations.

Article 20. Disposal of the Assets of Religious Organizations upon Termination of Activities

Following termination of the activities of a religious organization, those assets made available for its use by state or public organizations and by individuals shall be returned to their previous owners.

Upon termination of the activities of a religious organization, assets in its ownership shall be disposed of pursuant to its statutes (regulations) and existing legislation.

Assets of a religious nature belonging to religious organizations may not be subject to claims by creditors.

In the absence of a successor in rights, assets shall be transferred to state ownership.

SECTION IV.
RIGHTS OF RELIGIOUS ORGANIZATIONS AND CITIZENS CONNECTED WITH FREEDOM TO CONFESS A FAITH

Article 21. Religious Rites and Ceremonies

Religious organizations shall be entitled to establish and maintain freely accessible places of divine service or religious congregation, and also religious shrines (places of pilgrimage).

Divine services, religious rites, and ceremonies shall be conducted in houses of worship and on adjoining grounds, at places of pilgrimage, at establishments of religious organizations, at cemeteries and crematoria, and in flats and homes of individuals.

The commanding officer of a military unit shall not hinder participation in divine services and performance of religious rites by service personnel in their free time.

Divine services and religious rites in hospitals (including military), homes for elderly or disabled persons, places of remand detention, and penal institutions shall be conducted at the request of persons in them. Administrations of such establishments shall render assistance in inviting members of the clergy and determining the time and other conditions for the conduct of divine services, rites, and ceremonies.

In other circumstances, public divine services, religious rites, and ceremonies shall be conducted in the procedure stipulated for gatherings, rallies, demonstrations, and processions.

Religious organizations shall be entitled to propose the conduct of divine services for citizens in hospitals (including military), homes for elderly or disabled persons, and penal institutions.

Article 22. Religious Literature and Items of a Religious Nature

Individuals and religious organizations shall be entitled to acquire and utilize religious literature in the language of their choice, and also other items and materials of a religious nature.

Religious organizations shall be entitled to produce, export, import, and distribute items of a religious nature, religious literature, and other information materials of religious content.

Religious organizations shall enjoy the exclusive right to establish enterprises issuing divine literature and producing items of a religious nature.

Article 23. Charitable, Proselytizing, and Educational Activities of Religious Organizations

Societies, brotherhoods, and other associations of citizens may be established under the auspices of religious organizations to engage in charity, the study and distribution of religious literature, and other educational and proselytizing activities; they may have their own statutes, registered in the procedure stipulated for public organizations.

Religious organizations shall be entitled to engage in works of charity and mercy independently and also through public foundations.

Donations and payments made for such purposes shall be exempt from taxation.

Article 24. International Links and Contacts of Believers and Religious Organizations

Citizens and religious organizations shall be entitled, on an individual and group basis, to establish and maintain international links and direct personal contacts, including travel abroad to take part in pilgrimages, gatherings, and other religious events.

Religious organizations may send citizens abroad for study in theological educational establishments and may receive foreign citizens for the same purpose.

SECTION V.
WORK AND EMPLOYMENT IN RELIGIOUS ORGANIZATIONS AND THEIR ENTERPRISES

Article 25. Labor Relations in Religious Organizations

A religious organization shall be entitled to receive citizens to work for it.

Terms of labor shall be established by agreement between a religious organization and employee and shall be set out in a labor contract to be concluded in written form.

A religious organization shall be obliged to register labor contracts according to the established procedure.

Documents determining terms of remuneration of members of the clergy shall be registered according to the established procedure.

Citizens working for religious organizations under labor contracts may be members of trade unions.

Article 26. Labor Rights of Citizens Working for Religious Organizations

Labor legislation shall apply to citizens working for religious organizations under labor contracts in the same way as to workers and employees of state-sector and public enterprises, establishments, and organizations.

Taxation of incomes earned by citizens working for religious organizations, by members of the clergy included, shall be levied at the rates established for workers and employees of state-sector enterprises, establishments, and organizations.

Article 27. Labor Relations of Citizens at Enterprises and Establishments of Religious Organizations

Legislation on labor, taxation, social insurance, and social welfare of workers and employees of state-sector and public enterprises, establishments, and organizations shall apply to citizens working at all enterprises and establishments of religious organizations and at charitable institutions founded by them.

Article 28. Social Welfare and Social Insurance of Citizens Working for Religious Organizations

Citizens, including members of the clergy, working for religious organizations shall enjoy social welfare and social insurance as the equals of workers and employees of state-sector and public enterprises, establishments, and organizations.

To this end, religious organizations, their enterprises, and institutions shall make payments to the state social insurance fund and state pension fund of the USSR in the procedure and to the extent stipulated for public organizations, their enterprises, and establishments.

All citizens working for religious organizations shall be accorded and receive an ordinary state pension in accordance with existing legislation.

SECTION VI.
STATE AUTHORITIES AND RELIGIOUS ORGANIZATIONS

Article 29. State Authorities for Religious Affairs

The state authority of the USSR for religious affairs shall be a center for information, consultation, and qualified advice. In this capacity it shall:

- maintain contacts and coordination channels with equivalent establishments in union and autonomous republics and abroad;

- create a data bank on religious organizations in the USSR and on compliance with legislation on freedom of conscience and religious organizations;

- create a council of experts consisting of scholars of religion, representatives of religious organizations, and specialists on human rights issues to provide expert religious opinion and, when necessary, official conclusions in response to requests from government authorities and courts of law;

- render upon request from religious organizations assistance in achieving agreements with state authorities and necessary assistance on issues requiring decisions by state authorities;

- promote mutual understanding and tolerance between religious organizations of differing denominations within the country and abroad.

The state authority of the USSR for religious affairs shall be established by the Council of Ministers of the USSR.

State authorities of union and autonomous republics for religious affairs shall be established and function in accordance with legislation of the USSR, union, and autonomous republics.

Article 30. Liability for Violation of Legislation on Freedom of Conscience and Religious Organizations

Officials and citizens guilty of violation of legislation on freedom of conscience and religious organizations shall be liable as stipulated by legislation of the USSR, union, and autonomous republics.

Article 31. International Treaties

Should an international treaty to which the USSR is a signatory stipulate rules other than those contained in legislation on freedom of conscience and religious organizations, such treaty shall prevail.

President of the Union of Soviet Socialist Republics

M. Gorbachev

Moscow, the Kremlin, 1 October 1990

Law of the Russian Soviet Federative Socialist Republic on Freedom of Worship

Freedom of worship is an inalienable right of the citizens of the RSFSR, guaranteed by the Constitution and international obligations of the RSFSR.

This law arises from the provision, contained in international treaties and pacts, that the freedom to hold religious or atheist beliefs and to act pursuant thereto shall be subject solely to those restrictions that are established by law and essential to uphold the rights and freedoms of other persons.

I. GENERAL PROVISIONS

Article 1. The Purpose of This Law

The purpose of the Law of the RSFSR on Freedom of Worship is to regulate societal relations arising in the given sphere with the aim of ensuring observance and uniform application throughout the RSFSR of the principles of freedom of conscience enshrined in the Constitution of the RSFSR, and also of guaranteeing the rights of citizens to exercise such freedom.

Article 2. Legislation on Freedom of Worship

Legislation of the RSFSR governing freedom of worship shall consist of this law and other legislative acts of the RSFSR issued in accordance therewith.

Article 3. The Scope of Freedom of Worship in the RSFSR

Freedom of worship, enshrined in the Constitution of the RSFSR, shall include the right of each and every citizen to freely select, possess, and disseminate religious and atheist beliefs, to confess any faith or no faith, and to act in accordance with his or her beliefs, while observing the laws of the state.

Article 4. Principal Forms of Application of the Right to Freedom of Worship

Citizens of the RSFSR, foreign citizens, and stateless persons shall enjoy the right to freedom of worship on an individual or shared basis, by way of founding appropriate public associations. Religious and atheist public associations shall be founded and shall function on the basis of their statutes (regulations), which shall be registered in the proper procedure as stipulated in this law. The activities of public associations founded for purposes of exercise of the right to freedom of worship should not entail assault upon the person or infringements upon the rights and freedoms of citizens, nor other breaches of the law.

Article 5. Guarantees of Freedom of Worship

The fundamental guarantees of freedom of worship in the RSFSR shall be:

- equality of citizens irrespective of attitude to religion;
- separation of religious and atheist associations from the state;
- the secular nature of the state education system;
- equality of religious associations before the law;
- legislation ensuring the exercise of freedom of worship and establishing penalties for infringement thereupon.

Article 6. Equality of Citizens Irrespective of Attitude to Religion

Citizens of the RSFSR shall be equal before the law in all spheres of civic, political, economic, social, and cultural life irrespective of their attitude to religion.

Indication in official documents of a citizen's attitude to religion shall be prohibited. Any form of direct or indirect restriction of the rights of or granting of direct or indirect advantages to citizens in connection with their attitude to religion, the incitement in this respect of enmity and hatred, and also the insulting of citizens in connection with their religious or atheist beliefs shall be punishable by law.

Insults to the religious sentiments of citizens, and also the desecration of items, buildings, and sites venerated by a religion, shall be punishable by law.

Article 7. Civic Duty and Religious Beliefs

Attitude to religion shall not justify refusal to perform or evasion of civic duties established by law.

Substitution of one civic duty with another shall be permissible in circumstances provided for by legislation of the RSFSR. Persons who on account of religious beliefs cannot serve in the armed forces in a combatant role shall, on terms and in the procedure established by law, be permitted to serve in a capacity unconnected with the use and bearing of arms.

Article 8. Separation of Religious and Atheist Associations from the State

Religious associations in the RSFSR shall be separate from the state. Authorities and officials of the state shall not interfere in the formation by citizens of their attitude to religion nor in the lawful activities of religious associations and shall not instruct the latter to perform any functions of the state. Within the RSFSR neither state authorities nor offices of state may be formed for the explicit purpose of directing, managing, or deciding upon the exercise by citizens of freedom of worship. The lawful activities of religious associations shall be protected by the state.

Religious associations may not interfere in the affairs of the state and shall participate neither in elections of state and government authorities nor in the activities of political parties; however, members of religious associations shall be entitled as all other citizens to participate on a personal basis in political life.

Religious associations shall be entitled to participate in the social and cultural life of society pursuant to legislation governing the activities of public associations in the RSFSR.

Public associations formed for purposes of joint study and dissemination of atheist beliefs shall be separate from the state. The state shall not provide them with any material or ideological assistance and shall not instruct them to perform any functions of state.

Article 9. The Secular Nature of the State Education System

The state system of education and instruction shall be of a secular nature and shall not attempt to mold any attitude to religion.

Religious instruction and religious education may take place in nonstate establishments, privately at home, or under the auspices of a religious association, and also on an optional basis by representatives of religious associations with registered statutes in any preschool and educational establishments and organizations.

Instruction in religion and the fundamentals thereof and also of religious philosophy that is not accompanied by the performance of religious rites and that is of an explanatory nature may be included in the curricula of state educational establishments.

A child shall be entitled to freely express his or her opinion and shall be entitled to freedom of thought, conscience, and religion. The state shall respect the freedom of a child and of his or her parents or lawful guardians to ensure the religious and moral upbringing of their choice in accordance with their beliefs.

Article 10. Equality of Religious Associations Before the Law

All religions and religious associations shall be equal before the laws of the state. No religion or religious association shall enjoy any advantages or be subjected to any restrictions relative to others. In matters of freedom of worship and belief the state shall be neutral, that is, shall not favor any religion or outlook.

Article 11. State Supervision of Compliance with Legislation on Freedom of Worship in the RSFSR

State supervision of compliance with legislation on freedom of worship in the RSFSR shall be effected by Soviets of People's Deputies and also the appropriate law enforcement agencies in accordance with their terms of reference as established by law. Such supervision by other state authorities or by political parties and officials shall be prohibited.

Registration of the statutes (regulations) of religious associations pursuant to the rules stipulated by this law shall be exclusively within the terms of reference of the Ministry of Justice and its agencies in localities.

Article 12. The Advisory Council of the RSFSR Supreme Soviet Committee on Freedom of Conscience, Religion, Compassion, and Charity

An Advisory Council shall be formed under the auspices of the RSFSR Supreme Soviet Committee on Freedom of Conscience, Religion, Compassion, and Charity and shall consist of representatives of religious associations, public organizations, state authorities, experts on religious affairs, lawyers, and other specialists in freedom of conscience and religious denominations. The composition of the council shall be endorsed by the Presidium of the RSFSR Supreme Soviet upon submission by the said committee.

The Advisory Council shall:

- establish a data bank on religious associations registered in the RSFSR;

- advise the Committee on Freedom of Conscience, Religion, Compassion, and Charity and other committees of the RSFSR Supreme Soviet on the application of this law;

- provide legal and religious expert opinion and also official conclusions upon request by state and government agencies and courts of law.

Article 13. Liability in Respect of Breach of Legislation on Freedom of Worship

Persons guilty of breach of legislation on freedom of conscience and worship shall bear criminal, administrative, and other liability as established by legislation of the RSFSR. No person may be prosecuted for beliefs arising from his or her attitude to religion.

Confidentiality of confession shall be protected by law. Members of the clergy shall not be questioned upon and shall maintain in strict confidence all information known to them from confessions heard of citizens.

Article 14. State Authorities and Religious Holidays

Upon request by public religious associations, state authorities in the RSFSR shall be entitled to declare major religious holidays additional nonworking days.

II. THE RIGHT TO RELIGIOUS BELIEFS AND RELIGIOUS ACTIVITIES

Article 15. The Right to Religious Beliefs

Pursuant to the Constitution of the RSFSR, each and every citizen shall have the right to select and hold religious beliefs and to freely change them. A citizen of the RSFSR may individually or jointly with fellow believers confess any faith, perform religious rites without let or hindrance, voluntarily join and leave religious associations. A citizen of the RSFSR shall be entitled to proclaim and disseminate religious views and beliefs in oral, printed, and any other form, on condition that such activity shall not violate this law or public order and shall not entail assault upon the person or infringement of the rights of citizens.

Hindrance with or without the use of coercion of the assumption or rejection of religious beliefs and of the joining or leaving of a religious association shall be punishable by law.

Article 16. The Entitlement to Perform Religious Rites

Hindrance of the performance of religious rites that are not in breach of legislation of the RSFSR shall be punishable by law.

The conduct of atheist events in places used by believers pursuant to this law for the purposes of worship shall be prohibited.

Article 17. Religious Associations

A religious association shall be a voluntary alliance of adult citizens, formed for the purposes of joint exercise of the right to freedom of worship, including for joint worship and the promotion of a faith.

Worship and promotion of a faith shall be understood to include the performance of rites, the dissemination of one's beliefs in society directly or via the mass media, missionary work, acts of compassion and charity, religious instruction and education, ascetic establishments (monasteries, retreats, etc.), pilgrimage and other activities as defined by the appropriate system of beliefs and provided for by the statutes (regulations) of the given association.

Religious associations may be regional or centralized, with their own administrative bodies and other structural units as provided for by their statutes (regulations).

Article 18. The Religious Association as Juridical Person

A religious association of not less than ten adults shall assume the status of juridical person upon registration of its statutes (regulations) in the procedure stipulated in Article 20 of this law.

A religious association enjoying the status of juridical person may found other religious associations with the status of juridical person.

Article 19. The Statutes (Regulations) of Religious Associations

The statutes (regulations) of a religious association that has assumed the status of juridical person shall conform to the appropriate requirements of civil legislation.

Statutes (regulations) submitted for registration should indicate the following:

- the name and location and place of activities of the given association;

- the aims, goals, and general forms of the given association's activities;

- the procedure in which the given association shall be founded, its structure and administration;

- the sources of finance and the property arrangements both within the given association and between it and other associations with which its statutes (regulations) envisage collaboration;

- the procedure for making amendments and additions to the statutes (regulations).

All religious associations in the RSFSR, irrespective of the nature of their relationship, as set out in their statutes, to religious associations beyond the borders and authority of the RSFSR, shall operate in compliance with the legislation of the RSFSR.

Article 20. Registration of the Statutes (Regulations) of a Religious Association

Citizens who have founded a religious association shall, in order for it to gain the status of juridical person, submit an application with the statutes (regulations) attached to the Ministry of Justice of the RSFSR or its local authority (depending on the area within which the given association will conduct its activities).

Affiliation to a regional or centralized religious association shall be indicated in the statutes (regulations) and be confirmed by such association; in such circumstances the agencies of the Ministry of Justice shall be obliged to effect registration within one month.

In the absence of confirmation by a regional or centralized association, the appropriate agency of the Ministry of Justice shall consult the Advisory Council of the RSFSR Supreme Soviet, in which case the time limit for registration may be extended to three months.

Statutes (regulations) may be denied registration only should their contents contravene this law and other legislative acts of the RSFSR. A religious association may appeal in a court of law against refusal to register its statutes (regulations).

Article 21. Termination of the Activities of a Religious Association

The activities of a religious association may be terminated:

- upon decision by a general assembly of its founders, by the congress (conference) that founded it, and also in the event of its self-liquidation (collapse);

- by order of a court of law, should the activities of the religious association contravene its statutes (regulations) and existing legislation. Breach of legislation by individual members of a religious association shall not lead to liability of the association as a whole.

Article 22. Religious Rites and Ceremonies

Religious associations shall be entitled to found and maintain freely accessible sites for services or religious gatherings and also sites held in veneration by religions (places of pilgrimage).

Citizens and religious associations shall be entitled, without let or hindrance, to conduct services, religious rites, and ceremonies in houses of worship and on adjacent grounds, at places of pilgrimage, in establishments of religious associations, at cemeteries and crematoria, and in citizens' houses and flats.

Citizens shall be entitled to receive, acquire, and utilize holy artifacts and religious literature and also to perform and participate in religious rites at military units of all branches of the armed forces, in hospitals and clinics, in homes for the elderly and the disabled (of all categories), in children's homes and boarding schools, in remand detention centers and places of deprivation of freedom (including punishment and other cells).

The administrations of such establishments shall be obliged to ensure that citizens be able to exercise the freedom of worship, including by way of making available separate premises for the performance of rites and ceremonies, assisting in inviting members of the clergy and enabling them to converse freely with citizens.

In other places religious rites and ceremonies shall be conducted in the procedure established for gatherings, rallies, processions, and marches.

Article 23. Religious Literature and Items of a Religious Nature

Religious associations shall be entitled to produce, acquire, export, import, and distribute religious and holy artifacts and religious literature and other printed matter.

Religious associations shall enjoy the exclusive entitlement to found enterprises to produce literature for services and holy artifacts.

The issue of periodical publications of a religious nature and other religious literature not intended for use during services shall be effected pursuant to legislation on the press and mass media.

Article 24. Charitable, Cultural, and Educational Activities by Religious Associations

Religious associations shall be entitled to engage in charitable activities both independently and via public organizations (foundations). They shall be entitled to found cultural and educational organizations and also mass media outlets, including radio and television, on the conditions and in the procedure established for public associations in the RSFSR.

Article 25. International Communication and Contacts

Citizens and religious associations shall be entitled, on a group or individual basis, to establish and maintain international communication and direct contacts, including for pilgrimages, participation in gatherings and other religious events, in order to receive religious education; for such purposes they may invite foreign citizens.

III. THE ASSETS AND FINANCES OF RELIGIOUS ASSOCIATIONS

Article 26. The Assets of Religious Associations

Religious associations may own buildings, holy artifacts, sites of a productive, social, charitable, cultural, and educational nature, cash, and other assets essential for their activities.

Religious associations shall enjoy rights of ownership of assets acquired from their own or donated means, bequeathed by citizens, or transferred by organizations or the state, or otherwise lawfully acquired.

Religious associations shall be entitled to own assets abroad.

Terms for the maintenance by religious associations of sites and artifacts that are historical and cultural landmarks shall be agreed upon with the appropriate cultural authorities (departments). The state shall render financial assistance in the restoration of houses of worship that are of historical and cultural import.

Article 27. Use of Assets Belonging to the State, Public Associations, and Citizens

Religious associations shall be entitled to use for their own needs and pursuant to their statutes (regulations) grounds, buildings, and assets made available to them on a contractual basis by the state and public organizations and also by citizens.

The use of land by religious associations shall take place in the procedure established by legislation of the RSFSR.

Article 28. Production and Commercial Activities of Religious Associations

Religious associations shall be entitled, pursuant to their statutes (regulations) and legislation of the RSFSR and members of the federation, to establish enterprises with the status of juridical person for purposes of manufacturing, restoration, artistic, agricultural, and other activities.

Article 29. Labor Relations of Citizens in Religious Associations, at their Enterprises and Establishments

Religious associations, and also enterprises and establishments founded by them, shall be entitled to employ people to work for them.

Remuneration and other terms of labor of employees shall be determined by the religious association in question upon agreement with the employee and be indicated in the employment contract. The religious association shall be obliged to register the employment contract in the proper procedure and effect the established deductions to the state budget.

Labor legislation shall apply to citizens working to contract at religious associations in the same way as to workers and employees of state and public enterprises, establishments, and organizations.

The incomes of citizens, including members of the clergy, working at religious associations and their enterprises and establishments shall be subject to taxation at the rates in force for employed persons.

Article 30. Taxation of Religious Associations

Assets and financial means donated to religious associations, and also all money donated by citizens, shall not be subject to taxation.

Profits from manufacturing activities on the basis of assets of religious associations, with the exception of proceeds allocated for charitable, cultural, and educational purposes, shall be subject to taxation pursuant to legislation of the RSFSR in the procedure established for enterprises of public organizations.

Article 31. Social Provision and Social Insurance of Employees of Religious Associations

Citizens, including members of the clergy, working at religious associations and enterprises and establishments thereof shall enjoy social provision and social insurance equal to workers and employees of state and public enterprises, establishments, and organizations.

To this end, religious associations and their enterprises and establishments shall make payments to the state social insurance and provision funds in the procedure and amounts established for public organizations.

All citizens working at religious associations and enterprises and establishments thereof shall be assigned and receive an ordinary state pension.

Article 32. Disposal of the Assets of Religious Associations upon Closure

Subsequent to the cessation by a religious association of its activities, assets made available for its use by state, public, and other organizations shall be returned to their former owners.

Upon cessation by a religious association of its activities, assets in its possession shall be disposed of pursuant to its statutes (regulations) and existing legislation.

Upon the absence of a successor in rights, assets shall be transferred to the state.

First Deputy Chairman of the RSFSR Supreme Soviet

R I Khasbulatov

Moscow, RSFSR House of Soviets, 25 October 1990

Ministry of the Internal Affairs of the USSR

Guidelines for Correctional Labor Facilities Relating to Relations with Religious Organizations and Ministers

1. In accordance with Article 55 of the USSR Constitution, every citizen of the USSR has the right to profess any religion and to conduct religious worship. However, to this day, existing correctional labor legislation and the USSR Ministry of Internal Affairs normative acts do not define how convicted persons can exercise their right to freedom of conscience. At the same time, correctional labor facilities of some Ministries of Internal Affairs and Departments of Internal Affairs, interacting with religious organizations and ministers in order to provide moral support to convicted persons and to help their social adjustment after release from prison, have provided positive results.

2. Determining the guidelines for interaction with religious organizations, the USSR Ministry of Internal Affairs recommends that they be based on the following principles:

2.1. Cooperating with religious ministers and using their potential in ways that do not run counter to the USSR Constitution, when disseminating among convicted persons basic elements of enlightenment for their moral education, and by eradicating attitudes that are not in line with the socialist way of life.

2.2. Freedom of conscience and religion.

2.3. Making it possible for every convicted person to choose a religion or to be an atheist, to profess or not to profess any religion.

2.4. Voluntary participation on the part of representatives of religious organizations in providing social assistance to convicted persons in correctional labor facilities and to people exonerated from punishment.

2.5. Noninterference on the part of religious organizations or their representatives in the administration of the correctional labor facilities in order to enforce criminal convictions.

2.6. The established regime for the serving of the sentence and the requirements of the internal regulations of the correctional labor facilities must be complied with during religious worship and ceremonies, and the rights of other persons in correctional facilities must not be impinged upon.

2.7. In providing social assistance to convicted persons, all religious organizations and their representatives must practice *glasnost* in their work and have equal opportunities.

2.8. Forms of cooperation in the framework of joint programs must be instituted.

3. Convicted believers cannot be barred from religious worship or from using objects of worship. In accordance with the established internal regulations for correctional labor facilities, they can wear crosses and other similar objects of worship made from non–precious metals. They can have religious books published in the USSR, given by clergy or by their relatives during their visits to correctional labor facilities, or received in parcels and packages that do not exceed the permitted weight.

In accordance with the established order, every convicted person has the right to request religious organizations to arrange a meeting with religious ministers.

Minors can be involved in religious rites and practices only with the consent of their parents or guardians and with the consent of the adolescents themselves.

Meetings with religious ministers are not counted as visits legally permitted to the convicted person.

4. Convicted persons do not have the right to invoke their religious convictions in order to shirk their civic duties and violate the requirements of the regime or for the serving of their sentence, or in order to avoid the daily schedule of the correctional labor facilities.

5. Representatives of registered religious organizations may visit correctional labor facilities to provide moral education for the believers on an individual basis.

A minister who has arrived for a meeting with a convicted person submits to the administration of the correctional labor facility a certificate proving that he is registered as a religious minister, made out by an authorized person from the Council for Religious Affairs, as well as an ID.

When representatives of religious organizations visit correctional labor facilities, the administration informs them of the established procedure for the meeting and ensures their security.

6. The administration of the correctional labor facility should recommend to the ministers that they work to create a favorable moral and psychological climate among the convicted persons and concentrate their efforts on the most difficult cases in terms of their educational potential.

Minister, Lieutenant General V. Bakatin
November 1989

Religion in Politics
and Culture

Clergy in Soviet Parliament

In 1989, for the first time since the October Revolution, seven clergymen were elected to the Soviet parliament, the Congress of People's Deputies. Patriarch Pimen of Moscow and All Russia (who died in 1990); Metropolitan Alexis of Leningrad and Novgorod (now Patriarch Alexis II of Moscow and All Russia); and Metropolitan Pitirim of Volokolamsk and Yuryev received their mandates from public organizations. Supreme Patriarch and Catholicos of All Armenians Vasken I; leader of the Muslims of Transcaucasia Sheikh-ul-Islam Allahshukur Pashazade; Mufti of Central Asia and Kazakhstan Mukhammadsadyk Mammayusuf; and an Orthodox priest from the Moldavian capital, Kishinev Pyotr Buburuz, were elected People's Deputies by direct vote in territorial districts. After the death of Patriarch Pimen, Metropolitan Filaret of Minsk and Belorussia was elected.

The Congress of People's Deputies, then the supreme organ of Soviet political power,[1] comprised 2,250 deputies. One-third of them were elected for a five-year term from public organizations and two-thirds by direct vote—750 from territorial electoral districts and 750 from union and autonomous republics, and autonomous regions and districts. The Congress was to meet once a year to address major constitutional, political, social, and economic issues. From among its members the Congress elected the Supreme Soviet, a bicameral body, comprising the Soviet of the Union and the Soviet of Nationalities. The latter was a standing legislative, executive, and supervisory body of state power that held its sessions in spring and fall.

Its predecessor, also a bicameral parliament, merely rubber-stamped decisions made by the Soviet leadership. Elections to it were conducted on a one-candidate-one-seat basis, which rendered the elections meaningless. By contrast, in elections held in the spring of 1989, electors could choose their deputy from among several candidates. The new approach dealt a devastating blow to a number of top Communist Party functionaries. Thus, Yuri Soloviev, alternate member of the Communist Party's Politburo, lost the election and soon resigned his job. Many of his colleagues from other major cities met the same fate. Throughout the country, over thirty first secretaries of regional party committees suffered defeat. Before long the very nature of proceedings in parliament changed; now there were heated debates, sharp exchanges, and a thorough consideration of future decisions in many commissions formed by deputies.

Events following the coup attempt in August 1991 and the changing relationship between the Union and Soviet republics have led to further change in the structure of political power, and it will be interesting to see how church/state relations develop. The election of clergy to Soviet parliament was perhaps a historical first step in ongoing and increasing cooperation.

Biographies and Platforms of Clergy elected to the Congress of People's Deputies

SUPREME PATRIARCH AND CATHOLICOS OF ALL ARMENIANS VASKEN I

Supreme Patriarch and Catholicos of All Armenians Vasken I was born on 20 September 1908 in Bucharest. He graduated from a German evangelical school in 1924 and Bucharest University in 1936. In 1943 he became a monk and was ordained archimandrite. At this time, he headed the Armenian diocese in Romania. In 1951 he was appointed bishop. In September 1955 he was elected the 130th Supreme Patriarch and Catholicos of All Armenians.

The election of an Armenian hierarch deputy gives yet another opportunity to raise at the highest state level matters of concern to our church, to speak about its pressing problems, and to solve them positively in accordance with the law.

Issues relating to our church have been and remain central to us. We raise them, keep them alive, and address them. With more than two million Armenians scattered throughout the world, high on our agenda is the task of promoting stronger ties with the spiritual center, the Holy Echmiadzin, with Armenians living abroad, with numerous public and cultural organizations of the diaspora. A major line of our work is, of course, our participation in the relief operations after the earthquake in Armenia. We have to make the best use of all the foreign aid we have received, in particular, from Armenian communities. It must be used effectively for the good of our people in reconstructing the damaged cities.

The processes described as *perestroika* and democratization are very dear to my heart. Their main objective is true socialism and a just society. This, of course, agrees with our Christian doctrine. As Christians, we believe that of all ideologies the idea of socialism comes closest to the Christian gospel.

I would like to make the following point on the subject of democracy. Democracy, of course, means that every citizen has the right to express himself freely. However, democracy has another dimension that we sometimes overlook: every citizen must respect the views of others, sometimes different from his own. That is to say, democracy has two aspects, and no one can claim that only what he says is true.

It is my belief that the conflict between the Armenians and the Azerbaijanis is not a quarrel between Christians and Muslims. We respect Islam as one of the world's major religions and believe that Muslims also have respect for Christians. As a Christian and head of the church, I wish with all my heart that fraternal and friendly relations between the Armenians and the Azerbaijanis be restored in the spirit of internationalism, which has been one of the pillars of the Soviet state from the very first day of its existence. Of course, the spirit of internationalism must be properly understood and justice must triumph. We Armenians, no matter where we are—in or outside Armenia—must reject extremism and intolerance, be it nationalistic or religious. Intolerance of any kind does not have and cannot have any future in the world. It represents ignorance, backwardness, and sometimes even barbarism. It is unhealthy and transient. The future belongs to peace, harmony, patient dialogue, and creative work by nations and governments.

PATRIARCH ALEXIS II OF
MOSCOW AND ALL RUSSIA

Patriarch Alexis II of Moscow and All Russia (known secularly as Alexey Ridiger) was born in 1929 in Tallinn, in Estonia. In 1953 he graduated from the Leningrad Theological Academy with a degree in theology. He was professed in 1964 at the Holy Trinity-St. Sergiy Laura. That same year he became a bishop and soon after that an archbishop. In 1968 he was ordained metropolitan. At different times he served as bishop in the Department of the External Church Relations of the Moscow Patriarchate, in the Education and Pensions Committees of the Russian Orthodox Church, and as the administrator of the Moscow Patriarchate. In 1986 he became metropolitan of Leningrad and Novgorod and manager of the Tallinn diocese.

In 1990, upon the death of Patriarch Pimen, he was elected Patriarch Alexis II of Moscow and All Russia. Patriarch Alexis is a permanent member of the Holy Synod of the Russian Orthodox Church.

He was a candidate of the Soviet Mercy and Health Fund.

The most important lesson that our society has learned from its recent past is that there is an intimate link between morality and social progress. As is known, our history has borne out the old truth that coercive methods, disregard for human morality, conscience, intellect, moral choice, and inner freedom doom even the most fascinating social projects. That is why the sorry plight of our economy and public life today has not been brought on by ill will or bad expert advice. Rather this has happened because our society has become spiritually impoverished.

Relying on the force of morality and moral precepts, we shall bring down the barriers that divide people and win back alienated souls. This will bring together brothers and sisters in the quest for a happy future for us and our children. With reborn morality, we shall be tolerant of one another and kind to the needy, the sick, the disabled, the old, and the lonely; we shall treat nature with care, because contemptuous abuse of nature is a clear sign of egoism and a sick soul.

METROPOLITAN PITIRIM

Metropolitan Pitirim of Volokolamsk and Yuryev (his secular name is Konstantin Nechayev) was born on 8 January 1926 in the city of Kozlov (now Michurinsk), Tambov region, to the family of a priest. He graduated from the Moscow Theological Academy. In 1957 he was ordained bishop. In 1961 he became archbishop, and in 1987 metropolitan. He heads the Publishing Department of the Moscow Patriarchate. Metropolitan Pitirim is a member of the Central Council of the Union of the Soviet Friendship Societies, vice-president of the Italy-USSR Friendship Society, member of the board of the USSR-Australia and USSR-Sweden Friendship Societies. He is also a member of the Council of Directors of the International Fund for the Survival and Advancement of Mankind.

Since 1986 Metropolitan Pitirim has been on the board of the Soviet Culture Fund.

Both spirituality and dignity find expression in specific manifestations of the individual's moral potential—in concrete actions, and in one's attitude toward nature, people, and the material world. It is painful to acknowledge that both these concepts, which I can hardly differentiate—spirituality and dignity—have lost much of their value. Relations among many people are in disarray. Ethnic problems have reached conflict proportions. We see priceless cultural landmarks lying in ruins, many with no hope of being restored.

However, our principal asset is people. That is why resurrecting the individual endowed with a boundless potential to create is our top priority.

Rather than complain about darkness, better to light one candle. This truism fully applies to the task of reviving and cultivating the human soul, uplifting human dignity. If the land is returned to its original owners, the peasants, I am sure that people will be strong enough in body and spirit to rebuild their ancestral homes, to make the land fertile again, and to reawaken the moral sense. People can be kind, merciful, and hard working, radiating into the world around them the warmth of the soul. Hardships of daily life, no matter how severe, cannot break a strong spirit. The history of Russia is a never-ending story of a people waging a courageous battle for their souls and morality in the face of external calamities.

Many millions of our country's citizens have accumulated and preserved a vast spiritual potential through faith. However, when the church could not play an active social role, this potential was artificially frozen and in fact went to waste. I am convinced that the creative energy of believers can help bring about a spiritual rebirth of the nation. However, to achieve this, the teaching of the church must become accessible to everyone from childhood.

By way of a specific example I would like to refer to a program of cooperation being elaborated for the monastery and church parishes of Volokolamsk and the outlying areas of the Moscow region. This program, when fully implemented, can promote across-the-board development of central Russia—the historical and spiritual center for the unification of the nations and nationalities of our homeland.

In the past Russian monasteries were places where spiritual life and mercy flourished; they were eloquent examples of the rational use of nature; here cultural landmarks saw the light of day and morality has been kept alive. Today, if conditions are right, they can also contribute toward our common cause of *perestroika*.

The problems of soldiers back from Afghanistan pain our conscience. It is our duty to help all of them without exception to participate fully in creative work. To this end, among other things, a national rehabilitation center for war invalids should be established.

ARCHPRIEST PYOTR BUBURUZ

Archpriest Pyotr Buburuz was born on 27 September 1937 in the village of Durleshty in the Strashenk Region of Moldavia into a family of Orthodox Moldavian peasants. In 1965 he graduated from the Leningrad Theological Academy. Since 1968 he has been a clergyman at Kishinev Cathedral and has been in charge of the Kishinev diocese archives.

In 1972 he received his Master of Theology degree for his thesis, "The Apostolic Tradition of St. Hippolytus of Rome." From 1975 to 1978 he was a trainee at the Catholic Institute in Paris.

In January 1989 he was elected member of the board of the Moldavian Culture Fund.

My manifesto is based on the three aspects of the concept *ecology:* the ecology of the soul, the ecology of nature, and the ecology of culture. That is why, being a son of the church and my country, I shall champion the following:

1. An atmosphere in society promoting true freedom of the spirit and conscience. In this respect a new law on the freedom of conscience must play a major role. This process must run parallel to the formation of a state based on the rule of law in which adopted legislation is equally binding for all members of society, regardless of rank or position.

2. A greater role for the church in social life through religious instruction and education so as to help eradicate evils destructive to the personality and society, such as corruption, nepotism, enmity, egoism, greed, hypocrisy, falsehood, deception, alcohol abuse, and other vices well known to us from our everyday life.

3. Easing the lot of those who suffer, the disabled, the lonely elderly, orphans, war veterans, widows, and all ill-fated people. By taking care of fellow human beings we shall be manifesting love for our neighbors and thereby fulfilling the evangelical beatitude—blessed are the merciful, for they shall obtain mercy.

4. Preservation, renovation, and restoration of historical and cultural landmarks of the people. They represent our spiritual legacy, and we must preserve it well and hand it over to those who will come after us. The churches and monasteries that are still closed down must be returned to their true owner—the people, who perhaps were materially poor at the time they were built but were rich in spirit. All articles of church art (ancient manuscripts, books, icons, shrouds of Christ, church plates) must be returned to those who made them and to whom they properly belong.

5. Revival of cultural and educational traditions of the Russian Orthodox Church in Moldavia; the printing of a new edition of the Bible and other church educational literature; the publication of a church journal and calendars in the Moldavian language; the opening of a theological academy in Kishinev; the establishment of a church and archaeological museum and a museum of ancient church books, as well as an iconographic center to study icon-painting traditions in Moldavia and to meet current needs of churches and believers; the opening of Sunday and other schools where theology can be taught.

6. Clean water, land, and air. Only a healthy environment can nurture pure human souls and save us from the risk of direct or indirect poisoning.

7. Peace throughout the world, not only somewhere in other countries, but in my homeland, our cities and villages, and in our souls. I shall advocate peaceful and fair solutions to international problems. We must all live in peace; faith and religion fill us with love for one another and move us to mutual understanding.

8. I shall advocate that our country, just as all civilized countries, respect religious festivals, that people be given two to three days off to celebrate Christmas and Easter when they can forget their daily worries, stay with their families, or visit their relatives, especially those who are sick or elderly. This would promote the revival of national traditions, consolidate people, and help them know each other better and trust one another more.

SHEIKH-UL-ISLAM ALLAHSHUKUR
PASHAZADE

Sheikh-ul-islam Allahshukur Pashazade was born in 1949 in the village of Gil in the Lenkoran region of Azerbaijan, on the border with Iran, into the large family of an orthodox Muslim. After graduating from high school he entered the Mir-Arab madrasah *(high religious school) in Bukhara and graduated from it in 1971. In 1975 he completed his education at the Imam al-Bukhari Islamic Institute in Tashkent. He was deputy head, and in 1980 he became head, of the Spiritual Directorate of the Muslims of Transcaucasia.*

Sheikh-ul-islam Allahshukur Pashazade has been elected corresponding member of the Jordanian Royal Academy of Islamic Civilization.

For me serving my country and my people is a sacred duty and a great honor. The words of the Prophet (may Allah bless and greet Him!) come to mind: loving our country is part of our faith.

Today, to love our country means to face up to the tough challenges confronting it, for every person to make a real contribution to *perestroika*. Our life and the future of our children depend on the success of *perestroika*. If we do not grasp this truth, our dreams for a better life will remain just that—dreams.

I believe that my mission as a People's Deputy is first of all to do my best to advance *perestroika* and, consequently, to raise the level and quality of the people's life.

How do I see my work as a People's Deputy? In the first place it should not be assumed that since I am a man of religion I shall look out only for the interests of believers. As sheikh-ul-islam, I am duty bound to do this in any case. It is a different matter that as a deputy I shall be in a better position to fulfill my duty.

However, a People's Deputy must represent all his fellow citizens, without drawing a distinction among them, making the interests and aspirations of all people his own. The interests of a nation are made up of the interests of each individual. To be attentive to peoples' needs, to help them solve problems of concern to them—this, I believe, is the mission of a deputy.

To be a People's Deputy means to share the concerns of the entire republic. Today's principal challenge is to stabilize the situation in the region and to prevent ethnic conflicts. Every effort must be made to eliminate the differences in our society. We should remember that prosperity and peace on earth begin with prosperity and peace at home.

We have plans to build an old people's home at a mosque and take full charge of the people there. Of course, this is not enough. I think that it is necessary to elaborate an integrated program of Mercy. Thousands and thousands of grateful people who need daily help would benefit from it.

MUFTI MUKHAMMADSADYK MAMMAYUSUF

Mufti Mukhammadsadyk Mammayusuf was born in 1952 in the Andijan region of the Uzbek Republic into the family of an imam-khatyb of the local mosque. He studied at the Mir-Arab madrasah *in Bukhara and later at the Imam al-Bukhari Islam Institute in Tashkent. He continued his religious education in Tripoli. After his return to Tashkent, he worked for two years in the International Department of the Muslim Religious Board for Central Asia and Kazakhstan. In 1982 he became prorector of the Imam al-Bukhari Islamic Institute in Tashkent, and in 1987 he was appointed its rector. In 1989, when Mufti Babakhan resigned, the Tashkent* kurultai *(meeting) elected him Mufti, Chairman of the Muslim Religious Board for Central Asia and Kazakhstan.*

I would strive to ensure that Soviet Muslims make an important contribution to the survival of humankind, the preservation of the sacred gift of life, the prevention of a nuclear catastrophe, and a general improvement in international relations. We shall work to implement these goals through active involvement in the activities of Soviet and international peace, Muslim, and other religious organizations.

On the home front ethnic relations are at the top of my agenda. We shall promote friendship between all nationalities since our religion preaches fraternity and unity of nations. Under no circumstance shall events similar to those that have occurred in Nagorno-Karabakh [the location of recent bloody conflict between Armenians and Azerbaijanians] be allowed to happen. Religious figures can and must participate actively in solving ethnic problems that have accumulated.

I am deeply concerned by the grave environmental situation in Central Asia, and as a deputy I intend to work to radically improve it. I advocate greater material aid and spiritual guidance to orphan children and the adoption of specific measures to bring down infant mortality rates in the republics of Central Asia.

My program includes better religious instruction in the family, the publication of the Holy Koran in the Uzbek language, and assistance to the faithful on their pilgrimage. I have promised my electors in two densely populated districts of Tashkent that I will take steps to increase the pace of housing construction there. I will consider keeping this promise one of my most important responsibilities as deputy.

METROPOLITAN FILARET OF
MINSK AND BELORUSSIA

Metropolitan Filaret, newly elected member of the Soviet Parliament (after Patriarch Pimen's death), was born in Moscow in 1935 (secular name Kirill Vakhromeyev), graduated from Moscow Seminary and then the Academy. Later he became rector of both theological schools. For a time, His Eminence held the posts of Patriarchal Exarch to Western Europe, and chairman of the Department for External Church Relations of the Moscow Patriarchate. Metropolitan Filaret is a permanent member of the Holy Synod of the Russian Orthodox Church.

A critical moment has arrived, demanding that people think and act in a new way. We are in dire need of social, scientific, and moral bearings and values, which would serve as a sound basis for determining how we should act in the changing conditions of our existence. We need further socioeconomic development of society and perfection of democracy.

Our pastoral activities are largely devoted to strengthening the civic responsibility of religious people, their conscientious attitude toward work, the undeviating observance of high ethical standards in family and public life.

Religion and Charity in
Soviet Society

MOTHER TERESA
OPENS THE DOOR TO MERCY

There is no question that the revival of mercy in Soviet society was made possible due to *perestroika*, which opened a new dimension of humanism in social relations. But in practical terms, the efforts of Mother Teresa laid the foundations for such charitable work.

For decades, mercy and charity were taboo in the Soviet lexicon. Western propaganda of compassion for the sick and the unhappy was regarded as a ploy designed to distract the working people from revolutionary struggle. Mercy and charity were condemned as leftovers for the poor from the table of the rich. In line with the official policy it was assumed that in the socialist society the sick and the needy were to be taken care of by governmental and local institutions. The church was officially barred in 1929 from contributing to the cause of mercy and charity. It was argued that the church would use charity to strengthen its influence, perpetrate wickedness, and encroach upon the state of workers and peasants. When Mother Teresa was awarded the Nobel Peace Prize in 1979, her name was not even mentioned in the press. Instead the mass media gleefully reported news about crooks who were making millions under the smoke screen of charity.

What has happened since then could only happen at a time of *perestroika*. The Soviet Peace Committee invited Mother Teresa to come to Moscow in 1986. The conference hall was packed. She spoke in a slow and quiet voice, but there was profound silence as the audience listened to every word she said. She reminded listeners that humanity hungers not only for bread, but also for love. She spoke of people afflicted with leprosy and AIDS, who are rejected by society, abandoned even by their relatives, and in great need of help and compassion. Even small gestures are enough, she said, but they should manifest love. Great deeds, she concluded, grow from modest actions and bear good fruit.

Welcoming Mother Teresa on her first visit to the Soviet Union, Metropolitan Filaret of Minsk and Belorussia noted that clergy in the Soviet Union previously knew very little about her work or "the great mission" of mercy for the good of man. "Let me be quite frank and say that the example of your service has generated new thoughts and emotions in us," he said.

Some governmental and Communist Party bureaucrats were shocked when Mother Teresa proposed to send four sisters to work permanently in the Soviet Union, but she would not give up. She was firm yet tactful and skillfully used her diplomatic prowess to have her way. By the time that her project had begun, several new charitable initiatives had already been launched in Moscow.

THE ARMENIAN EARTHQUAKE OF 1988

The Armenian earthquake on 7 December 1988 also helped to change the attitude toward relief programs in Soviet society. In 1966, when a similar earthquake hit the city of Tashkent, the Soviet Union flatly rejected any help from foreign countries. Even the number of victims was a closely guarded secret. In 1988, the situation was radically different. Doctors, rescue teams, and later construction workers came from all parts of the world. The generous help provided by all religious organizations in the Soviet Union and abroad was received with much gratitude.

Among the first volunteers to Armenia was, of course, Mother Teresa. Together with her sisters she set up a charity center in the city of Spitak, which had been completely destroyed. Later she organized a twenty-four-hour service at a hospital in the city of Yerevan, where the victims of the earthquake had been taken for treatment. In recognition of her great service, the Supreme Patriarch and Catholicos of All Armenians Vasken I awarded Mother Teresa the Order of Narses Shurali, the highest distinction of the Armenian Apostolic Church.

When the situation in Armenia had improved, Mother Teresa, accompanied by five nuns, went to the city of Tbilisi in Georgia. Numbers of people there had sustained injuries when troops had used violence to disperse a peaceful demonstration in the center of the city. Here too Mother Teresa set up a charity center. In the Sioni Cathedral, His Holiness and Beatitude Catholicos-Patriarch Ilia II awarded Mother Teresa the Order of St. George, the highest distinction of the Georgian Orthodox Church.

Back in Moscow, Mother Teresa and her sisters also set up two centers in hospitals and pledged to support a home for the elderly. When Mother Teresa left for Calcutta, the sisters stayed behind to carry on their noble work of mercy and charity.

From such a start, charitable work in Soviet society is growing rapidly—buoyed in particular by support from religious communities.

SOVIET MERCY AND HEALTH FUND

When the Soviet Mercy and Health Fund was set up, several religious leaders were among the first people elected to sit on its board: Metropolitan Alexis of Leningrad and Novgorod (now Patriarch of Moscow and All Russia), permanent member of the Holy Synod of the Russian Orthodox Church; Mufti Talgat Tadjutdin, chairman of the Muslim Religious Board for the European Part of the USSR and Siberia; and Pastor Mikhail Kulakov, chairman of the Council of the Adventist Church of the Russian Federation. Regional branches of the fund have now been set up all over the country, and many religious leaders have been elected to serve on the governing bodies of these organizations. These religious leaders are active in efforts to collect money, to provide help to those who need it, and to promote better understanding in Soviet Society of charity issues.

Professor Svyatoslav Fedorov, a leading specialist in eye microsurgery, has been elected chairman of the board of the Soviet Mercy and Health Fund and has put forward a radical program of action. Says Fedorov: "The Soviet Mercy and Health Fund has been set up, first of all, in order to provide social assistance to the needy and to patch up the holes in the fabric of our society that have appeared because the theoretical tenets of socialism have not been properly thought out. Second, it has been set up to help more people become friends and make them understand that a person who helps another is the first to benefit from the good work."

Apart from the Soviet Mercy and Health Fund, other charitable organizations also have emerged. One such agency is the Soviet Children's Fund named after V. I. Lenin, whose chairman is writer Albert Likhanov.

CHRISTIAN CHARITABLE ORGANIZATIONS

In the Lithuanian city of Kaunas the first constituent congress of the women's Catholic organization Caritas took place. Delegates spoke about their duty as Christian believers to alleviate people's suffering; help old people, orphans, and the sick; to fight alcohol abuse, drug addiction, and prostitution; and to assist people in distress. The congress decided to uphold the family, promote motherhood, and condemn abortion. Delegates emphasized that it is necessary to work toward a healthy society and to promote the moral education of the younger generation. For this purpose, they recommended that classes of religious instruction should be introduced into school curricula and high school students should be taught a course in ethics. The chief doctor of the central hospital in the city of Kaunas told the congress that he would open the hospital's doors to nuns and priests and all members of Caritas who were prepared to offer help to the sick.

In 1989 a charitable organization called The Latvian Christian Mission was set up in the Baltic Republic of Latvia. Its president is Pastor Vadim Kovalev, Presbyter of the Church of the Evangelist Christian Baptists in the city of Ogre. The official emblem of the mission is both simple and expressive. It features the Latin letter *M*, the first letter in the words *mission* and *mercy*, inside the contours of the human heart with a superimposed cross, the symbol of Christianity. So far the mission has about three hundred members—Lutherans, Baptists, and Pentecostals—who work in hospitals, kindergartens, and old people's homes. The mission has been providing free food for about four hundred people. It has begun work with convicts serving prison sentences, and the results have been very encouraging. Also, the mission has launched a three-year course for Christian nurses. In addition to medical subjects, the curriculum includes lectures on biblical and moral subjects.

A fund for social assistance named after Doctor F. P. Gaaz has been set up in the Ukrainian city of Odessa on the Black Sea coast. Christians from different denominations participated in setting up this fund. Its mission is to alleviate the plight of the elderly and to provide help and medical aid to disabled persons, orphans, and mothers with many children. A mercy center is being set up in an ancient two-story building, which will be used as a boarding house for the elderly and as a research center to study the social, psychological, and medical problems of old age. In the kitchen situated on the premises a qualified dietitian will supervise the preparation of food to be distributed among elderly persons who live alone.

Eighteen sisters of the Moscow Baptist Church have been involved in charity and relief work at the gerontological department of the Kaschenko Psychiatric Clinic in Moscow. At first, the volunteers were divided into two groups, with two women alternately working morning and evening shifts in every department and spending an average of six hours a day in the clinic. However, it soon became clear that the number of nurses was not enough, and during church services preachers made frequent appeals to the members of their congregations to volunteer and to devote themselves to the service of those who suffer. The number of Christian sisters who decided to become nurses began to grow rapidly. They helped to clean up rooms, clothed and fed the patients, and took them out for walks. Sisters spent a lot of time with them talking, reading the Bible, and praying together.

Recently, Moscow's Baptists have launched a new project. They are now offering help to the Children's City Hospital Number 41, where boys and girls with genetic face and jaw deformities receive treatment on an in-patient basis. Some of the children in the hospital have been abandoned by their parents. About thirty male and female nurses work shifts, feeding and clothing children and taking them out for walks. On Easter each child is given toys and other gifts.

In February 1989 the presbyter of the Moscow Church, Mikhail Zhidkov, received a delegation of children from Boarding School Number 28. Nearly 50 percent of the six hundred children living there had been abandoned by parents. The principal of the school asked the Baptist Church for help, and twenty members of the congregation immediately answered his appeal. They assist the staff, bathing children, taking them out for walks, and reading books to them. The church has also offered help in repairing wheelchairs, organizing an amateur woodworking shop, and collecting books for a library.

The Seventh-Day Adventists are also contributing to the cause of mercy and charity. Adventists support the neurological department of the Moscow City Clinical Hospital Number 4, where they work as nurses on a day-to-day basis. In the Yasnogorsk district of the Tula region Seventh-Day Adventists have built a new building for the Zhelibinsk boarding school for mentally retarded children. In addition to classrooms, the new building also houses a spacious gymnasium. But the church now has other far-reaching plans, including a rehabilitation center for disabled children, a food factory, and an agricultural cooperative, which will provide food not only for members of the congregation, but also for many other people in hospitals and in homes for the elderly.

ORTHODOX CHRISTIAN
CHARITABLE EFFORTS

The Council of the Hierarchs of the Russian Orthodox Church, held in time for the celebrations of the four hundredth anniversary of the Russian Patriarchate in 1989 put a heavy emphasis on the charitable mission of the church, its involvement in the struggle against alcohol abuse, drug addiction, and other social problems. Many Russian Orthodox diocesan administrations, parishes, and monasteries are increasingly involved in charity programs, and new Orthodox charitable organizations are forming.

Doctor Alexey Masteropulo heads a new charitable association of Orthodox Christians. According to Masteropulo, early appeals from the Orthodox clergy for the faithful to dedicate themselves to work in clinics and hospitals drew predominantly retired people and thus mercy services could not be sustained.

"It was then that the idea of an association, a charitable public organization, was put forward by a group of intellectuals belonging to the Orthodox Christian Church," said Masteropulo. "Significantly enough, when young orthodox believers with different educational and professional backgrounds read our charter, they were ready to leave their jobs and work in the association full time. It is hard to say whether their decision represented a form of protest against the domination of the state and was motivated by religious considerations, or whether it was prompted by the desire to do charitable work side by side with people who share their ideals."

To get income to undergird its charitable acts, at present, the association is setting up several enterprises in which over 50 percent of the jobs are given to disabled persons and all profit donated to charity.

The association plans eventually to set up its own polyclinic and diagnostic center, a home for the elderly, a shelter and workshops for drug addicts and a sisterhood of Christian mercy with a medical vocational school attached to it.

OTHER MINISTRIES

In recent years churches in the Soviet Union and the United States have cooperated in organizing seminars on the church and alcohol and drug abuse. Seminars have been held in both Moscow and New York. The Russian Orthodox Church has also launched a major campaign to fight drugs and alcohol abuse on a national scale. Several clergy attended the All-Union Conference of Chief Narcologists and Chief Doctors of Narcological Clinics, which was held in the city of Volgograd at the beginning of October 1989.

Since 1989 the Russian Orthodox Church and the Baptist and Adventist communities have been providing moral support for convicts serving prison sentences. Here is Hieromonk Sergiy, one of the pioneers of this noble service, relating his impressions after his first visit to a prison.

"It was time for dinner, and as we walked in, accompanied by prison guards, profound silence fell in the mess hall. I placed myself at an iron-barred window. The light of the setting sun was on the faces of the people sitting at the tables. Wrinkled foreheads, gloomy eyebrows, hard-set mouths, and an earthy color of the skin, something you do not see anywhere else—the visible signs of prison life. There was a mixed reaction to my sermon. Some prisoners smiled in disbelief, others looked as if they could not care less. But there were still other people whose eyes showed repentance and long-suppressed pain, not because there were no words to give vent to it, but because there was nobody who was prepared to listen and alleviate their suffering. I saw those eyes and I realized that I was needed.

"Not only convicts needed me. I saw that the prison authorities were very excited about my visit. This came through very clearly in their warm welcome and the respect they showed for me. They readily accepted my proposal to work together to win the minds of the convicts, and I know they were sincere when they invited me to come again.

"I believe our help in prisons would prove beneficial not only for convicts. Prison guards work under tremendous stress, because their job is among the least prestigious in society today. They need the word of the clergy and the beneficent assistance of the church too. Without either their hearts will not stand the strain, or they will turn into stone. When I visited old people's homes and watched the staff go about their work there, I drew the conclusion that they are either profoundly religious people filled with compassion for their patients, or they have turned into stone and are no longer moved by any suffering. I think that in prisons the situation is largely similar."

Religious Programs
on Radio and Television

Today, central and local radio and TV stations openly broadcast religious programs in the Soviet republics. This is a remarkable contrast to times prior to *perestroika* when the rare use of clergy by the media was generally an occasion for sensationalism and propaganda. But still problems exist. There is criticism that the media, particularly central television, gives preference to Christian programming over that of Muslims, Jews, or other religious groups.

RADIO PROGRAMMING

In January 1989, Radio Moscow World Service began broadcasting regular Russian language programs for Christians. They air every Sunday afternoon and are rebroadcast three times on Monday. They can be received throughout the Soviet republics and abroad.

The first broadcast began with an address by His Holiness Patriarch Pimen of Moscow and All Russia, who said,

> The past year has been marked by significant events. Relying on the processes of *glasnost* and democratization, our country is reconsidering many things in its life. This process influences favorably relations between the church and the state. There has been a marked improvement in the international situation. The new thinking is becoming firmly established in politics and diplomacy.

The program includes the Sunday sermon, which usually runs for about eight to ten minutes. Sermons are prerecorded and address a wide range of subjects. Religious holidays, acts of Jesus Christ, and stories of holy people have all been treated as sermon topics. Sermons have been read by representative clergy from Orthodox, Baptist, Seventh-Day Adventist, and other churches.

Vitaly Kulikov, the pastor of an Evangelical Christian Baptist Church, began a recent Easter sermon this way: "Dear brothers and sisters, recently the whole

Christian world celebrated Christ's Easter. . . . Allow me therefore to extend to you an ancient Christian greeting: Christ is risen!"

After preaching from Luke 24 on the hope provided Christians through the resurrections, Pastor Kulikov concluded,

> Let the Resurrection of Christ live in the hearts,
>> And let it dispel doubt and fear.
>> He is risen,
>> And the darkness of the night has perished forever.
>> He is truly risen in his glory!
>> Amen!

After the Sunday sermon, the program usually includes some material on the life of the church. For example, recent broadcasts have included the Divine Service from the Volokolamsk cathedral, an interview with the mother superior of the Tolga Convent Varvara, and a story about the life of seminarians. Church participation in humanitarian actions is also featured prominently. Upon agreement with the Publishing Department of the Moscow Patriarchate, reviews of the weekly *Moscow Church Bulletin* are broadcast regularly.

Moscow Radio kept its listeners informed about the election of religious figures to the Congress of People's Deputies, provided extensive coverage of their participation in the work of the Congress, and broadcast interviews with them when that supreme organ of Soviet state power was in session.

TELEVISION PROGRAMMING

Virtually every day national television broadcasts various programs in which clergy participate. They include a variety of discussion, roundtables and intercontinental satellite links. In time of major religious festivals reports come on the air live.

At present the possibility of regular religious programs on national television is being considered. Viewers have already had an opportunity to watch the Sunday sermon by Metropolitan Pitirim of Volokolamsk and Yuryev.

Metropolitan Filaret of Minsk and Belorussia, a permanent member of the Holy Synod of the Russian Orthodox Church and head of the Department for External Church Relations of the Moscow Patriarchate, had the following comments to make about these changes:

"For a long time our bureaucrats—and there is no shortage of them in the country—could not understand that the human spirit needs to communicate with the church. Today there is awareness of this need. . . . Suppose the time will come when the church is given (television) airtime. What will it offer its viewers? First of all, of course, informational programs. There are many bedridden believers in our

country. For them, television is the only window on the world, and they also want
to watch liturgies and know how a specific religious holiday is celebrated.

"There is a word in the language that is rarely used in the secular world. It is
catechization, which means 'enlightenment.' It would be good to have programs on
the fundamental truths of faith in the Orthodox, Catholic, and Evangelical confessions, and to provide each church with an opportunity to tell its story—its history
and role in world culture. This would be interesting and educational for nonbelievers
and would probably become an integral part of believers' viewing. Today, thinking
about a state based on the rule of law, we should start with the little things. If my
fellow countrymen, indifferent to religion, can always find something they want to
see in the programming, believers, as citizens enjoying full rights in their homeland,
must also have a similar right to choose. Religious programming will restore equality
among members of the society, and television programs will meet their most diverse
spiritual needs."

Religious Groups in
Today's Soviet Republics

Divine service at the Kiev-Pechery Laura, founded in 1051 and returned to the Russian Orthodox Church in 1988.

The Russian Orthodox Church

Statistics: The Russian Orthodox Church has some 50 million believers; 12,000 churches; 13,000 clergy; 107 active monasteries with more than 2,500 monks; and 26 seminaries and academies with more than 3,000 students.

Organization: The Church is run by the Holy Synod headed by Patriarch Aleksis II, elected at the 1990 Local Council. The Local Council is the supreme body of power, but according to new rules, a number of key questions are now to be decided by the Bishop Council. The administrative center of the Church is located in St. Daniel's Monastery, which is also the residence of the Patriarch.

Brief History: The Russian Orthodox Church marks its beginning and the spread of Christianity through Russia from the Baptism of Rus in 988, a year after St. Grand Prince Vladimir accepted the faith. The Russian Church was initially under the jurisdiction of the Church of Constantinople and had the status of a Metropolinate. In 1589 it became autocephalous.

After the Russian Revolution the Church was brutally victimized. By the beginning of the Second World War there existed only a few temples, the Holy Synod did not function, and there were only two bishops free. The authorities ceased to support even the obedient schismatic renovation church. During the war the Church began to regain its status, but in the early sixties it suffered a fresh blow, with the closing of more than half of its acting temples. Under *perestroika*, many temples, monasteries, and theological schools began to open, and religious literature came out in large editions.

Current Situation and Problems: Clergy are now taking part in the political and social life of society on all levels. The church hierarchy is being renewed, although most bishops served before *perestroika* days. Lately some Russian Orthodox communities have been distancing themselves from the jurisdiction of the Moscow Patriarchate and joining the Russian Church abroad. There have been disputes over church property and a large number of temples in the Ukraine have been put under the jurisdiction of the Ukrainian Autocephalous Orthodox Church.

Declaration of the Holy Synod of the Russian Orthodox Church

3 April 1990

God-loving archpastors, pastors, and all the faithful children of the Russian Orthodox Church,

In our life, the time has come when everybody must realize their responsibility before the Lord for our Mother Church and its historical destiny.

The rapid changes taking place in the country have not bypassed the church and have posed serious challenges. For decades the church has been artificially separated from the people and largely separated from the life of society, but now it attracts close attention from various social forces and movements. Not infrequently, these forces and movements find themselves bitterly opposed to one another and each would like to see the church among their allies and to have the church support their understanding of the objectives and purposes of the spiritual, political, social, and economic transformation of the country and the solution of ethnic problems. We are called upon to be the guardians of the church tradition and be guided by the will of the First Bishop Tikhon, the Patriarch of All Russia, and other confessors of Christ's faith in our century, and we emphatically state: The Orthodox Church cannot be on the side of any group or party interests; it cannot link our destiny with politics. The church is the mother of all its faithful children, and she embraces all of them, irrespective of their political outlooks, with love, demanding from them the purity of the Orthodox faith and faithfulness to their Christian calling. It is this position that gives the church the right to make a moral evaluation of the developments that are currently taking place and the problems that concern our society. In doing so, the church is guided solely by the word of God and the apostolic tradition that it preserves.

One acute problem involving ethnic conflicts prompted the bishops of our church to convene a council in January of 1990 and to address all the children of the church with an appeal, which we hope has received an appropriate Christian response from you.

But our country is still facing many difficult problems that directly affect all of us: the need for spiritual renewal of society through practical measures of the upbringing of children and youth; the task of reviving our fatherland's culture, whose many monuments have been criminally destroyed or neglected, and calling for immediate measures to save them; the protection of the environment, which is in a catastrophic state in some regions of the country due to barbaric methods of economic management; and, finally, the need to pay attention to the social sphere, which has been greatly damaged by both the economic policy and the heartless attitude of many people. Today, society expects the church to take practical and effective steps to help resolve all these problems in the shortest period of time.

However, we should admit with humility that in many respects our church community, including the hierarchy, the clergy, and the laity, has turned out to be unprepared to respond appropriately to present challenges. The difficult decades have not gone by without leaving their mark. For many years the church was perceived as an ideological force that posed a threat to society. The open reprisals, which began in the difficult years of the Revolution and continued in the 1920s, the 1930s, the late 1950s, and the early 1960s, were all aimed at the church's elimination. During some periods its influence on people was curbed by means of covert encroachments and attempts to compromise it through organized propaganda. The interference of state agencies in the policy of the selection of the leaders of the church and the administration of parishes was also designed to achieve the same objectives. As a result, the church was forced out of the life of society, its activity was limited strictly to performing Divine Services in cathedrals, its testimony was weakened by constant pressure on the clergy, and its material base was severely undermined. Looking back over the past decades and the tragic experience of life and the testimony of our fathers and mothers, brothers and sisters, and attempting to understand our own experience, we can state that the church has survived not by its power or human wisdom, but by the power of its spirit and the gift of Divine Grace. This gift of grace has strengthened the weak forces of hierarchs, clergy, and all the faithful and has helped the church to preserve its faith in Christ and to continue along the road of the cross. Today, some people believe that some who walked along this road did not do as they should have done. With surprising ease judgment is passed on those who were subjected to scorn, open oppression, or covert pressure and who, throughout all those difficult years, tried to remain faithful to their calling as far as their understanding and strength would allow. We should all remember that human judgment is limited to the possibility of analyzing only those facts that are accessible to history, and in this sense even the most just judgment must always be qualified. Only God, who understands all hearts, knows "the hidden things of darkness," and only he "will make manifest the councils of the hearts" (1 Cor. 4:1–5). For this reason the evaluation of our Church's modern history which is being made in church circles today should be as impartial as it should be ethical. It should serve the spiritual renewal of all of us, it should unite and not divide the children of the church, and it should be Christian in its spirit and its meaning.

But the past, no matter how difficult it was, does not relieve us of responsibility for the results of our service today. It is absolutely clear that many people have grown accustomed to the situation of forced social inactivity and, whether they want it or not, continue to remain aloof from the changes taking place and do not use the possibilities now opening for the church. However, there is another extreme. Church representatives are now taking part in the activities of public organizations and elected bodies of power, speaking in the press and other media, yet not all representatives of the church realize their responsibility and by their statements give cause for passing judgment both in the religious and the secular spheres. It is absolutely clear that there is temptation in the church just as there is very frequently in our secular community to replace deeds with rhetorical statements and posturing designed to produce effect.

The difficult conditions in which the church was forced to exist made it difficult for it to manifest the main principle of church administration, that is, the principle of *sobornost* or conciliarity. Having unity in the sacraments, we have not always retained the living links with each other and mutual understanding in our approach to solving important questions in the life of the church community and evaluating our church's past. The current sentiments represent the sad result of the weakened conciliarity of church life. These sentiments have been aggravated by the passivity on the part of some members of the clergy and believers who have grown accustomed to think about the church only in terms of the performance of the Divine Service, on the one hand, and, on the other, by the increased activity of certain groups of the clergy and the laity, some of whom call themselves in a totally inappropriate manner, given Orthodox teaching, "the independent church public." The activities of the latter are largely aimed at stirring up criticism (which, incidentally, is entirely deserved in many cases) of the past and the present in the life of the church, but this criticism only exacerbates existing tensions. These activities are perceived by the overwhelming majority of the hierarchy and the clergy as an antihierarchical and anticanonical phenomenon that—whether we like it or not, despite the visible difference and seeming dissimilarity—pursues the same objectives as the ill-famed schism of Renovators (*obnovlentsy*).

Nevertheless, it is absolutely clear that under certain conditions the tensions that have emerged inside the body of the church can serve a creative and constructive purpose. They can promote a genuine revival of the mission of the church, the organization of religious and moral education of children and adults, and the cause of charity and the participation of the church in solving problems facing our people today. The most important of these conditions is preserving the canon order and the unity of the church and renouncing the secular political methods of struggle and mutual recriminations and suspicions. We should not repeat the sad history of the religious schisms of the 1920s. Today, as never before in recent years, we must consolidate the efforts of all the healthy forces of the church community. We must resolve the urgent problems of the internal organization of church life without delay.

The Statute of Administration of the Russian Orthodox Church, adopted by the Local Council in 1988, and the decisions of the Council of Hierarchs of 1989 contain a program of priority action. At the same time it should be emphasized that as the conciliar foundations of church life are strengthened, church legislation itself should be improved to meet the ideal laid down by the Local Council of 1917–1918.

By speaking about the problems facing our church today, we repeat what has already been said by the Council of Hierarchs and emphasize the need for a revival of the parish as a genuine church community. Without such a revival we will not be able to resolve the problems of the organization of spiritual enlightenment, charity, and normalization of the life of the church community.

There is no question that the introduction of the new statute has improved the situation in many parishes and created possibilities for the normal development of newly created communities. However, much more work is still needed calling for an active and responsible attitude on the part of the bishops and the clergy, on the one hand, and the parishioners, on the other.

In accordance with the statute we must strengthen conciliar foundations at the diocesan level. The parish cannot exist in isolation from its local church, that is, the diocese. A speedy creation of effective structures of diocesan administration on the broad conciliar basis not only will help resolve the problems facing parish communities and make it possible to promote the cause of spiritual enlightenment on the diocesan level, but also through the involvement of the best church forces will make it possible for the clergy and the laity to rally around their archpastors in the clear understanding that they represent one church community.

Finally, we must carry out a profound reorganization of the structures of our supreme church administration, which frequently come under deserved criticism from the Councils of Archeries and broad sectors of the church community. This reorganization should be carried out in the administrative sphere, external church relations, and in the spheres of economic and publishing activity by synodical agencies. We must carry out radical transformations in our spiritual school, which is called upon to train erudite and zealous pastors and profound religious scholars capable of conducting scientific research into many problems faced by the church in the teaching of its faith, education, pastoral, canonical, and social activities. All these questions call for a genuinely broad-based discussion within the framework of the church community, and we call on the bishops, the clergy, and the laity to take part in it. To organize this discussion and prepare recommendations for a practical solution of the problems facing the church in the sphere of religious-moral education and the social service, the Holy Synod, which met in session on 3 April of this year, set up a special Commission on the Revival of Religious-Moral Education and Charity. The commission has been entrusted with the task of organizing a broad-based dialogue with the participation of bishops, clergy and laity, and representatives of the church public concerned about the questions of religious-moral education and social service of the church. The Holy Synod expresses the hope that the work of the commission will promote the consolidation of all healthy church forces in overcoming the problems facing our church in this crucial period in it history.

The profound changes taking place in the life of our society have affected the sphere of church-state relations. The process of democratization has created the necessary preconditions for full normalization of these relations. In this connection the Holy Synod calls for attention to the importance of an early adoption of a new law on the freedom of conscience and religious organizations by the USSR Supreme Soviet. In the course of preparing the draft of this law the Holy Synod has on two occasions made an official statement of its position and put forward specific proposals. This position was presented first to the Council for Religious Affairs at the USSR Council of Ministers and then to the Presidium of the USSR Supreme Soviet. Its main principles were formulated on behalf of all the bishops by the Council of Hierarchs last October, and appropriate documents were also published. Unfortunately, the ideas and amendments suggested by the church were virtually ignored in both the draft submitted by the USSR Council of Ministers and its later version. It is to be regretted that, compared with previous versions of the draft, every subsequent version of the draft law known to the church is increasingly at variance with the position of the church. In this connection the Holy Synod has deemed it necessary to send a message to the chairman of the USSR Council of Ministers, N. I. Ryzhkov, in which it stated the official position of the Russian Orthodox Church. In particular, the message expressed the hope that the draft submitted for the consideration of the Supreme Soviet would reflect sufficiently the aspirations of those whose rights it was called upon to guarantee, that is, the believers of our country. On the eve of the discussion of the draft law in the USSR Supreme Soviet the Holy Synod believes it is an appropriate moment to make known to the religious and secular communities the thrust of its position in the hope that it will be understood by all those who are concerned about putting into practice human rights and freedom of conscience in our state. At the same time we draw attention to the fact that this position, as stated below, does not contain any amendments regarding the equal status of religion and atheism in the USSR. As is known, we introduced these amendments earlier, and their absence in the following list does not mean that the position of the Holy Synod has changed. Limiting the list of proposals relating to the content of the draft law, we emphasize that the most important objective of the new law is to ensure genuine religious freedom. In the opinion of the Holy Synod the law on the freedom of conscience and religious organizations should reflect the following provisions:

1. Legal recognition by the state of any religious organization as one indivisible system, comprising hierarchical structure, constituent components, and agencies, which should be granted the rights of a legal entity.

2. Recognition of the charter (statute) of such an organization as the source of law for the system of government agencies.

3. The right of a religious organization to carry out religious education and upbringing of children and adults in all forms and at different levels.

4. The possibility for voluntary study of the fundamentals of different religions in educational establishments outside the curriculum of popular education.

5. The right to publish and disseminate freely theological and religious education literature; access to all mass media; and the possibility of setting up editorial boards, publishing houses, and mass media by religious organizations.

6. The exclusive right to publish theological and Divine Service books and also make holy and church utensils.

7. The right of religious organizations to property, assets, leasing, and land ownership and use in accordance with the existing general legislation without discrimination.

8. Abolition of the existing taxation of enterprises (shops) in accordance with the income taxes imposed on the population. We believe that for this purpose it is expedient to determine that tax payments of these enterprises to the state budget should be equal to those of enterprises belonging to public organizations and funds minus the means donated to charity, mercy, and assistance in connection with calamities and other extraordinary circumstances.

9. The reaffirmation of the fact that the income (profits) of religious organizations are not subject to state taxation. The earned income of all persons employed at religious organizations, including those involved in the performance of religious rites (the servants of the church), should be taxed on the general terms established by legislation. All kinds of social insurance should also be extended to all these individuals.

10. The legalization of all forms, expressions, and manifestations of charity and mercy activities, both independently and in conjunction with social funds and organizations; the right to create societies to this end attached to religious organization and the possibility of receiving financial and other material donations for these purposes.

11. The determination of the terms of reference of state agencies for religious affairs so that any interference in the internal life of the church and the resolution of the questions of church existence is totally prevented. The task of such agencies should consist in giving assistance and help to religious organizations in ensuring the rights of citizens to freedom of conscience.

12. Control and supervision over the implementation of legislation on the freedom of conscience and religious organizations on the same basis as the control and supervision over other laws of the country. In this connection it is unjustified to give special powers to local soviets to exercise control over the compliance with legislation on the freedom of conscience.

The adoption of the new law will represent an important but not the only measure aimed at improving the relations between church and state. In the practical sphere of these relations everything that does not correspond to existing legislation and causes conflicts and tensions should be eliminated.

In the first place this relates to the so-called registration of clergy by authorized officials of the Council for Religious Affairs. Such registration has no legal grounds and represents direct interference by government officials in the internal affairs of the church.

District council public commissions on the supervision of legislation on religious cults should also be dissolved, because they have become obsolete. At present their activity has continued to breed conflict and in a number of instances has provoked justified dissatisfaction of believers in some areas.

Despite the concern of the church and secular public, the problem of the preservation of church buildings that represent our sacred monuments of history and culture has not been resolved, and their destruction has continued. Large sums of money are needed to carry out restoration, but the church does not have this money. Also, restoration of profaned shrines and the protection of historical monuments should become an act of national repentance and have an important spiritual-moral and educational significance. Therefore, the collection of means for these purposes should be participated in not only by the church but also by state and public organizations, including the USSR Ministry of Culture. We believe that cooperation with them is very important today.

Historical reality has faced the church with new challenges, but at the same time it opens new possibilities, which can and must be used with only one purpose—to help modern man acquire fullness of life and gain salvation. The church does not and cannot have any other aim. This is its calling and this is the calling of every one of its servants and every member of the church. Let us renew our calling and our responsibility for the destiny of the church, and let us remember the words of the apostle: "I therefore . . . beseech you that ye walk worthy of the vocation wherewith ye are called, . . . endeavouring to keep the unity of the Spirit in the bond of peace" (Eph. 4:1, 3).

Will the Lord Help Us?

An Interview with Patriarch Alexis II of Moscow and All Russia

His Holiness Alexis II, Patriarch of Moscow and All Russia, was elected to the patriarchate in 1990, having formerly served as the Bishop of Leningrad and Novgorod. He is a theologian and community leader and in 1989 was voted into the Soviet Parliament. He is dedicated to Christian unity and has participated in ecumenical ventures within the Soviet Union and internationally. He granted this interview to the *Literaturnaya Gazeta* in 1990.

Correspondent: Your Holiness, when Metropolitan Tikhon was informed of his election to the patriarchy several days after the 1917 October Revolution, he said, "Your news of my election is for me the scroll on which is inscribed 'lamentations and mourning and woe.' Many will be the tears I will have to swallow and the moans I will have to utter in the office of patriarch, especially in these grim times!" Did you want to say anything similar when you were ordained patriarch? After all, the present times are also grim.

Patriarch: And yet 1990 is not the same as 1917. The words that you have quoted were taken by Patriarch Tikhon from the prophet Ezekiel. Both their destinies were remarkably similar. In the days of Patriarch Tikhon, as in the days of the prophet Ezekiel, the captivity of their peoples was only beginning, and in both cases that captivity lasted seventy years. In both cases, the captivity resulted from the people's falling away from God, and the immediate religious danger was the subjugation of believers to the religious views of their new rulers, that is, to ancient or new paganism.

The prophet Ezekiel and Patriarch Tikhon addressed either the apostates or those on the verge of apostasy. I will remind you of the words the Lord had spoken to his prophet before he handed him that bitter scroll: "I send thee to the children of Israel, to a rebellious nation that hath rebelled against me: they and their fathers have transgressed against me, even unto this very day. For they are impudent children and stiffhearted. . . . And they, whether they will hear, or whether they will forbear . . . yet shall know that there hath been a prophet among them. And thou, son of man, be not afraid of them, neither be afraid of their words. . . . And thou shalt speak my words unto them. . ." (Ezek. 2: 3–7).

It seems to me that today, quite the contrary, people are looking for the road leading to the church; therefore it would not be appropriate to address the above stern words to them.

As for my own attitude, I would define it by quoting a church precept that says you don't ask to be crucified, nor can you escape from the cross. If fate decrees that I share Patriarch Tikhon's fate, I will accept it, but I would not be so audacious as to compare myself with him.

Moreover, at the time you speak of, the blow was aimed especially at the church and the patriarch. Today, however, the church and the patriarch will have to bear only the suffering that will fall to the lot of the entire nation. Therefore, today the patriarch should not single out his special cross.

Corr.: What does today's society look like to you? Could you give a brief moral definition of it?

Pat.: My definition is based solely on the experience that I as a pastor can have, and that experience brings me principally into contact with people who turn to me. And once a person turns to the church that means that the moral and spiritual elements in him have come awake. On the whole, it is the aim of the pastor to see what is best in a man and hope that it will develop. Certainly, the information that comes from all sides sometimes drives one to despair. But I repeat that the encounters my brother clergymen and I have had are most comforting, especially as regards the children who study in Sunday schools. I hope we are not going to lose that generation.

The English writer and Christian Gilbert Chesterton said once that all people are divided into two categories. The first, and the best, are simply people. Happily, these make up the greater part of society.

The past has certainly left its imprint. Everyone knows of the vices of our social life. As for religious life, it can easily be described as religious barbarization. Christianity had been banished from the life of the people, but paganism is coming to take its place, what with all the sorcerers, healers, a surrogate of Oriental wisdom, and the deification of extraterrestrials. . . . And it may very well be that this paganism will be harder to overcome than the paganism of a thousand years back.

Corr.: People are demanding that the Communist Party of the Soviet Union repent of the oceans of sorrow and suffering that it brought to the people. Do you feel that the Russian Orthodox Church has anything to repent of?

Pat.: The Reverend Isaac Sirin said, "The whole church is a church that sins, the whole church is a church that repents." The church is not holy of its own holiness but of the holiness of Christ, who lives and acts within it.

If we do not multiply this talent, we sin. Every one of us has sinned against God and against our neighbor.

But, apparently, your question has a different meaning: you want to know whether the Russian Orthodox Church has sinned against the Russian people, isn't that right? But what is the Russian church if not the Russian people themselves taken in their striving for the spiritual? And the Russian church as a whole has no sins that are separable from the Russian people.

If you wish me to be more concrete, I can say that we do not believe that the position taken by Metropolitan Sergius in 1927[1] and later by the church leadership has brought harm to the church or the people. There are many debates regarding the declaration made by Metropolitan Sergius in 1927. However, the declaration does not mark a turning point in the history of our church in the decades of Soviet power. Adopted in the hope of stopping persecution, it did nothing to stop it. As for its contents, it was neither the first nor the most far-reaching attempt at straightening out things between the church and the authorities who had deprived it of the right to exist.

In these attempts at explanation, the church had to give the authorities the tribute of loyalty that they demanded. The church had to explain that it would not use its authority to aggravate the confrontation between the people and the authorities or to stir up political feeling. That is why Metropolitan Sergius said in the declaration, "We wish to be Orthodox and at the same time to realize that the Soviet Union is our civil motherland, whose joys and achievements are our joys and achievements, and whose failures are our failures." This formula has been much attacked in church circles. But did not Tertullian, one of the first Christian theologians, say the same thing to the Roman emperor, also a godless man and a persecutor of the Christians? "When the state is shaken by calamities, we suffer together with all its citizens, and though the crowd considers us strangers, it appears that calamity will not pass us by" (Tertullian, *Apologia* 31.3). Alas, this time also calamity did not bypass the Christians though they stressed pointedly they wanted no discord with the government on political grounds.

In Metropolitan Sergius's formula there is a certain fine point that many people refuse to see. It is the joys and sorrows of the motherland, and not those of the atheistic government, that he considers as his own. What is more, he used the term *motherland* at a time when the word was as good as prohibited. Therefore, the statement in the message from the synod of the Russian Orthodox Church abroad that "the declaration made by Metropolitan Sergius regarding the identity of the interests of the church and the godless government deprives the Moscow patriarchate of freedom to this day" (*Russkaya Mysl*, no. 3711, 2 December 1988) does not correspond to the truth. If anything, it was not the declaration that deprived the patriarchate of freedom.

The words pronounced sixty years ago are not the crux of the matter; they have no magic power. I repeat that the declaration of 1927 did not bring immediate results. But the course mapped before that by Patriarch Tikhon and developed after him by Metropolitan Sergius helped, nevertheless, to preserve the church to this day. That course was to commit a smaller sin so as to avoid a bigger one. For instance, during the war a soldier kills enemy soldiers and that is a sin, but as the church sees it it would be an even greater sin for him to abandon his kith and kin to the enemy. Sometimes one has to sacrifice one's personal sinlessness for the sake of others. A patriarch or metropolitan who would deliberately endanger his flock by laying it open to reprisal would have sinned far more before God and man, and Russia than if he shielded them through compromise. And the church leaders had to shield the church in many different ways, and one of them was declaration of loyalty.

That was painful. But many millions of Orthodox Christians under totalitarian government could not vanish into catacombs. Yes, we have sinned, but not against the people, for it was for their sake, for the sake of being together with hundreds of millions of people that the hierarchies of the church committed the sin of silence, the sin of untruth. And we have always done penance to God for that sin.

Moreover, our refusal to take the church into the catacombs has borne purely spiritual fruit: we, members of the Russian Orthodox Church, did not cultivate within us hatred and thirst for revenge. I am afraid that the psychology of the catacombs would have developed that feeling in us.

Corr.: Don't you think that the church bore too meekly the villainy to which the murderers and sadists subjected it and the entire nation? It is known that in connection with the campaign to expropriate church valuables that started in February 1922, there were up to two thousand trials throughout Russia and more than ten thousand faithful liquidated by shooting squads. Among the victims were a number of hierarchs, Metropolitan Veniamin of Petrograd, for one. He is today considered a candidate for canonization just like an earlier victim of Bolshevik terror, the Grand Duchess Elizaveta Fyodorovna, mother superior of the Martha and Maria Convent, not considering the countless losses incurred by the church during the Stalin rule. Yet, the church is not known to have voiced any sharp protests, addressed to the international public or the like. Even in Brezhnev's time when no shooting threatened, the church did not raise its voice in protest to defend the victims of tyranny. (I am not speaking of the individual priests who raised their voice in protest.)

There had been moments, especially in the time of Patriarch Tikhon, when the people were prepared to see in the church their last bulwark, to rally round it in order to withstand the bloody tyranny. But there was meekness instead of confrontation.

It is difficult to imagine that the Catholic Church of Poland could have been so docile.

Pat.: Initially, our "meekness" was connected with the feeling that the church and Russia were accepting their bitter cup from the hands of God. And the persecutors themselves were seen as the instruments of God's scorching and healing touch. Let us remember the message of Patriarch Tikhon or, say, the verses of Maximilian Voloshin of the civil war times. The latter wrote, "I believe in the right of the higher powers that have unchained the ancient elements, and out of the depth of the charred Russia I say; 'You are right to have judged thus!'"

Catholicism has its own traditions, certainly. Political realism also refers to these traditions. The Catholic Church did not lead the struggle against communism either in the Baltic republics or in postwar Poland, Germany, Hungary, Czechoslovakia, or Rumania. Moreover, the Catholic communities in these countries found their place in socialist conditions far easier than we did, and they did not evoke the persecutions that fell to the lot of the Russian Orthodox Church.

The position adopted by Patriarch Tikhon, who did not call for armed resistance, is deeply ingrained in Orthodox tradition. Indeed, it was not his personal decision. Rather, through him the faith of the entire church—all its two thousand years of experience—found expression. I will not go into the spiritual significance and the substantiation of this behavior; I will say only that being a genuine Orthodox he could not act otherwise. Let us remember the feat of the first Russian saints, the martyrs Boris and Gleb.[2]

Corr.: Do you bear a grudge against the Communist Party of the Soviet Union and the Soviet government for cruelly tormenting the church so many years?

Pat.: Our Savior has bidden us to pray for our enemies, and prayer is always a constructive concentration of goodwill. It is a powerful active desire of your soul for genuine welfare and goodness and salvation for the one you are praying for. Certainly, that is why spiritually it is impossible to hate the one whom you wish to bring to his senses through your prayers. These people have themselves chosen to be our enemies, while we have not permitted ourselves to feel hatred or ill will toward our persecutors. If we had succumbed to the temptation it would have meant our spiritual capitulation because it would have meant that the forces of evil had entered our hearts and, through hatred, put us on the same plane with our persecutors.

The Orthodox faith preaches that it is a sin to hate, and one should love the sinner. I can and I am duty bound to condemn (give a moral assessment of) a person's evil deed. But I cannot put the equation sign between the misdeed and the person. I can say, "The man has told a lie," and that will be a permissible reprimand. "The man is a liar" would be a sinful condemnation. While we never condoned the sin of persecuting the church on the part of the government and ideological inspirers of the persecution, we always tried to see living men in these persecutors. Believers and priests who have been in concentration camps say that in some cases they succeeded in leading their jailers and investigators to Christ. It was of these devoted Christians that Voloshin wrote, "Under torture we learned to believe and pray for our tormentors. We understood that each one was a captive angel in devil's guise."

Corr.: Why do you think the Marxists have stopped their long struggle against the church? Did they simply come to realize the impracticability of such a struggle, or were they moved by some deeper workings of the mind and heart?

Do you hope that the restored church will be able to contribute to the solution of the problems facing our society today? Do these hopes seem exaggerated to you?

Pat.: First of all, we always offer thanks to God, the giver of life and goodness, for all the good changes in our lives. His will is manifest in the people's urge to seek goodness.

The changes now taking place are inevitable, for the thousand years of Christianity in Russia could not disappear altogether and because God could not forsake the people who had loved him so in their previous history. Though there had been no gleam of hope for decades, we never stopped praying and hoping—hoping against hope. We know the history of humanity and we know God's love for his children. And in this knowledge we derived the assurance that the time of trial and the reign of darkness would come to an end. Thank God, the people and the authorities have come to realize that to war with the church and religious faith means to war with one's own soul.

Moreover, the burden of unresolved social problems makes a large number of people assume that somewhere outside their milieu, people have experience resolving these problems. That is, somewhere in other countries or in the church that was thrown out of active social life.

As for possibilities of the church helping society, we have to take into consideration the fact that though the church has accumulated vast experience in helping an individual human soul, it has no recipes for society as a whole or for the solution of economic, political, or ecological problems. In this area we must think and search together. This is an area for dialogue (as distinct from the church sermon and the saving of souls).

Today the church is conducting this dialogue through participating in the country's Parliament and in other government bodies, through conferences, schools, and the periodical press. We believe it is very important to give secular experts in all areas of science an opportunity to get acquainted with the fundamentals of the Christian view of the world and man, so that proceeding from this view they could themselves search in their professional activities for solutions consonant with the initial premises and goals of Christianity.

That is why it is so important for us (and I'm sure for our entire society) to have optional instruction in Christian doctrine and the foundations of spirituality and morality allowed in secular educational establishments, of course, in keeping with the wishes of the parents and the students.

Corr.: It is a fact that there is a rapid growth of church parishes throughout the country. Does it make you happy? On the one hand, the increase is truly staggering, but on the other, what are eleven thousand parishes for two hundred million Russians? Where do you get the priests for the newly opened parishes? If the country is suffering from a shortage of good physicians, good teachers, and good engineers, where is it to get good priests? That means that the rapid growth of parishes is no reason for rejoicing, is it?

Pat.: The spirituality of a man, a priest, in the church's understanding, is the genuineness of his religious life, his love of God, prayer, liturgical worship, the church, and its aims. From that arises his love for others. I am certain that the majority of our clergy possess this love of God and all humankind. Because if the clergy lacks spirituality, the church disintegrates and its end approaches. However, the revival that our church is going through today is evidence of the contrary; it shows that my confreres have not stopped being true pastors.

Things are more complicated where educational and cultural standards are concerned. Thousands of churches are opening and there is a great need of priests. The seminaries are able to satisfy only one-third of that need. Even before *perestroika* not all priests had a theological education, and today that number is even smaller. Today bishops are obliged to ordain persons whose great desire to accept priesthood is not backed by necessary training. Unfortunately, the gap is growing between the demands that society makes on the church and the abilities of a clergy that is not sufficiently prepared for dialogue and is too small numerically for the two hundred million people who are gradually returning to the faith.

The more obvious need is to distinguish between the statements by individual priests (especially in matters concerning culture and social life) and the position of the Orthodox Church as a whole.

We do have educated persons who combine a good knowledge of modern culture and adherence to Orthodox tradition. What is more, believers who work in secular establishments of science and culture and who need no longer to conceal their religious feeling openly cooperate with the church, while many of them join the priesthood. The standards of our religious academies are rising, too. With the combined efforts of theologians, the Holy Synod is working out the positions of the church on major problems of present-day life. Therefore, if a priest may find it difficult to give the necessary advice, it does not mean that the church as a whole does not have the answer. The church has different sections; hence there are questions the answers to which should be sought in monasteries, questions that are to be answered in religious academies, and still other questions— the ones most basic and necessary for the people—that parish priests should answer.

We shall try to make up for the shortage of skilled pastors by publishing books and periodicals. When not every priest is capable of being a competent teacher and preacher, we hope that television and other media will help us spread the Word of God.

We also hope that theologically knowledgeable laymen will share the work of reviving parish life. In this we should not be satisfied only with the efforts by the hierarchy and priests. We should demonstrate in practice that ours is a *soborny* church (meaning unity in multiplicity and multiplicity in unity) and that the concerns of the church are the concerns of every Christian, every parishioner. The teaching of religion, the history of religion, the fundamentals of spirituality and morality to laymen should become the norm. However, I would like to warn people against the appearance of imposters who will preach alien views under the guise of Orthodoxy, or who will simply be lacking the knowledge necessary to preach well. Therefore, we believe that laymen should take up the work of religious enlightenment only after receiving the blessing and approval of the parish priest or bishop who can ascertain the quality of the material to be taught. On the other hand, laymen who invite representatives of the church to deliver a course of lectures in secular educational or cultural establishments would do well to ask the would-be lecturers if they have been authorized to do so by the church.

I hope that the development of catechizing and preaching will soon draw into the church new people who will be capable of mending the ills of our church life, ills that we in our own lifetime perhaps shall not be able to overcome. The emergence of church fraternities that choose the task of instruction in the faith are a sign of the times and the answer to the needs of the church.

Corr.: Today, when there is no peace either outside or in the souls of people, many are looking to the church with hope, expecting to see it as an example of wisdom and quiet dignity. And the church speaks of peace, love, and mutual forgiveness—but only in sermons. In reality, the church has also been caught up in the general epidemic of hatred, struggle, and confrontation. Hostility is flaring among the different confessions; the Russian Orthodox Church is being attacked by the Karlovichi, the Ukrainian autocephalists. We have all witnessed the frenzy of hate that broke out during your recent visit to Kiev. What is the explanation for it?

Pat.: There exists abroad an emigrant Orthodox Church that, regrettably, is unwilling to associate with the Russian Orthodox Church and accuses it of political and very possibly religious compromises. Of course, there are no grounds for accusing us of religious or doctrinal changes, with the exception of our refusal to maintain that the monarchy is the only possible system of government for a Christian society. In the area of politics . . . I do not believe the man to be morally impeccable who comes up to a badly beaten fellow and instead of rendering assistance showers him with reproaches, saying, "Why didn't you shout and call for help when they were beating you?!" He should have understood that the victim had been beaten so hard that he couldn't even shout.

On the other hand, think of what would have been if in the times of the Mongol yoke (in the 13th to 15th centuries) some church members would have acted against the policy of Alexander Nevsky and Metropolitans Alexis and Peter, which was aimed at achieving truce with the Golden Horde, and would have demanded the organization of an immediate uprising? Would the dissent have brought closer the hour of liberation?

Or what would have happened if in Byzantium the church had started a dissent on account of political sympathy or antipathy for one or another emperor?

We have no need of theological-political inspection from abroad to check whether we believe as we should, pray the Orthodox way, or whether our church life bears the stamp of God's grace. But we will accept with joy all attempts to share with us the spiritual experience accumulated by Orthodoxy abroad, its experience of life in conditions that differ greatly from ours but that are now gradually becoming our own.

We are prepared to unite on an ecclesiastic and not a political basis. However, it is political declarations and gestures that are demanded of us. If this continues we may soon reach a point when a person who comes to be baptized asks the priest about his political affiliations and, if they don't coincide with his own, goes in search of another parish to be baptized in.

You have to agree it would be absurd to have a Russian Monarchic Orthodox Church, a Russian Constitutional and Democratic Church, a Belorussian Ecological Orthodox Church, and so on.

But seriously, since olden times the church system has been territorial. What I mean is that the bishop of New York has no more right to set up a parish in Ryazan than the bishop of Tashkent.

We consider all those who agree to be united with us in the faith, all those who wish to move toward Christ together with us, to be one of us, and we do not want state borders or political prejudice to separate brothers.

As for the Ukrainian autocephalists, they wish to see in Christ, not their Lord and Judge, but an ally, an ally in their political struggle. Two thousand years ago people also treated Christ as a political figure: some regarded him as a political leader, while others feared him as they would a dangerous political criminal. And together they crucified him in the end. The subjugation of the interests of the church to political interests and the conversion of the church into a political instrument have always meant coercion with regard to faith and have always led the church to Calvary.

Only a person of shallow faith, not a genuine Christian, can use faith to achieve mundane or political gains. But what is sin for one person is also sin for a group of people or a party. If the Ukrainian autocephalists could explain clearly why unity with the Russian Orthodox Church hindered their spiritual salvation or how they would grow spiritually richer by separating from their Russian brothers, I would try to understand them.

The Ukrainian Orthodox Church has its specific difficulties and its traditions. Being well aware of the fact we have granted it independence in matters of management. But we cannot take them seriously when people wish to ban the use of church Slavonic in liturgical worship on the grounds that it is Moscow's intrigue against the Ukrainian language. They should know that in Moscow we do not pray in Russian either, but it is not a question of politics but theology, and it would be wrong to regard that as the church's discrimination of the Russians.

In any case, it is not worthwhile to use the language of ultimatums, accusations, and hate in church.

Corr.: The situation in the country is growing more critical every day. Could you tell me—if it is not a secret—what you are praying for nowadays?

Pat.: Obviously, that is your concluding question and so in order to sum up our talk, I would like to quote the words that Father Georghy Florovsky used to end his book, *The Roads of Russian Theology:* "The mistakes and failures of the past should not put us out of countenance. The historical road has not been traversed to the end, the history of the church has not ended. The Russian road has not closed, either. It is open, though it is difficult. The stern historical sentence should regenerate into a creative appeal to complete what has been left undone. And it is meet that we enter the Kingdom of Heaven through many sorrows."

NOTES

1. Metropolitan Sergius took a position that was loyal to the new Soviet authorities.

2. Boris and Gleb, two sons of Prince Vladimir of Kiev, were killed by hirelings of their brother Svyatopolk in the eleventh century.

The Church and *Perestroika*

Metropolitan Kirill of Smolensk and Kaliningrad

The church, founded by our Lord Jesus Christ, serves a salvific eschatological purpose. This purpose is to save people and show them the way into the Kingdom of God. This can be fully achieved only in the world to come. However, the spiritual elevation of people, the work of their salvation, is implemented here on earth within the framework of human history, and the church, which combines the temporal and the eternal, the human and the divine, the visible and the invisible, is involved in this history through things temporal, human, and visible. It shares the world's historical fate, and at the same time it is the leaven that is to spiritually renovate and transform the human family.

As is well known, over the past few decades not many of our compatriots heeded the prophetic voice of the church. Predominating in our society was an erroneous and most dangerous stereotype regarding religion and the church as deplorable "vestiges of the bourgeois system" incompatible with socialist morality. The building of the new society was associated with the idea of eradicating "religious prejudices." Varied methods were employed to this end, from reprisals and crude administrative methods to abusive propaganda and suppression of information.

As a result, the church found itself ousted from public life. It was assigned a narrow and obscure place beyond the margins of that life in order to demonstrate "massive" withdrawal of citizens from religion. Closed cathedrals in the centers of our cities and tiny churches overcrowded with elderly women somewhere in the suburbs were the vivid symbols of the place of religion in our society. They were intended to show that there is no room for the church in the dynamic life of our society today and, consequently, in the future. Obscure backyards were its supposedly proper place. And its frock, backward old men and women who clung to their religious prejudices because of lack of education. And though by its years of humble sacrifice the church had convincingly proved its bond with the people and loyalty to patriotic traditions, there were ideologists in our society who questioned the sincerity of the church and regarded it as a secret and dangerous enemy; they were ready to interpret in this sense any word pronounced by the church if it failed to conform with their understanding of public benefit. Society not only refused to listen to the voice of the church but also denied it the right to raise its voice except in cases when the pronouncements of the church corresponded to the official political stand and were considered useful.

CHURCH RENEWAL AND POLITICAL REFORM

The current changes in the Soviet Union have involved relations between the church and the state. Believers rejoice at the registration of thousands of parishes, the reopening of churches and monasteries, the opening of new theological schools. The main thing is, however, that the visible revival of ecclesiastical life is a result of profound reforms in our society. Without these reforms the outside changes would be merely cosmetic and would not guarantee the irreversibility of the process. The older generation remembers the unfortunate experience of the "cosmetics" of the postwar years when the opening of a considerable number of churches was stopped. The late 1950s and early 1960s witnessed their mass closing and even their destruction. The significance of the present situation lies in the fact that changes are taking place not only on the external practical level but also, and this is especially important, on the level of theory and public psychology. A new pattern of relations between the church and the socialist state is emerging, and the principle of freedom of conscience, proclaimed by the Revolution, is being filled with real content. Radical changes are taking place in the views of the role and significance of religion, the church, and believers in the life of our society. Believers are no longer regarded as second-rate citizens and their religious convictions as vestiges of the past impeding social progress. It has been acknowledged that religious beliefs promote personal and social morality; help improve international relations, family ties, and conscientious work; and combat drunkenness and crime. The celebrations marking the millennium of the baptism of Russia promoted the recognition of the church's role in the development of natural culture and the assertion of moral ideals. A very important inner process is underway which is transforming and renovating the principles of our public life.

As a result the church is gradually coming out of the "obscure backyards" to become a partner in a dialogue. For the first time in long decades society is opening up and can hear the voice of the church. That means that the church is again able to fulfill its pastoral service in full, at the personal and public levels. The new situation presents new challenges to the church. The public wants to know the church's view on issues of personal and public morality, politics, economics, ecology, culture, education, relations between ethnic groups, upbringing of the younger generation, the family and marriage, and so forth. The church's view should, of course, be essentially pastoral and based on a thorough theological analysis. It should be first of all addressed to members of the church, but not to them alone, because the problems our society faces today cannot be overcome without the joint efforts of believers and nonbelievers. The church, therefore, should speak a language that can be understood not by Christians alone. And at the same time it should be the pastoral voice of the church because this is what the public expects to hear. The current change is also characterized by society's very positive attitude to the church's practical participation in solving a number of specific problems, such as charity, participation in the elected bodies of government, the revival of national culture and rural life, the development of an interethnic dialogue, and filling the gaps in religious education.

A NEW ROLE FOR THE CHURCH

The church's new role in Soviet society is not at all simple. It places new tasks before the central bodies of church administration, the hierarchy, theologians, and clergy, and before theological schools, monasteries, and parishes. It requires hard theoretical work, changes in church practices, stronger ties binding us together in Christ, prayerful and spiritual efforts, and striving for moral perfection.

The church's pastoral word should manifest concern for social justice. This concern is based on people's equality before God as having but one nature and one common origin. Equality, however, is not the same as egalitarianism. People differ from each other in spiritual and moral potential, in intellectual and physical abilities. Our social system should offer everybody equal opportunities for the free development of his or her talents. At the same time society should take special care of and render particular support to those who are unable to attain adequate living standards without such support. The principle of citizens' social security, which is basic in our society, is often distorted. That refers primarily to single elderly people, invalids, and in some cases to youth. This seems to be the sphere where the witness and service of the church can be especially effective.

Social justice and prosperity cannot be achieved if there is no respect for the law and if people ignore their civic duties. The socialization of life results in personal prosperity depending to an ever greater extent on the prosperity of the whole society. Crimes against society and a desire to prosper at the expense of others ultimately weaken society as a whole. Society cannot develop successfully without discipline in public relations, without law and order, without people feeling responsible for whatever they do.

Duty, however, is a moral notion. It is the overcoming of egoism and the subordination of your personal interests to those of your neighbor. The sense of duty cannot be introduced from outside or enforced. It grows from morality and is regulated by morality and consciousness. It should also be kept in mind that the sense of responsibility is strong when living conditions do not undermine one's dignity and instead correspond to one's vocation, when social structures ensure everybody an access to decision making. Such notions as morality, democracy, and economics merge in creating the commonweal, that is, the totality of conditions that ensure the improvement of both personality and society. To serve the church today also means molding a sense of responsibility for the commonweal, encouraging a conscientious attitude toward work, and the overcoming of personal and collective egoism. The church should pay attention to the economic conditions of people's life and to the development of democratic institutions so that external circumstances would help both the individual and society foster moral and social virtues.

A special accent is placed in our society on economics. The hopes for better living conditions and the solution of social problems are justly associated with the success of economic reform.

It is important that economic reform should develop within the limits of moral responsibility, that it not spiritually disfigure, oppress, or exhaust man, that it not promote the concentration of power in the hands of individuals or groups of individuals or result in feckless exploitation of natural resources and pollution of the environment or cause social tension and conflicts. At the same time an economic system should be flexible enough to provide everybody the opportunity to show reasonable initiative, to reveal one's talents, to work freely and creatively and thereby efficiently create values indispensable to both self and society. An economic system should combine two main dimensions: efficiency and justice. The key to a vital and humane economy lies in a balance between the two. It would, of course, be inhuman to forget about justice by raising economic efficiency through whatever means available. That would lead to both overt and covert exploitation, loss of the right to work, success of one at the expense of another, trampling upon human dignity. Justice, however, is likewise senseless without economic efficiency. Such a justice turns into equality of all in poverty, loss of initiative, social stagnation, and, finally, violation of justice in a broader than merely economic or social aspect.

THE CHURCH AND CULTURAL DEVELOPMENT

Culture and cultural development trends occupy a prominent place in the current public discussion. It is obvious that the rapid changes in society caused by the scientific and technological revolution have a great impact on culture. Such phenomena as industrialization, urbanization, and the development of transport, communication, and mass media promote mutual cultural penetration and the emergence of new cultural forms. Not everything is that simple in the new cultural situation. On the one hand, the increasing cultural exchange facilitates mutual enrichment of cultures and the creation of cultural forms able to express the unity of human race. On the other hand, however, there emerges the threat that national cultures reflecting the spiritual wealth and diversity of human family will be obliterated under the domination of a unified, so-called mass, culture.

The church has always supported genuine culture, which promotes man's integrity, and opposed anticulture, the destruction of that integrity under the guise of culture. The church's concern for the cultural situation should be part of its general pastoral concern for man. That concern, however, cannot be based on the artistic tastes, sympathies, or antipathies of certain individuals or guided exclusively by adherence to certain historical cultural forms or genres. In the course of two millennia, living in various conditions, the church is known to have used and consecrated various cultures of many peoples. Opposing evil and temptation and inspiring morality, the church has been impregnating cultural creativity and helping that creativity to emancipate and elevate man. And today it is called upon to continue that service using this rich tradition, the beauty of the Divine Service, the strength and attractiveness of the moral ideas of the Gospels. Its word can help many of our contemporaries both to express through culture their understanding of beauty and truth and to find in genuine culture the support it needs on the hard road to spiritual perfection.

Our church can and must occupy a special place in preserving the national cultural heritage, which will help modern man gain access to the spiritual wealth and wisdom of previous generations, to enter the living tradition of their history. In this connection the restoration of ruined and defiled churches and the preservation of the tradition of church singing and icon painting have not only practical ecclesiastical but also tremendous cultural significance.

Responsible before God for the spiritual state of its people, each local church is called upon to preserve, protect from destruction, and foster all spiritual values contained in a people's culture and customs. Imbued with this concern, a local church serves the cause of consolidating moral principles in the people's life because the popular tradition carries within it the centuries-old experience of mastering the moral ideal.

Our local church is a multinational church, and as such it is called upon to include in itself and its witness different cultures. It is also called upon to unite people of different nationalities, filling human relations with Christian virtues, and to nurture all "till we all come . . . unto the measure of the stature of the fulness of Christ" (Eph. 4:13).

At this time marked with a growth of national self-identification and with an aggravation of national contradictions, the witness and service of our church should include a special concern for international relations. With the experience of its inner life the church shows society an example of international relations free from sinful pride, intolerance, and alienation. Without joining in the political discussion or identifying its position with that of opposing sides, the church can carry the word of reconciliation in an attempt to heal open wounds, to unite and not divide people, and to help them understand or maybe even forgive each other in order to restore justice and peace among themselves. To achieve that our church can use the opportunities offered in the field of ecumenical dialogue with other confessions and non-Christian religions. To achieve national reconciliation our church should be still more open to the cultures, languages, and faith traditions of its members so that each Christian, regardless of his or her nationality, would not feel like a stranger in the church and could glorify the name of God and grow spiritually in his or her native cultural milieu.

The new situation in our country broadens the opportunities for the church not only to pass moral judgment on various aspects of public life, but also to participate directly in that life. This refers primarily to charity and dissemination of religious knowledge.

LEGISLATION ON RELIGION

Believers look to the new law on freedom of conscience to guarantee the irreversibility of current processes which help them to feel themselves equal members of society whose convictions no longer invite covert discrimination or public condemnation.

The church's social programs and methods of religious education depend to a great extent on the new law. Both activities are part and parcel of professing the Christian faith and are already approved in well-known international legal acts signed by the USSR.

Neither forms nor methods of church charity should be restricted, leaving it to the believers to respond to society's demands according to sound reason and possibilities. Such forms can and must be diverse: participation in governmental and nongovernmental social programs and funds, establishment of joint church-state, church-cooperative, or purely church charity organizations. The law should meet religions halfway and encourage selfless service to those in need of human assistance and support.

In connection with the problem of religious education it should be recalled that a decree adopted by the Council of People's Commissars in 1918 proclaimed the possibility of private religious education. Unfortunately the term *private* was interpreted so freely that all organized religious education was eliminated and outlawed. Religious instruction was prohibited in churches (Instructions of the People's Commissariat of the Interiors and the People's Commissariat of Justice of Belorussia of 5 May 1928) and even at home (ibid. and Article 11 of Resolution 83 of the Central Executive Committee of Georgia of 8 October 1938). The new law should, in my opinion, provide a proper interpretation of the term *private*. In other words, the term means "without organizational, financial, or any other support by the state or mass organizations." It follows from the letter of the decree that religious education should be realized by those interested in such education. It seems important that the new law promote a free realization of this clause of the decree, thereby offering opportunities for various models of religious education: from voluntary studies of religion in the auspices of educational establishments to parish schools and circles. The question about where, when, and who will realize religious education and who will finance it should be solved by those interested in such education.

The Decree of People's Commissars of 3 January 1918 proclaimed the principle of separation of the church from the state and deideologized the state because Orthodoxy was no longer the state religion. The separation meant that the state acknowledged its being religionless, that is, free from the religious postulates of any one particular group. Neither the said decree nor any other law has proclaimed any other ideology to be the state ideology. The state ideology, that is, ideology obligatory for all citizens, was replaced with freedom of conscience, presupposing the right to "profess any religion or not to profess any." This Leninist interpretation of the freedom of conscience was further formalized in the 1918 Constitution of the Russian Federation: "All citizens enjoy the freedom of religious or antireligious propaganda" (Article 13). The deformation that followed distorted the principle of freedom of conscience proclaimed by the decree. The Stalin Constitution of the USSR (1936) changed Lenin's wording and thereby violated the balance inherent in it: "All citizens may exorcise religious cults and enjoy the freedom of antireligious propaganda" (Article 124). The imbalance was preserved in the 1977 Constitution of the USSR and even supported politically: atheistic propaganda began to be carried out at the expense and with the help of the state, and atheism became an obligatory subject to be studied at state educational establishments. To make scores of millions of Soviet religious citizens realize that the state they live in is not atheistic, the new law should state clearly that the freedom of conscience is, in particular, the freedom to choose between religion and atheism, and propaganda of corresponding beliefs, including religious and atheistic education, should be put in equal conditions.

PARISH LIFE

The situation in the church itself is another obstacle to the utilization of present opportunities. For many long decades our parishes have been deprived of the right to engage in social activities, and the habits and forms of such work have been consigned to oblivion. Under certain conditions they could be restored rather quickly, but the problem is that the parish itself has changed under the impact of well-known historical circumstances: it is not always a genuine community where each member finds recognition and support. More often than not, especially large parishes in cities consist of people who hardly know each other. But even in small parishes where people do know each other they have no sufficient experience of communication and joint efforts for the benefit of the entire parish. Most of the parishioners do not associate with the parish any other obligations than those related to liturgy.

It should be emphasized that our believers are not to blame for that. They represent the third or even the fourth generation of people for whom parish life was strictly limited to liturgy, and many of them just have no idea of its other forms. The same is true for priests as well. The problem emerged as soon as the church was given an opportunity to expand its charitable activity. Wherever new donations alone were requested, people readily cooperated, but where people's efforts were required with some elements of self-organization and collaboration, difficulties appeared.

Parishioners who have proved able to organize brotherhoods, sisterhoods, or other voluntary associations to help the afflicted deserve great respect and gratitude.

Such associations should become a norm of our everyday parish life. Individual initiatives, including those by hierarchs, are not sufficient; they can inspire only individual acts of charity. What we need, instead is a revival of genuine *diaconia* on all levels of church life. Like liturgy, *diaconia* should stem from the very nature of Christian community, feeding on its spiritual energy and at the same time replenishing that energy.

Despite current difficulties, we have reason to hope that our church will prove able to revive the service of charity and love. What provides grounds for such a hope? The fact that, by divine providence, our church, having been deprived of many things, has preserved the main thing. And that main thing has helped it to survive. The church has preserved the sacred grace-bestowing life with the Eucharist as its center through which the Holy Spirit transforms human community into the body of Christ. It is precisely in this respect that a church community differs from any other group of people or collective, and herein lies its strength, its spiritual potential, and, consequently, its vitality. And, together with the apostle Paul, in the humility and simplicity of our hearts, we can answer the question of whether the Russian church is able to meet the challenges of our hard times in the following way: "The foolishness of God is wiser than men; and the weakness of God is stronger than men" (1 Cor. 1:25). The church's highest priority today is, through parish life, to reveal the spiritual potential of our faithful and to direct that potential toward creating and multiplying moral values in society. Primary efforts should be aimed at building community life, developing relations between members of parishes, and drawing believers into parish work.

Joint work in church unites people, which is exemplified by the newly open parishes. It seems very important, therefore, that parishioners be involved in taking care of their church building and discussing issues of parish life. Pastoral work outside of liturgical time also seems desirable. It can include various meetings, talks, and circles. A special note should be made of work with various age groups: children, teenagers, middle-aged adults, and aged people. Acts of charity should be carried out first of all in parishes. Concern for "widows and orphans," that is, all those in need, should become part and parcel of everyday parish life. It is only in this way, by moving from the small to the big and relying upon the entire parish rather than on its individual members, that *diaconia* can be revived, catechistic work can be organized, and the spiritual needs of our people can be met on the scale of the entire church.

LEADERSHIP TRAINING

The prospects for a revival of parish life make the problem of training clergy very urgent. It is not theological schools alone that need new curricula in pastoral theology. Parish priests who lack experience in this kind of work also need relevant training. The problem could be solved by organizing pastoral seminars in dioceses or deaneries. Such seminars could provide an opportunity for priests to exchange experience and to learn methods of parish work and catechetical instruction.

The life of the church community provides for the close ties and mutual enrichment of all its members. The church principles of *sobornost* (community) involve all people of God in church life and cement the unity of pastors and flock. Decisions made in this spirit run no risk of being rejected by everyday reality. Having traversed a difficult historical path, our church is entering a period when the external conditions become favorable for restoring the principles of *sobornost*, and it is important that, by hard work and prayer, those principles be indeed restored and consolidated.

Hopes and disappointments come and go, but our church continues to stand by its people as it has always done. And the task of paramount importance in its relation to society today may be, as always, ardent prayer that the nation's historical road become a road of purification.

Rehabilitation of
Stalinist Reprisal Victims

In 1990 Soviet President Mikhail Gorbachev announced that all victims of Stalin's terror, including clergy, would be rehabilitated. This act was the result of the struggles and combined efforts of different church and public organizations for many years.

In 1989, the Holy Synod set up a special commission to study materials related to the rehabilitation of clergy and laity of the Russian Orthodox Church who were subjected to reprisals after the Revolution. The commission is chaired by Metropolitan Vladimir of Rostov and Novocherkassk, Head of the Chancellery of the Moscow Patriarchate, who issued a statement that said, in part, "Innocent victims who suffered for their faith in Jesus Christ deserve to be revered by the church as martyrs and confessors. All of them were citizens of their country and did not commit any crimes against it. Frequently people were persecuted for the mere fact of their being members of clergy or for being believers. We must exonerate the clergy and laity who suffered for their faith. There is no question that their civic rehabilitation is, first and foremost, the responsibility of the state and society as a whole, which, thank God, have now realized this. On its part the church is prepared to do everything in its power to assist in this noble endeavor. . . . It is clear that the church cannot be held responsible for what took place during reprisals, nor is it legally bound to compensate people subjected to reprisals for ruined health or loss of providers. However, it is a matter of religious duty and mercy to try to assist these people. . . . The Synod Canonization Commission has been collecting and studying materials that can be used to canonize new martyrs. Chapels are being built over the graves of reprisal victims. Numerous commemorative plaques bearing the names of the clergy and laity subjected to reprisals will be installed in churches and cemeteries. We are trying to preserve the memory of every innocent victim. To identify each of them name by name is our duty and the duty of all society. It is a duty that we owe to our conscience and our morality."

STALINIST REPRISALS

Reprisals against the clergy and religious leaders in the 1920s, 1930s, and 1940s were carried out on a massive scale under the slogan, "The struggle against religion is the struggle for socialism!" In the period from 1918 to 1940, 207 bishops, 42,000 clergymen, and millions of believers either were killed or perished in concentration camps, prisons, and internal exile.

The next wave of reprisals against the clergy and laity swept the country in 1921 and 1922, when church valuables were seized during the famine in the area of the Volga river. Reprisals were taken not only against those who opposed the seizure, but also against all people considered politically unreliable. The seizure of valuables and the backlash of the clergy were frequently invoked as a pretext for all sorts of arbitrary actions. One case in point is the death sentence passed on Metropolitan Veniamin of Petrograd in 1922 in the course of a trial marked by blatant violations of the most elementary standards of justice. In the late 1920s and the early 1930s, the policy of forced collectivization in the countryside was also used to close down many churches and to carry out reprisals. In the bloody year of 1937, many people who had survived previous purges or lingered in camps or internal exile were not spared.

Speaking at an international scientific religious conference held in Moscow in 1988 Archbishop Ioann of Kuybyshev and Syzran cited the following statistics on the number of clergymen subjected to reprisals since 1925:

1925	—	20 hierarchs
1926	—	11
1927	—	7
1928	—	6
1929	—	6
1930	—	8
1931	—	16
1932	—	1
1933	—	9
1934	—	6
1935	—	14
1936	—	20
1937	—	50

By the end of 1939 only four ruling hierarchs were still free: Metropolitan Sergiy (Starogorodsky), Metropolitan Alexiy (Simansky), Metropolitan Nikolai (Yarushevich), and Archbishop Sergiy (Voskresensky). Several bishops were in retirement or were acting as superiors of cathedrals. By the end of the 1930s, the Russian Orthodox Church was virtually destroyed and sessions of the Holy Synod were banned. On 7 April 1925 Patriarch Tikhon, who himself had spent many years in prison, passed away, but the authorities did not permit the convening of a local council to elect a new patriarch. A number of locum tenentes of the patriarch's throne were imprisoned. Several months before his death Patriarch Tikhon wrote a bequest in which he expressed his concern about succession in the church hierarchy and the canonical structure of church administration. He wrote,

> In the event of our death, our patriarch's rights and responsibilities are temporarily granted to His Eminence Metropolitan Kirill, until a new patriarch is legally elected. If he is not able to discharge the above-mentioned rights and responsibilities, they shall pass to His Eminence Metropolitan Agafangel. If this metropolitan is also unable to exercise them, then our patriarch's rights and responsibilities shall be transferred to His Eminence Pyotr, Metropolitan Krutitsky.

The bequest of His Holiness was read out at a session of Russian Orthodox hierarchs during the burial of Patriarch Tikhon, after which the following document was drawn up:

> Having satisfied ourselves that the documents are authentic and taking into account the fact that (1) under the given circumstances the deceased patriarch had no other means of preserving the succession of power in the Russian church and that (2) neither Metropolitan Kirill (Smirnov), nor Metropolitan Agafangel (Preobrazhensky) are currently in Moscow and can assume the responsibilities with which the above-mentioned document invests them, we, the hierarchs, recognize that Metropolitan Pyotr (Polyansky) cannot disobey the order given to him and in compliance with the will of the deceased patriarch must assume the responsibilities of the patriarch's locum tenens.

This document suggests the following conclusions: Metropolitans Kirill and Agafangel had been imprisoned, and Metropolitan Pyotr, mindful of their plight, tried to evade superior orders.

Subsequent developments proved that Metropolitan Pyotr's misgivings were entirely justified. He faced enormous problems from the beginning. The patriarchal church was not granted legal status by the new government, and for that reason it could not function normally in accordance with the administrative organization of the local church. The patriarch had failed to win legal recognition for the Russian Orthodox Church although he had spared no effort. For this reason, a deep divide soon emerged between the church hierarchy and Russia's bishops. Every Orthodox bishop ran his diocese as he pleased. Left-wing extremists in the church, who called themselves the *obnovlentsy* ("renovators"), refused to obey the orders of church authorities. The government supported them, and their influence began to grow, particularly in central and northern Russia and the southern Ukraine.

On 1 October 1925 the renovators convened an ecclesiastical council. It was attended by 78 bishops, 105 clerics, and 131 lay persons. All were granted the right to vote. The council attacked the traditional Orthodox hierarchy, accusing it of political intransigence and of abandoning Christian ideals and the mission of the church. What the renovators wrote and said about Metropolitan Pyotr clearly implied that he was a man who maintained links with monarchists abroad and that he belonged to the reactionary Black Hundred organization.

On 10 December 1925 Metropolitan Pyotr was arrested on charges of anti-Soviet agitation. After eleven years of imprisonment and internal exile, the metropolitan died in 1936, and it is not known where he died or where he was buried.

In accordance with a bequest left by Metropolitan Pyotr, Metropolitan Sergiy (Starogodsky) began to rule the Russian Orthodox Church as deputy of the patriarchal locum tenens on 14 December 1925. On 8 December 1926 he was arrested. His arrest followed an attempt by Russian hierarchs to elect a new patriarch; they were secretly collecting signatures to hold a ballot. On 20 March 1927 Metropolitan Sergiy was set free, probably because he had given assurances of loyalty to the Soviet regime.

Metropolitan Sergiy was given permission to set up a provisional Holy Synod, which comprised Metropolitan Arseniy of Novgorod (Stadnitsky), Metropolitan Serafim of Tver (Aleksandrov), Archbishop Silvestr of Vologda (Bratanovsky), Archbishop Alexiy of Khutin (Simansky), Archbishop Sevastyan of Kostroma (Vesti), Archbishop Filipp of Zvenigorod (Gumilevsky), and Archbishop Konstantin of Sumy (Dyakov). On 29 July 1929 Metropolitan Sergiy and the members of the synod adopted a declaration, which was published in the government newspaper *Izvestia TsIK* three months later. The declaration pledged total loyalty to Soviet authorities, and, at the same time, it stated that from that time on not only the joys and achievements of the state but also its setbacks would be regarded as the joys and misfortunes of the faithful. This reversal in the policy of the church was totally unexpected for many believers and was condemned by them, because the reprisals against the clergy and laity continued unabated. Ninety percent of all parishes rejected the declaration. In the fall of 1926, when the reprisals against the clergy and bishops were stepped up again, a group of hierarchs imprisoned on the Solovetskie Islands in the far north of the country, headed by Archbishop Illarion (Troitsky), sent a special message addressed to the Soviet government. In it the hierarchs clearly stated why in that situation good relations between the church and the state were impossible:

"The church recognizes the existence of the spirit, which is the beginning of everything; communism denies this. The church believes in the living God, the Creator and the guiding force of the universe, who determines lives and destinies; communism does not admit his existence and sees arbitrariness in the existence of the universe and the absence of any reasonable finite causes in its history. The church believes that the purpose of human life is in the celestial predestination of the spirit; it always reminds believers about their celestial fatherland, even if they enjoy the highest development of material culture and highest levels of affluence. Communism does not admit of any other goals for man other than his well-being on earth. From the heights of this philosophical controversy the ideological difference between the church and the state descends into the sphere of direct practical significance and the sphere of moral principles. The church believes in the inviolable moral principles of justice and law; communism believes them to be a conditional result of the class struggle and evaluates moral phenomena only in terms of expediency. The church preaches love and mercy, while communism preaches comradeship and ruthless struggle. The church preaches meekness, which elevates man; communism makes him proud and humiliates him. The church protects the purity of the flesh and the sacredness of childbearing; communism regards marital relations only as the satisfaction of instincts. The church regards religion as a life-giving force, which not only ensures the attainment of man's eternal predestination, but which also serves as the source of everything great in human creativity, the foundation of well-being on earth, happiness, and the health of peoples; communism regards religion as an opiate, which intoxicates people and saps their energy and is the source of their afflictions and poverty. The church wants religion to prosper; communism wants it to be destroyed. Given this profound divergence in outlook between the church and the state, there can be no internal movement toward each other or reconciliation, just as there can be no reconciliation between affirmation and negation, between yes and no, because the soul of the church, the condition of its being, and the meaning of its existence are the very things that communism categorically denies. Given this irreconcilable ideological rift between the church and the state, which is inevitably reflected in the life and activities of these organizations, a collision in their day-to-day work can be prevented only by consistently implementing the law on the separation of the church from the state, in accordance with which neither the church should impede the civilian government in its effort to increase the material well-being of the people, nor the state should constrain the church in its religious and moral work.

"Unfortunately, seldom does reality match this wish. Both in legislation and in administrative practice, the government does not remain neutral in matters concerning faith and atheism. It clearly sides with atheism, throwing all its weight to impose, develop, and disseminate atheism as a counterbalance to all religions. It is the religious duty of the church to preach the gospel to all, including the children of believers. However, law deprives it of the right to discharge this duty in relation to minors.

At the same time, in schools and youth organizations, the principles of atheism with all the logical consequences thereof are forcibly instilled in young children and adolescents. The fundamental law grants citizens the freedom of religious beliefs. Yet this right clashes with another law under which a religious community cannot act as a juridical person and therefore cannot possess any property, even objects of no material value but which are sacred to believers solely because of their religious significance. In the interests of antireligious propaganda this law was invoked to move remains of saints from cathedral to museums.

"In its administrative policy the government takes all measures to suppress religion: it has been using every pretext to close down churches and turn them into places of public entertainment and to shut down monasteries despite the introduction of some elements of work in them. It imposes all sorts of constraints on the clergy's everyday life, prevents believers from teaching at schools, and prohibits public libraries from lending religious books and even books of idealistic philosophy. On many occasions top government officials have stated that even the limited freedom that the church still enjoys is temporary and a concession to the centuries-old religious customs of people.

"The law on the separation of church from state contains two separate clauses. It prohibits the church from participation in politics and civilian government, but it also contains a pledge on the part of the state not to interfere in the internal affairs of the church, its religious teaching, service, and administration.

"In full compliance with this law the church is hoping that the state will conscientiously discharge its responsibilities in good faith and preserve the freedom and independence of the church.

"The church is hoping that it will not remain without any rights in this difficult situation. It is hoping that the legislation on the teaching of the law of the Lord and the legal status of religious associations will be reviewed and amended for the benefit of the church and that remains of the saints revered by the church will not be profaned any more and will be returned from museums back to cathedrals.

"The church is hoping that it will be permitted to organize a diocesan department, to elect a new patriarch and members of the Holy Synod acting under his supervision, and, when it seems necessary, to convene for that purpose a diocesan congress or an all-Russia Orthodox council.

"The church is hoping that the government will refrain from any open or secret attempt to influence the election of delegates and members of the council, that it will not limit the freedom of discussion on religious issues at these meetings or require any preliminary obligations that would predetermine major decisions.

"The church is also hoping that the activities of the religious organizations thereby created, the appointment of bishops, and the election of the Holy Synod will be free from the influence of the government clerk appointed to exercise political control over them.

"In submitting this memorandum for the government's consideration, the Russian Orthodox Church feels compelled to stress once again that it has been completely sincere in stating to the Soviet authorities the difficulties that prevent the establishment of mutually benevolent relations between church and state. . . . Being profoundly convinced that a strong and trustful relationship can only be based on full justice, it has stated openly and without any deviations or recriminations what it can promise to the Soviet authorities and what it cannot abandon because of its principles and what it expects from the government of the USSR."

This important and profound document was made public by Archbishop Ioann at an international religious conference in Moscow in 1988. Its authors perished in Stalinist prisons, but their ideas laid the foundation for new relations between the church and the state today.

WORLD WAR II BRINGS RELIEF

The reprisals and antireligious propaganda did not end until the beginning of the Second World War when Stalin needed wider support in Soviet society. After July 1941 the magazine *Bezbozhnik* ("Atheist") was no longer published. Some churches reopened. It is now known that during that period some clergymen were set free. That kind of partial rehabilitation of the church met the needs of the millions of people who had lost their fathers, husbands, brothers, and sons on the battlefield and longed for the consolation that the church could offer.

During 1942 talks with Vyacheslav Molotov, who was the second most important person in the Soviet state, the Allies called for the Komintern to be dissolved and the Russian Orthodox Church restored in its rights. It should also be noted that the Stalinist leadership was uneasy about reports that churches and monasteries were being reopened in the territories occupied by German troops. For example, the monastery at the Kiev-Pechery Laura, closed down in the early 1930s had reopened. Stalin realized that his policy toward the church had become very compromising politically, and he ordered a turnaround. In 1942 a book was published, allegedly by the Moscow patriarchate, denying the facts of religious persecution and ascribing rumors of such facts to "Goebbels' propagandists." The same book described in great detail atrocities committed by German troops and carried photographs of a monastery near Moscow that had been destroyed by German troops.

The situation began to change rapidly, and on 4 September 1943 Stalin invited Metropolitan Sergiy (Starogorodsky), Metropolitan Alekxiy (Simansky), and Metropolitan Nikolai (Yarushevich) for a meeting. As a result of their talks the church was given permission to convene a council and elect a new patriarch, resume religious publications and the education of clergymen, and reestablish contacts with foreign churches. The Council for the Affairs of the Russian Orthodox Church was set up under the Soviet of the People's Commissars, which was later incorporated into the Council for the Religious Affairs under the Council of Ministers of the USSR.

Although reprisals stopped and religious life began to revive, the state maintained strict control over all church activities. Under subsequent regimes the situation remained unchanged until the era of *perestroika*.

However, in the 1960s the situation again took a turn for the worse. Nikita Khrushchev ordered nearly one-half of the acting cathedrals, churches, and monasteries to be closed down. It was officially declared that the current generation of Soviet people would live under communism, and Khrushchev even said that communism would triumph by 1980. The leading ideologues of the time, specifically Mikhail Suslov, asserted that there was no place for the church in a communist society. Fortunately, there were no mass executions or reprisals, which already indicated a certain improvement.

After Stalin's death in 1953, large numbers of his victims were rehabilitated. The charges of espionage and subversion against many clergymen were dropped. However, the press remained biased against the clergy. It continued to publish materials about their counterrevolutionary activities against the Soviet regime, or it dismissed the whole issue of religion in society.

REHABILITATION

Only now are clergymen who were sentenced on trumped-up charges being rehabilitated. On 22 May 1989 more than one thousand people attended a memorial meeting in the hall of the Palace of Culture of the *Serp i Molot* plant. They came to commemorate victims of antireligious persecutions at a mass ceremony. Clergymen, writers, artists, and relatives of the people who perished in Stalinist prisons condemned antireligious persecutions and mourned their innocent victims. The meeting was organized by the Memorial Society, a new historical and educational public organization. A ten-meter-long stand with photographs, letters, and other documents was set up in the lobby. At the end of the meeting it was announced that the work to collect these materials would continue and that Memorial had set up a special center to keep the Soviet public informed about its activities.

The Local Council of the Russian Orthodox Church of 7–8 June 1990, resolved there was need for "special effort in preparation of materials for the canonization of martyrs who suffered for their faith in the reprisals to which our Church was subjected in the twentieth century." The Canonization Commission thereafter issued a document "The Stance of the Church on Martyrdom" elaborating the principles that guided the Church at different times in canonization, and the guidelines for further Commission activities in canonizing the new martyrs.

The two latest Commission sittings were devoted to studies of information for the prospective canonization of Vladimir, Metropolitan of Kiev and Galicia (in the world, Bogoyavlensky) and Benjamin, Metropolitan of Petrograd and Gdov (in the world, Kazansky).

Metropolitan Vladimir (1848–1918) was shot without any preceding investigation or trial at the Kiev-Pechery Laura on 25 January 1918. The Local Council active in Moscow at that time adopted a resolution concerning his death, which said, in part: "All Russia shall say prayers for the souls of all martyred for their faith at this bitter hour, on 25 January or the following Sunday." The Metropolitan was buried at the Church of the Apparition of the Cross, above the Near Caves of the Kiev Cave Monastery.

Benjamin, Metropolitan of Petrograd and Gdov (1873–1922), Archimandrite Sergius (in the world, Vasili Schein, member of the State Duma of the fourth convocation, and one of the Secretaries of the Local Council of 1917–1918), Yuri Novitsky, professor of criminal law at Petrograd University, and the lawyer Ivan Kovsharov were shot on 13 August 1922, on the sentence of the Petrograd provincial revolutionary tribunal for "organization of counterrevolutionary action and sabotage of the decree of 23 February 1922, on the requisitioning of church valuables."

As the Canonization Commission studied the files of Metropolitan Benjamin and the persons executed with him, many pronounced on their innocence. The Church appealed to the USSR Procurator-General's office for their posthumous rehabilitation. On February 11, 1991, Alexis II, Patriarch of Moscow and All Russia, received a reply from V. Ilukhin, Senior Assistant of the USSR Procurator-General, which said:

"From its studies of the investigation and court materials preserved at the archives, the office of the USSR Procurator-General concludes that V. Kazansky (Metropolitan Benjamin) and the other 58 persons were sentenced against the law. Their files do not indicate that they established an anti-Soviet organization and worked to undermine the Soviet system. The letters of Metropolitan Benjamin to the Commission for Aid to Famine-Stricken Areas and later to the Petrograd Provincial Executive Committee provide no grounds to assume criminal activities. In his appeal of 10 April 1922 to the Orthodox Christians of Petrograd, the Metropolitan called to the clergy and laity to make donations in favor of the famine-stricken localities, assist *ad hoc* commissions requisitioning church valuables, and prevent violence and resistance during requisitions.

"In this connection, A. Vasiliev, USSR First Deputy Procurator-General, addressed the Presidium of the RSFSR Supreme Court to revoke the court decision on V. Kazansky (Metropolitan Benjamin) and the other fifty-eight accused in absence of *corpus delicti*. His protest was satisfied on 31 October 1990, and all persons sentenced were rehabilitated."

On 22 February 1991, the Most Holy Patriarch Alexis II received from V. Lebedev, Chairman of the RSFSR Supreme Court, in reply to his later inquiry, a copy of the resolution of the Presidium of the RSFSR Supreme Court of 31 October 1990, which revoked the court decisions on Benjamin, Metropolitan of Petrograd and Gdov, and other persons in the absence of *corpus delicti* in their activities, and rehabilitated them. The Patriarch ceded the papers to the Canonization Commission, authorizing it to publish them.

Father Pavel Florensky,
Back from Obscurity

Archpriest Alexander Kozha

In January 1989 the Soviet Culture Fund held the first in a series of meetings on the "Return of Forgotten Names." It was devoted to Father Pavel Florensky (1882–1937?), a priest of the Russian Orthodox Church.

The past twenty years or so have seen a steadily growing number of Father Pavel's works being published. A philosopher and theologian, mathematician and art critic, inventor and historian, he was a person of encyclopedic learning. Working in most diverse spheres of human culture and having enriched each of them with his discoveries, Father Pavel was one of those who paved the way to a comprehensive world outlook of the future.

In each of the fields of learning he pursued, Father Pavel's focus centered around substantiating and commenting on the main dogma of faith—the Holy Trinity. All his theological and philosophical premises were derived from the Orthodox concept of the Holy Trinity.

The core of Orthodox teaching about the Trinity is the principle of triunity. The world can be regarded as consisting of beings externally related to each other and mutually linked in time and space. The philosophy of triunity asserts that all creatures are inseparably linked with each other internally, ontologically. It regards the world as an organic whole and recognizes humankind's unity not only genetically, but also truly ontologically. People are brothers and sisters, not because descended from Adam and Eve but intrinsically.

Pavel Florensky wrote in his book *The Pillar and Affirmation of the Truth,* "To love means to accept divine energy and help it to open itself through the outer world . . . just as it acts in the triune God himself." This understanding of love is ontological rather than psychological, and it is much higher and deeper than the category of morals.

Father Pavel Florensky revered life in all its spiritual plenitude. He wrote, "All nature is animate and alive in the whole and in parts. . . . Everything is closely linked. The energies of things flow into other things, and each lives in all and in each" (*The General Human Roots of Idealism*). Because united with the entire world, humankind is responsible for all creation. In other words, theologically, the ecological problem must be solved, not in strictly scientific terms but in religious and moral ones.

Thus, the main contribution of Father Pavel Florensky's work lies in the fact that he consciously introduced the principle of unity, borrowed from the sphere of pure theology, into the metaphysics of the created world. This has made it possible to apply the principle of unity in all spheres of modern theology and philosophy.

Having graduated from the Department of Physics and Mathematics of Moscow State University in 1900 by defending his thesis, "The Idea of Discontinuity as an Element of World Outlook," Pavel Florensky decided to continue his studies at the Moscow Theological Academy. He finished a course of study there in 1908 and remained as a lecturer in the history of philosophy. Between 1908 and 1919 he taught several original courses on the history of classical philosophy, Kantian philosophy, and the philosophy of religion and culture. From 1912 to 1917 he headed *Bogoslovski vestnik* ("Theological Herald"), which in many respects determined the Russian cultural atmosphere at the start of the century.

After his ordination in 1911, Father Pavel became a connecting link between the Moscow Theological Academy and Moscow intellectuals who sought spiritual support in the church, because he was accepted by both groups.

The Revolution of 1917 was not a surprise to him. He had written much about the deep crisis of bourgeois civilization, and he often spoke about the approaching collapse of the established principles of life. He held no illusions about personal risks brought about by the social upheaval, but he never considered leaving his country. When Paris offered a brilliant career in science and international recognition, Father Pavel chose Solovki because emigration was alien to his nature.

He was among the first priests who combined his church service with secular jobs. Until 1929, the year of "the Great Change," in Stalin's terminology, Father Pavel wore his cassock in his office and in scientific laboratories, and members of the "new intelligentsia" called him a "learned priest."

He felt that it was his moral duty and vocation to do all he could to preserve the foundations of spiritual culture for the sake of future generations. He splendidly expressed this idea in a letter written in 1917:

> Everything that is going on around us, is, of course, excruciating. But I believe and hope that, having exhausted itself, nihilism will prove worthless, bore everybody to death, become hateful, and then, after the collapse of all this vileness, all hearts and minds will turn to . . . Holy Rus, not sluggishly and circumspectly as they used to, but eagerly. I am sure that the worst is still ahead and not behind us and that the crisis has not yet passed. But I believe that the crisis will clear the Russian atmosphere,

even the world atmosphere spoiled as far back as in the seventeenth century.

In 1918 Father Pavel became a member of the commission for the protection of objects of art and old culture in the Holy Trinity-St. Sergiy Laura. Quickly an inventory was made of all the wealth of the laura, and priceless articles were thereby saved for posterity. The commission conducted preparatory work leading to the signing of the decree by Lenin turning the Holy Trinity-St. Sergiy Laura into a museum.

In an attempt to preserve still-functioning monasteries as centers of spiritual culture Father Florensky suggested the concept of a living museum, preserving each article in its original surroundings. Today this concept is widely accepted by museums all over the world.

In 1921 Father Pavel was elected professor of the Higher Artistic and Technical School.

When various new trends (futurism, constructivism, abstractionism) flourished in art, he tried to vindicate the spiritual value and significance of universal forms of culture. In his works *An Analysis of Space and Time in Works of Art, Inverse Perspective, The Iconostasis,* and *At the Watershed of Thought,* he showed that there were no criteria of choice within the confines of culture itself. He stressed that the assessment of values lay beyond the confines of culture as such; religion was a matter of necessity.

At the same time Father Florensky was engaged in intensive studies in applied physics and technology. He helped to elaborate the nation's electrification program, the GOELRO Plan, and he worked at the Committee on Electrotechnical Norms and Rules. He set up the country's first materials testing laboratory, published the book *Dielectrics and Their Technical Applications,* and was among the first to promote synthetic resins production. And he did all this in the Russia of the 1920s, in a country torn apart by the Civil War, amidst a dislocated economy and a fierce, uncompromising ideological struggle.

He was a coeditor of *The Technical Encyclopedia* and a member of the Presidium of the Bureau on Electroinsulating Materials and the Commission on Standardization.

In 1922, in his book *Imagery in Geometry,* he deduced from Einstein's general theory of relativity the finiteness of the universe, with humanity in the center of it as the summit of creation.

He also continued his studies of religious consciousness. He suggested setting up a religious and philosophical academy in Moscow where representatives of all religions could work together. In his *Philosophy of Cult* he posed the question of such cooperation, stressing that religion is an inherent attribute of humankind although it takes many forms.

Persecutions of Father Pavel began in 1919–1920 with attempts to denounce the work of the commission for the protection of the Holy Trinity-St. Sergiy Laura as a counterrevolutionary scheme designed to "create an Orthodox Vatican." He was also accused of attempts to organize an "idealist coalition" among fellow lecturers. Pseudoscientific attacks followed of his book *Imagery in Geometry* and his article "Physics at the Service of Mathematics," in which he described an electrointegrator, a prototype of modern analog computers. Father Pavel was painted as an enemy in disguise, thereby turning public opinion against him.

In the summer of 1928 Father Florensky was banished to Nizhni Novgorod. Three months later he managed to return and, with the help of friends, to resume his work. The situation was such, however, that he said, "I was in exile and returned to penal servitude."

In February 1933 Father Pavel was arrested again, given a ten-year sentence, and deported to eastern Siberia. As convicts were used on building projects in permafrost areas, Father Pavel studied both permafrost and building construction. Soon he was sent to a permafrost research station. Eighteen months later, however, he was deported to the special Solovetsky prison camp. There he worked at an iodine factory, studied the extraction of iodine and other substances from algae, and made more than ten scientific discoveries and inventions, which were all patented.

In the summer of 1937 the Solovetsky camp was turned into a special prison. Father Pavel's last known letter dates from that period. Probably he perished in 1937, although the official date was listed as 15 December 1943. (Dates of death of the victims of reprisals were distributed evenly over a number of years to conceal the massive scale of the reprisals.)

In one of his last letters Father Florensky summed up his life in this way: "The worst thing in my fate is the break in my work and the practical annihilation of the experience of my entire life, which has just reached a mature stage when it could yield genuine fruits. . . . But it remains an open question who, myself or society, has more to lose."

Judging by this and some other letters of the last period of Father Pavel's life, we can assume that he underestimated the true scale of the tragedy of the nation. He attached too much importance to speculative philosophical constructions and his own personality. He wrote, for example, "Glancing back, I see that I have never had really favorable conditions for my work, partly because of my inability to put my personal affairs in order, partly because of the state of our society, with which I have been out of step by at least fifty years. I was ahead of it, while to achieve success one should be not more than two or three years ahead." Or, "It is clear that the world is organized in such a way that in order to give it something you must pay with suffering and persecutions."

However strange it might seem, most people in those years underestimated the massive and determined scale of reprisals, thinking that others were punished for real crimes while they themselves were victims of circumstances. People in prison camps believed their cases would soon be reconsidered and justice would triumph. Many petitioned the authorities trying to prove that what they had been doing prior to their arrest was of great value to both the people and the state. Father Pavel was among them. He sent his petition in 1934, but to no avail. The construction of a new culture was in full swing, and there was no room in it for vestiges of the old world.

Father Pavel realized better than most that progress devoid of spirituality was doomed. He believed that the glorification of humanity untempered by suprahuman spiritual values would lead inevitably to a personality cult in politics, to a destructive and predatory attitude toward the environment, to a worship of "pure" knowledge and immoral experiments in science, and to extreme individualism in the arts.

It still seemed incredible at that time that the twentieth century would bring humankind to the brink of self-destruction. But today, decades after Father Florensky's predictions, we find them to be absolutely correct. And again, humankind turns to the quest for eternal truths, to the sources of genuine spirituality and universal values.

This is how Father Florensky, at the end of his life, assessed the inevitable course of human history: "Hateful is human stupidity, which has existed from the beginning of history and which, evidently, will last to its end. . . . The world is going mad and is raving in search of an elusive something, while clarity, which alone is required, is in its own hands."

In the summer of 1989 one of the streets in a village on the Solovetsky Islands, his last place of residence on earth, was named after him.

Revival of Traditions
at Russian Monasteries

Archpriest Alexander Kozha

Before 1917 there were more than a thousand monasteries in Russia. After the Revolution their number decreased rapidly, and on the eve of World War II not a single one remained open. Starting in 1943, several monasteries were reopened, including the Holy Trinity-St. Sergiy and the Kiev-Pechery lauras. However, in the early 1960s Nikita Khrushchev mounted a new offensive against the church, since he considered the church an ideological risk. Since the advent of *perestroika*, several ancient monasteries have been handed back to the church and new monasteries built. There are now 107 active monasteries.

Russian monasticism has always differed in some respects from its Western counterpart. Russian monks never fled public life *en masse* as did ascetics in Egypt in the early centuries of Christianity. Nor has their life been as strictly functional as life in an order in the medieval West.

Russian monasticism has always maintained close links between monks and Christians who lead a secular life. Old monks used to say that a full secular family life was like a vine, while the life of a monk was like the dry stick that props up the vine. If the prop is removed, the vine will fall to the ground and rot. Therefore, a vine generously covered with bunches of grapes needs a dry stick to support it. In this way Russian monasteries have provided a living embodiment of holiness, from which secular society can draw spiritual strength.

Russian asceticism acquired a special quality from the Byzantine Hesychasm, transformed in the prayers and meditative experience of Aphonite monasticism. The practice of Hesychasm flourished in Russia in the fourteenth century in the time of St. Sergiy of Rodonezh and his followers and had a remarkable influence on Russian icon-painting (St. Andrei Rublev), then after a certain decline, it came back to life in late eighteenth to early nineteenth centuries.

The spiritual life of this period is intense and diverse—the spirit soars to unprecedented heights in the knowledge of God (St. Serafim of Sarov), there is a strong preference for hesychastic prayers and meditation, and finally, a unique form of monasticism appears, known as *starchestvo*, represented by the *starets* or monastic elders, which complemented and enriched still further the traditional spiritual life.

One of the ancient monastic centers recently returned to the church is the Optina Hermitage. This hermitage has been recognized as a spiritual center and place of healing. People from all across Russia, from all walks of life and of all ages, the educated and illiterate, used to travel to the Optina Hermitage to consult with old monks there. The insight and holiness of the brothers even caught the eye of the Russian intelligentsia, writers and thinkers who rarely turned to the church for guidance.

This is what Father Pavel Florensky wrote in 1919 about the significance of Optina Hermitage:

> If one begins to trace in one's mind the diverse trends of Russian life in the realm of the spirit, directly or indirectly, we always come to Optina Hermitage as a spiritual focal point. Contact with it sets the spirit afire. . . . The cloister, remarkable not so much for its outstanding individuals as for the harmonious combination and interaction of the spiritual forces, has always been and continues to be today one whole, a place that, taken in its integrity, is a powerful generator of spiritual experience and, I even venture to say, the only place in Russia stimulating the spirit, at least in this way and with such force.

Is it possible to restore this spiritual center for Russia now that it once again belongs to the church? If so, we will need to train spiritual teachers. Strong spiritual ties can reemerge only in those places where there is an uplifting spiritual life and enlightened teachers to mold the spirit. One sign of hope that we may be able to restore the spiritual life of monasteries is that today more people want to enter monasteries than can presently be accommodated.

Not only the spiritual threads of monasteries were broken, but also their economic life. The monks of Optina Hermitage, for example, prospered economically until the beginning of the twentieth century. They tended a large garden and farmed several plots of land, kept stables, and tended a dairy farm. (They even raised a new breed of dairy cattle for which they were awarded a gold medal at an agricultural exhibition.) The monks built a cascade of twelve ponds, which abounded with fish. The monastery had a brickworks, a tile factory, a woodworking factory, a turnery, a metalwork shop, a saddle-making shop, an icon-painting and iconastasis-making studio, a large printing house, and other businesses. The monastery library received newly released books including works on natural sciences, from publishing houses around the country.

Unfortunately, these things were stolen, destroyed, or hidden.

Is it possible to restore all this? The Orthodox people have responded eagerly to the appeal for help made by the Russian Orthodox Church. The first contribution to restoring these landmarks was made by monks and novices themselves. Pilgrims put in considerable work under the guidance of monastery brothers, and believers have made significant financial donations. Icons, church plates, and books are arriving at the newly opened monasteries from acting monasteries, parishes, and individual believers. Restoration workers spend as much time as is necessary to restore ancient icons to their former appearance and significance.

But far greater resources are necessary. Installing central heating, running water, and electricity to monasteries entails considerable expense. In this respect help from local authorities and state organizations is invaluable. It is already clear that the church lacks both the people and the material resources to quickly and expertly restore the monasteries being returned to it. The question thus arises: should not the organizations that have reduced these national historical and cultural landmarks to this condition participate in restoring them? Unfortunately, the new laws on religion do not answer this question. This is a task for the entire nation. By saving our cultural heritage we ensure our survival as a nation.

Today, a number of prominent religious figures advocate putting together state-church and public-church programs to protect landmarks of culture, to study and extend our cultural legacy. Some experience has already been accumulated in the joint church-state use of the Holy Trinity-St. Sergiy Laura in Zagorsk, the Kiev-Pechery Laura in Kiev, the Novodevichiy Monastery in Moscow, and the Cathedral of the Dormition in Vladimir. As monasteries, they are places where church services are held, yet they also remain state museums.

There are other concerns as well. Who, for example, should live in the Valaam Monastery, on a small island in Ladoga Lake near Leningrad? In the past such island monasteries with agrarian land were settled primarily by Russian peasants who cultivated the land and lived off it. The garden of the Valaam Monastery had sixty different kinds of apple trees. Yet all of the cultivation was done by hand; monks and pilgrims carried earth on their shoulders. If the monastery is to revive its agriculture, someone will have to master anew agronomy, agrotechnology, gardening, and vegetable growing. And this is only one particular question relating to the conditions of life in one monastery.

Nevertheless, the mood predominant in society and the pace of restoration already taking place give us hope that the churches and monasteries that have been returned will be restored. As for the spiritual tradition, our challenge here is immeasurably tougher; it involves restoring in its integrity the world of holiness, purity, and selfless love for which the monasteries have traditionally stood and reviving their work of uniting the earthly with the divine.

The revival of the Russian Orthodox Church and the urgent need for renewed spiritual values felt today by millions of our compatriots hold out the hope that through divine grace the church will realize these aspirations and quench the thirst of its people's spirit.

An Armenian wedding.

The Armenian
Apostolic Church

Statistics: The Armenian Apostolic Church has more than 3 million followers. It has 62 churches, 13 monasteries, and 120 clergymen. The theological seminary and academy in Etchmiadzin have 80 students.

Organization: The Armenian Apostolic Church is headed by the Supreme Patriarch and Catholicos of All Armenians Vasken I. He holds the See of Holy Etchmiadzin and is the supreme spiritual head of all devout Armenians, the guardian and protector of the Armenian Church—its beliefs, rites and rituals, canons and traditions.

The hierarchical structure of the Armenian Church includes the historically established Catholicossate of the Great House of Cilicia (Lebanon), the Armenian Patriarchal See of Jerusalem, and the Armenian Patriarchal See of Turkey. "In the spiritual aspect," these three episcopal sees are under the jurisdiction of the Supreme See of Holy Etchmiadzin, but have international administrative autonomy.

Brief History: Armenia became Christian in A.D. 301. The Armenian Church, which belongs to the ancient Eastern Orthodox Churches, was established and developed as an independent Christian national church. Doctrinally, the Armenian Church bases its faith on the Bible, tradition, and the decisions of the first Three Ecumenical Councils. The Bible was translated into Armenian in the early 5th century right after the Armenian alphabet was created.

Many Armenian clergymen died and most churches were closed down during the years of the Stalin reprisals. The *perestroika* years have given the Armenian Church the possibility of restoring its positions.

Current Situation and Problems: In connection with the ethnic conflicts, the Armenian Apostolic Church is experiencing serious difficulties in Azerbaijan and Nagorny Karabakh, where a great number of Armenians reside.

Supreme Patriarch and Catholicos of All Armenians Vasken I and the Armenian Apostolic Church

In spite of the tragedy of the 1988 earthquake and the ongoing unrest and violence between Armenian and other ethnic populations, the head of the Armenian Apostolic Church looks to the future with optimism.

"If misery and martyrdom were the lot of the Armenian people, then we should know full well that it is also the nation's lot to endure, to win, and to survive," says Supreme Patriarch and Catholicos Vasken I. "Let us have faith in the moral force of the Armenian people. Let us have faith in the future of the Armenian homeland."

Vasken I does not intend his statement to fan ethnic unrest. He has, in fact, spent much effort struggling for religious tolerance and mutual respect among all people.

"The religions that emerged and evolved in the course of history enrich one another by their diversity, provided, of course, they are free from fanaticism and extreme intolerance," says Vasken I. "It would be wrong if all prayed from the same book. I am a Christian and my holy book is Christ's gospel. However, I also find it useful to read the Talmud and the Koran, and I find interesting ideas there."

In his opinion religions should not be viewed as separated by watertight partitions or opposed to each other, and their right to existence and development should not be denied. "One of the realities of our time is that different religions, national languages, and cultures mutually complement and enrich one another and help achieve mutual understanding. The spirit of internationalism is something that we Christians feel very strong about. I would like to point out that the first document expounding the idea of internationalism in the history of humanity was Christ's gospel.

"The differences that exist between religious confessions and teachings must not separate people or set them against each other. Every believer protecting his religious belief and his spiritual traditions should respect the spiritual and moral values of people of other religious convictions and everything that they treasure. This kind of religious tolerance can only be based on profound knowledge and understanding of life. It is the only sure sign of true spirituality that every true believer should have."

The Supreme Patriarch and Catholicos has called on Armenians and Azerbaijanis to respect each other's national identity, to uphold justice, and not to break their friendship. "Our peoples were destined to be neighbors and have been living side by side for centuries. There are over half a million Armenians in Azerbaijan and about two hundred thousand Azerbaijanis in Armenia. Let us face this reality. We have to find a way to live in peace and friendship in this world," said the Supreme Patriarch and Catholicos.

The Armenian Church is one of the oldest Christian denominations, and it has a unique national character. It belongs to the family of the ancient Eastern or Orthodox churches, which also include the Ethiopian, Coptic, Assyrian, and Indian Malabar churches. It was established and developed independently within the national borders of Armenia. Its holy book is the Bible, and it relies on the holy tradition and the decisions of the first three ecumenical councils held in Nicaea (A.D. 325), Constantinople (A.D. 381), and Ephesus (A.D. 431).

ARMENIAN CHURCH HISTORY

According to tradition, in the middle of the first century A.D., the holy apostles St. Thaddaeus and St. Bartholomew preached Christianity in Armenia (that is why the Armenian Church is called apostolic). The first Christian communities emerged at that time.

In 301, when Armenia was ruled by King Tiridates III (298–330) and St. Gregory the Illuminator was the first Armenian Supreme Patriarch and Catholicos (300–325), Christianity was proclaimed as the country's official religion. The Holy Echmiadzin, where the seat of the Supreme Patriarch and Catholicos of all Armenians was located, became its spiritual and administrative center.

In translation *the Echmiadzin* means "the only begotten has descended." According to tradition, St. Gregory the Illuminator had an apparition in which Christ with a halo around his head descended from heaven and with a fiery mallet pointed to a site where the church was to be built. The construction work was completed in 303. The altar of the descent was erected in the middle of the cathedral in the name of The Only Begotten Son of God.

For many centuries the Holy Echmiadzin was the center of moral and spiritual forces of the Armenian people, the fount of culture, science, and education. Here, in 406, Archimandrite Mesrop created the Armenian alphabet. The monastery promoted the development of Armenian literature, arts, philosophy, medicine, and astronomy. The founder of Armenian classical polyphonic music and the scholar of Armenian musical ethnography, Archimandrite Komitas; the founder of the new Armenian literature, Khachatur Abovyan; and poet Avetik Issaakyan studied and worked in this holy abode.

THE ARMENIAN CHURCH IN THE
TWENTIETH CENTURY

At present, about three million Armenians live in Armenia, and one and a half million live in other Soviet republics. Almost two million Armenians make up the diaspora—in the Middle East and the Persian Gulf area, the Balkans, western Europe, North and South Americas, and Australia. The diaspora began as a result of genocide perpetrated against the Armenians in Turkey in 1915, when several million people were killed. It continued again in 1920, when the Cilician Armenians were forcibly deported.

In the wake of those tragic events, which prompted a mass exodus of Armenians, the church emerged as a major force in promoting spiritual unity among the people and as the guardian of national culture and traditions.

The church went through many severe trials during the years of Stalin's rule. The 1930s were an especially difficult period for the nation. Many clergy were forced to abandon church life, while some of them were deported far beyond their native land. As a result, most churches were closed down. Religious life virtually ground to a halt or was severely restricted. Only a few monks remained at the Echmiadzin. In these tragic circumstances, in 1938, Catholicos Khoren I Muradbekyan died of a heart attack.

After World War II, the situation in the Armenian Church began to return to normal. Many churches were opened again, and destroyed cathedrals were put under restoration. The Religious Academy at the Echmiadzin reopened, and the publication of the journal of the catholicotate resumed.

THE ARMENIAN CHURCH TODAY

The current Supreme Patriarch and Catholicos has held his office since 1955. This is how he assesses the situation that has now evolved in his country: "I believe that after the difficult days and years of stagnation the Soviet society has entered on the path of moral convalescence. The most important thing today is to do everything to prevent a repetition of the past."

There has been a marked growth in the number of people attending Armenian churches. Many more people bring their children to be baptized, whereas thirty years ago this sacrament was administered to only about a quarter of all newborns. More and more young people want to be married in a church wedding.

"We want religion to help in the moral and spiritual education of young people and strengthen the moral foundations of the family," says the Supreme Patriarch and Catholicos. "The evangelical commandments often give us guidance in different situations we face in our life. We want to instill kindness, love, peace, mercy, and good in the young people who come to us."

During the years of *perestroika* many more young people want to devote themselves to spiritual life, and the competition among those who seek entrance at the Echmiadzin Religious Academy has now become much stiffer.

About forty students from the USSR and foreign countries study at this unique educational institution, which offers a five-year course of religious education. Students take classes in theology and Armenian studies. The curriculum also includes the Armenian, Grabar, Russian, ancient Greek, and English languages; the history of Armenia and the world; and the history of the Armenian and world churches. They study works of the fathers and teachers of the church; Armenian religious literature; philosophy; the Old and New Testaments; dogmatic, moral, doctrinal, and pastoral theology; apologetics; logic; psychology; homiletics; church music; and other subjects.

The octogenarian Supreme Patriarch and Catholicos has preserved a remarkable ability to work. He runs the church's day-to-day affairs and is a prolific writer. Soon after the terrible earthquake of 1988, he traveled to the United States to raise money for the victims and their families. How does he manage to do it all? Vasken I responds to this question with a piece of advice: "If you want to sleep well and feel good, live honestly."

Top left: Patriarch Alexis II of Moscow and All Russia.

Top middle: Metropolitan Pitirim of Volokolamsk and Yuryev.

Top right: Mufti Mukhammadsadyuk Mammayusuf, chairman of the Muslim Religious Board for Central Asia and Kazakhstan.

Bottom left: Archpriest Pyotr Buburuz, a Russian Orthodox clergyman from the Moldavian capital, Kishinev.

Bottom middle: Sheikh-ul-Islam Allahshukur Pashazade, leader of the Muslims of Transcaucasia.

Bottom right: Supreme Patriarch and Catholicos of All Armenians Vasken I.

A Muslim shrine in Central Asia.

The new center for Seventh-Day Adventists in Zaoksky village, Tula Region, some 75 miles from Moscow.

The Vilnius Cathedral, returned to the Lithuanian Catholic Church in 1989.

The St. Daniil Monastery in Moscow, returned to the Russian Orthodox Church in the 1980s.

An iconostasis in the Church of the Intercession of the Holy Lady, St. Daniil Monastery.

A Muslim celebration in the Volga Region.

The introduction of Archbishop Carlis Gailitis in Riga.

Buddhists after service.

The Russian Orthodox sacrament of baptism.

The Russian Orthodox sacrament of marriage.

A Russian Orthodox Sunday school class in Moscow.

The Moscow Choral Synagogue.

Krishnaites in the streets of Moscow.

Monks at the Ivolginsky Buddhist Datsan.

A Seventh-Day Adventist Baptism.

The Georgian Autocephalous Orthodox Church

Statistics: The Georgian Autocephalous Orthodox Church has about 3 million followers, more than 300 churches and 400 priests, ten monasteries, a theological seminary, and an academy.

Organization: The Georgian Autocephalous Orthodox Church is headed by His Holiness and Beatitude Catholicos-Patriarch of All Georgia, Ilia II, along with the Holy Synod. Apart from Georgian parishes, there are also Russian and Greek Orthodox communities that are under the jurisdiction of the Georgian Church. The Georgian Patriarchy has publishing, economic and financial, and foreign church relations departments, which are headed by the bishops.

Brief History: Georgia owes its final conversion to Christianity to the sermons of St. Nina, a Georgian by origin who came from the Georgian colony of Cappadocia. St. Nina converted the Georgian King Marian (265–342) to Christianity, and it was under his rule that Christianity became the state religion (324–326).

During the first centuries the Georgian Church was under the jurisdiction of the Antioch Patriarchate. It became autocephalous in the 5th century under King Vakhtang Gorgasali. In the early 11th century, its head was given the title of His Holiness and Beatitude Catholicos-Patriarch of All Georgia. In 1811 the Russian emperor eliminated, by non-canonical actions, the autocephalous jurisdiction of the Georgian Orthodox Church. Its independence was restored in 1917.

After the Russian revolution, the Georgian Church experienced the mass closure of churches and reprisals against clergy. It was only in the 1980s that the Church managed to greatly increase the number of functioning churches and monasteries, to resume its publishing activities, and to open a theological academy.

Current Situation and Problems: The Church suffers from a shortage of clergy and of religious literature in the Georgian language. A new translation of the Bible into modern Georgian was recently completed, but there is still a shortage of paper and production capacities. Ethnic conflicts also challenge the church.

In the Shadow of the Grapevine Cross

Since the advent of *perestroika*, the rapid pace of change in the Georgian Auto-cephalous Orthodox Church has caused its leaders great joy.

The number of churches and monasteries, for example, has doubled annually in recent years.

"Only yesterday, it was difficult to imagine that this kind of thing was possible in our situation," says Metropolitan David of Sukhumi and Abkhazia.

THE CHURCH'S BEGINNINGS

The Georgian Church ranks sixth among autocephalous Orthodox churches, following the Constantinople, Alexandria, Antiochian, Jerusalem, and Russian churches.

According to tradition, after the resurrection of Christ and the descent of the Holy Spirit at Pentecost, the apostles, together with Mary, the Holy Virgin, drew lots to determine where they were to go to preach the Gospel. Georgia was the lot of the Holy Virgin herself, but she heard a voice from heaven and sent instead the apostles Andrew the First Called and Simon the Canaanite. This explains why Georgia is sometimes referred to as the Holy Domain of the Heavenly Queen, while the Georgian Church is called apostolic.

It was through the preaching of St. Nina that Georgia later converted to Christianity. According to tradition, St. Nina received a grapevine cross from the Holy Virgin and came with it to convert Georgia. That cross is preserved in the Sioni Cathedral in Tbilisi and serves as the symbol of the Georgian Autocephalous Orthodox Church.

St. Nina was born late in the third century or early in the fourth century A.D. in Cappadocia, a Roman province in the east of Asia Minor, which at that time was a center of Christian learning. Accompanied by her sisters, St. Nina came to Georgia from Armenia in 318 or early in 319. She had to spend the winter on Georgia's southern frontier, but when summer came, she ascended the mountains and saw Lake Paravani. She was greeted by fishermen and herdsmen, who gave her food and shelter. Tired after her long journey, Nina fell asleep. In her dream she saw God's angel, who said to her, "Go to the city of Mtskheta and give this scroll to the pagan king sitting there, because it is for this that you have been sent."

The traveler continued on her way to the ancient capital of Iberia. In the valley of Borzhomi she descended to the Kura River and continued downstream until she came to the city of Urbnisi, where she stayed in Jewish homes for one month. The young virgin, who spoke the language of the Jews fluently, was graciously received and was given many attentions. When she came to Mtskheta, St. Nina first converted to Christianity the chief priest of the Kartlian Jews, then Queen Nana, and finally King Marian himself in 326. In the same year Christianity was adopted all over Georgia. At King Marian's request the Byzantine emperor Constantine sent a bishop and several priests to the newly converted Iberia. Christian churches were built everywhere. St. Nina was buried in the church of Bodbia in Kakhetia.

Many centuries have gone by since that time, and in 1989 a large group of young Christian believers decided to repeat the difficult journey of St. Nina, Equal to the Apostles. On 31 May the young men and women convened on the shores of Lake Paravani to hold a commemorative service. His Holiness and Beatitude Catholicos-Patriarch of All Georgia Ilia II gave his blessing to the young people before they set off on their long journey. The ceremony drew large numbers of people who put up colorful tents on the shores of the lake.

Many historical sites in Georgia are associated with Christian preachers, and large numbers of pilgrims visit them every year. The holy remains of a prominent Christian theologian, St. Maxim the Confessor, who died in 662, rest in the mountains of western Georgia in the village of Lechkhumi. The famous theologian Archbishop John Chrysostom of Constantinople, who was sent into exile to Transcaucasia, also found his resting place in Georgia. He passed away in 407 in Kamani, situated five kilometers from the city of Sukhumi, on the Black Sea coast. In 438 his holy remains were moved from Kamani to Constantinople, but the shrine, which used to contain his remains, is still carefully preserved in the cathedral of Sukhumi.

THE HEAD OF THE CHURCH

During the first centuries of its existence the Georgian church was under the jurisdiction of the Antiochian patriarchate. In the fifth century, under King Vakhtang Gorgasali, the Georgian church became autocephalous, and its first bishop was granted the title of Catholicos-Archbishop. At the beginning of the eleventh century, the primate of the Georgian Orthodox Church, Melkhisedek I, was awarded the title of His Holiness and Beatitude Catholicos-Patriarch of All Georgia. The official title of the current primate of the church is His Holiness and Beatitude Catholicos-Patriarch of All Georgia, Archbishop of Mtskheta and Tbilisi Ilia II.

His Holiness Ilia II (his secular name is Irakliy Shiolashvili) was born in 1933 in the city of Ordzhonikidze in the North Caucasian Mountains area into a devout Georgian family. He was baptized by Archimandrite Tarassiy Kandelaki, who was the secretary of the Catholicos-Patriarch of All Georgia, and came under his strong spiritual influence. In 1952 Irakliy entered the Moscow Theological Seminary, which he finished with distinction in 1956. The next year he was accepted at the Moscow Theological Academy and took his final vows under the name of Ilia. In 1960 he graduated from the academy with a Ph.D. in theology. His dissertation is entitled, "The History of the Iberian Monastery on Mount Athos."

In August 1963 Archimandrite Ilia was consecrated Bishop Shemokmedsky and appointed vicar to Catholicos-Patriarch Yefrem II. Elevated to the dignity of metropolitan, he was the ruling hierarch of the diocese of Sukhumi and Abkhazia. From 1963 to 1972 he worked at the Georgian Orthodox Theological Seminary. After the death of His Holiness and Beatitude Patriarch David VI, Metropolitan Ilia, the Locum Tenens of the Patriarchal Throne, was elected primate of the Georgian Church by the local council.

THE CHURCH IN GEORGIAN HISTORY

With the introduction of Christianity, Georgia was also introduced to much Christian culture. During the times when the country was constantly threatened by invaders, the church played an important role in preserving the Georgian language and national identity, promoting literacy, and developing literature and the arts. For example, in the fifth century Yakov Tsurtaveli, a priest at the king's court, wrote a religious book entitled *The Martyrdom of Saint Shushanika*, which is considered a masterpiece of ancient Georgian literature. Also, the Georgian Church promoted the development of the arts, hagiographic and hymnographic writing, lay literature, the crafting of jewelry, and icon painting.

The church preserved the spiritual force of the nation in the face of Islamic invasions. In the eleventh century, on the orders of the Muslim conqueror Djalal-ed-din, one hundred thousand Georgians were killed in one day alone because they refused to profane the icons of the Savior and the Mother of God even under the threat of death.

In 1801 Georgia became part of Christian Russia, and again the country underwent great trials. In 1811, by an edict of the Russian emperor, the autonomy of the Georgian Orthodox Church was terminated. In blatant violation of all the canons of religion the Georgian Church was turned into an exarchate subordinate to the Holy Synod in Petersburg. Government officials tried to use the church as a tool in their policy of russification, and it was not until the downfall of the Russian monarchy that the Georgian Church regained its independence.

After the autonomy of the Georgian Church had been restored, elections of the Catholicos-Patriarch were held and the Holy Synod was reconvened.

CURRENT EVENTS

At present, the church consists of fifteen dioceses. The Georgian church also exercises jurisdiction over the Russian and Greek Orthodox communities in Georgia. Priests are trained at the Theological Seminary and the newly opened Theological

Academy in Tbilisi, which preserves the traditions of the Gelati and Ikalta theological schools.

The Georgian Church publishes a journal entitled *Dzhvari vazisa* (*The Grapevine Cross*), which has been published for more than ten years and a continuing collection of articles entitled "Theological Works."

In 1989 a new translation of the Bible into modern Georgian literary language was completed. This work brought together a large number of people, both clergy and lay specialists, most of whom are professors at Tbilisi University.

Also in 1989, two separate baptismal ceremonies were held, each involving thousands of people. The first was an open-air ceremony convened May 14 near the church of the Holy Virgin and lasting from five o'clock in the evening until the early hours of the following morning. Among those baptized by the Catholicos-Patriarch Ilia II were many adults who had been prevented from being baptized when believers were persecuted. After the ceremony of baptism had been completed, in accordance with Georgian Christian tradition, the Catholicos-Partriarch hung thousands of little crosses on the necks of young boys and girls.

Later that summer a similar ceremony was held in Mtskheta where the Aragva and the Kura rivers meet, the place where King Marian and his family were baptized in 326. Catholicos-Patriarch Ilia II, assisted by many clergy, officiated at the ceremony reviving the ancient rite. Once again thousands of people entered the waters of the Kura carrying children in their arms. People from all parts of Georgia attended the ceremony; they carried flags of the church and of the Georgian state and sang hymns glorifying Jesus Christ. The date of the ceremony, 13 July, is of note since it is known as "Tsvetskhoveli," or "the life-giving pillar." This is also the name of the nearby cathedral.

CRISIS IN TBILISI

However, tragic events have marred the revival of the Georgian people's spirituality. Late at night on 8 April 1989 a large crowd of people gathered in the center of Tbilisi for a peaceful demonstration. People called for sovereignty, more democracy, and *glasnost*. They carried religious and national flags, sang songs, and danced in the streets. Many of them lit candles and knelt down in prayer.

Catholicos-Patriarch Ilia II was awakened in the middle of the night to learn that the people in the central square were facing a terrible danger. Troops had been called in, the approaches to the square were blocked by armored personnel carriers, and city hospitals were alerted to receive casualties. His Holiness went straight to the square. He pleaded with the people there to think about the danger they were facing and he implored them to disperse and to go pray in the city cathedral, but the square had already been sealed off.

Although few people had believed that bloodshed was actually possible, at four o'clock on the morning of 9 April a terrible crime was committed: soldiers wielding short army spades charged into the defenseless crowd, which included children, old men, pregnant women, and students exhausted by a hunger strike, and then used gas to disperse the crowd. Their barbaric action left nineteen people dead and hundreds of people wounded. It was indeed a miracle that the Catholicos-Patriarch's life was saved; people managed to take him to a safe place. A nearby church was turned into a refuge for those still in a state of shock. Priests administered first aid and provided spiritual support to people overcome with sorrow and pain.

Several days later the place was inundated by a sea of wreaths and flowers. His Holiness and Beatitude Catholicos-Patriarch gave his blessing to a *panikhida* (a commemorative service) in the square, and the square was sprinkled with holy water. Assisted by clergy, the Catholicos-Patriarch conducted a *panikhida* at the Sioni Cathedral. On the fortieth day after the tragedy, the wreaths and flowers from the square were brought into the cathedral, and the Catholicos-Patriarch commemorated the dead at a ceremony attended by large numbers of people and relatives and friends of the victims.

ETHNIC CONFLICT

There was more violence in the diocese of Sukhumi and Abkhazia, situated on the Black Sea coast. It was a bloody ethnic conflict involving Abkhazians and Georgians. However, innocent people were frequently the victims of those bloody clashes. The crisis came to a head when a large section of the Abkhazian population called for secession from Georgia and demanded that the Abkhazian Autonomous Republic be granted the status of a union republic (such as Georgia or Armenia). The scale and the intensity of the conflict forced the authorities to impose a curfew in the capital city of Sukhumi, and troops were called in to maintain law and order and to protect people's lives.

In that situation the clergy of the diocese of Sukhumi and Abkhazia, led by Metropolitan David, did all they could to defuse tensions and to restore the Christian principles of love and compassion for one's neighbor. They preached in churches and cathedral, pleaded with believers, and appealed for tolerance and compassion in their radio and television broadcasts. Said Metropolitan David, "Apart from Abkhazians, there are also Georgians, Armenians, Greeks, Russians, Ukrainians, and Jews living in the diocese. In the past different nationalities lived in peace and friendship. That was a tradition honored over many centuries. Even after what has happened, we believe that common sense will triumph, and Abkhazians and Georgians will reach out to each other. Generally speaking, we believe that in a multinational state like ours an atmosphere of friendship and cooperation is vital. The Georgian Orthodox Church is making its contribution to this noble cause."

Despite such tragic events, religious life in Georgia since 1989 has been continuing much as usual; services are regularly held, rituals are observed, and restoration work is proceeding in churches and monasteries. The Georgian patriarchate has moved to new premises because there was not enough room in the old building. And on the elevated left bank of the Kura River, in the historical center of Tbilisi, the local authorities have allocated a site for a new cathedral of St. Trinity. The Georgian Church, the Union of Architects of the Republic, and the Society for the Preservation of Ancient Monuments of Georgian History and Architecture have launched a competition for the best architectural design for the cathedral.

A Greek Catholic priest in Lvov.

The Greek Catholic Church

Statistics: The Greek Catholic Church has around a half million followers in the Western Ukraine. It has 1,906 churches, 12 monasteries, and 2 theological schools.

Organization: Pope John Paul II is considered the head of the Church, but the Church is guided by a Synod led by Cardinal Miroslav Liubachivsky, who has been proclaimed Patriarch of the Ukraine.

Brief History: The Greek Catholic Church came into being as a result of the 1596 Brest Union, which united the Orthodox and Roman Catholics living on the territory ruled by Poland. This took place at a council held in the Belorussian town of Brest, where Orthodox Bishops and believers recognized the authority of the Roman papacy, but continued the practices of Slavonic language services and Orthodox rites. In Belorussia the Union fell apart in the 19th century and it was abolished in the Ukraine at the Lvov Council in 1946 on Stalin's direct instructions.

Most clergy and believers went over to Orthodoxy, while those who remained were subjected to severe reprisals or went underground. Metropolitan Iosif Slipyi was thrown into a concentration camp. He was released and could go abroad only after twenty years of imprisonment.

In 1989 government authorities lifted the ban on the Greek Catholic Church and a considerable number of believers and clergy returned to its fold.

Current Situation and Problems: The need for redivision of church buildings and property between Greek Catholic and Russian Orthodox congregations now that the Greek Catholic faith is legal has led to sharp conflict, sometimes accompanied by violent actions. The situation is exacerbated in communities and congregations torn by internal conflicts. In this context, dialogue between the Russian Orthodox and the Catholic Churches is a matter of considerable importance.

The Greek Catholic Church
Is Given Legal Status

On 9 November 1989 it was announced that the Greek Catholic Church, also known as the Uniate Church, was given legal status in the Ukraine. The church had not been formally recognized since its ties with Rome were dissolved in 1946 during Stalin's regime.

The official press release said,

> "The Council for Religious Affairs officially declares that Greek Catholics can enjoy all the rights established by the law for religious associations, given strict compliance with the Constitution of the Ukrainian Soviet Socialist Republic and the legislation on religious cults.

> "Questions regarding the registration of the religious communities shall be resolved in accordance with the expressed will of the believers themselves. Any attempts to influence the choice of their faith are inadmissible. In order to determine the genuine desire of believers to set up a religious community with a view to practicing a given faith, it is suggested that in case of necessity a secret ballot should be held in towns and villages with guarantees of strict compliance with the standards of democracy and legality. In order to ensure objectivity and prevent attempts to exert pressure on believers it could be possible to set up observer commissions, or groups representing local authorities, the public, religious communities, and unofficial associations."

In Lvov, the metropolitan of the Greek Catholic Church, Vladimir Sternyuk, welcomed the decision of the authorities and promised that church members would do all that they could to see that the legalization would be implemented "in a humane and civilized manner without causing any harm to our brothers, the faithful of the Russian Orthodox Church."

The hierarch said that old grudges—those dating back centuries and those from more recent times—should be forgotten. And the church as a whole should not continue to be punished for the collaboration of some church leaders with the Nazis during World War II.

"In their turn the Nazis played upon the national and religious feelings of the local population who had not yet perceived the true identity of fascism. They deceived believers by their promises of freedom and broader rights for the church. This explains why some religious leaders of the Ukrainian Catholic Church were prepared to collaborate with the Nazis. All their hope proved to be illusory, and in the end they met with utter disappointment. However, for the sake of justice it is necessary to separate the truth from the lies, and it is wrong to identify the real culprits with all believers. From a historical perspective, this is the only way to assess the tragedy that befell the Ukrainian Catholic Church. Those individuals who were found to be guilty were severely punished, but their guilt was used to discredit the Ukrainian Catholic Church completely and later to impose an official ban on it. Thousands of people, in fact whole families, were thrown out of their homes and sent to cold Siberia, only because they believed in their God.

"We cannot consider the decisions of the Lvov Council, held in 1946, as just. In those harsh conditions there was little hope that the five million Greek Catholics living in the western Ukraine would be able to make their will known through democratic procedures.

"It is true that the local people go to pray in Russian Orthodox cathedrals, because they have reconciled themselves to the absence of their own churches. However, in their souls they have remained true to their faith. This accords with the decisions of the Second Vatican Council. Together with the Russian Orthodox Church we worship the same God, we have the same language and national traditions, we have almost the same rites, prayers, and symbols. The fundamental difference between us lies in the fact that Ukrainian Catholics recognize the power and the authority of Apostle Peter and his heir, the pope in Rome, which were established by Jesus Christ. We are part of the universal Catholic Church, which unites thirteen churches enjoying equal rights. One of them is the Eastern Church, to which we belong. Some of the believers of our church refused to compromise and maintained their faith underground during all these years. We do not blame or have any recriminations against those who have chosen the Orthodox religion. This is a matter for their conscience.

"Injustice has provoked bitter resentment on the part of some believers. If we remove injustice, resentment will disappear too. This is one of many possible alternatives that could satisfy all sides. For example, in Poland and some other countries Uniates and believers of other denominations worship in the same cathedrals in accordance with an agreed-upon timetable. Imagine a village inhabited by both Orthodox and Ukrainian Catholic believers but having only one church. Is it not possible for them to alternate hours and even days of service? This alternative can prove to be by far the most painless solution. We can coexist with the Russian Orthodox Church, and we harbor no hatred toward Orthodox believers. The latter cannot be held responsible for the actions of those who did evil to us in the past. In our statements addressed to the Soviet leadership we were quite sincere in declaring that we bless the policy of radical changes and social renewal and pray for Mikhail Gorbachev and his comrades in the leadership of the country. What people need most now are mutual understanding and kindness in the spirit of true Christian love and forgiveness."

UNIATE CHURCH HISTORY

The Ukrainian Greek Catholic Church was established at the end of the sixteenth century when a large part of Orthodox Ukrainians and Belorussians were placed under the jurisdiction of the Holy See in accordance with the terms of the Union of Brest-Litovsk in 1596. At a later period of time, as the Polish domination in the Ukraine and Belorussia gradually diminished, some Uniates returned to the fold of the Russian Orthodox Church. In Belorussia, reunification was completed in the nineteenth century. However, in the western Ukraine, the Greek Catholics preserved their faith. Formally, the union was abrogated by the Lvov Church Council in 1946. It is alleged by many that the council was stage-managed by Stalin. Some of the clergy returned to the fold of the Russian Orthodox Church, while others, including Cardinal Joseph Slypy, were subjected to reprisals. Uniate cathedrals were handed over to the Russian Orthodox Church. Thus staunch Uniates were forced to go underground. In the early 1960s Nikita Khrushchev ordered the mass closure of churches in the Soviet Union, including those in the Ukraine. This measure provoked widespread dissatisfaction and largely strengthened the authority of the Greek Catholic Church, which stepped up its activities in that new situation.

During the early years of *perestroika* attempts to restore normal religious life in the Ukraine met with strong opposition from the former leadership of the republic, headed by Vladimir Scherbitsky.

The international religious community has expressed mixed reactions to the situation in the Ukraine. Those motivated by the natural desire to uphold civil rights and human rights enshrined in international instruments have defended the Uniates. However, some religious leaders have adopted a negative or very cautious attitude to the problem. On many occasions representatives of different religious denominations have spoken out against the restitution of the Uniates and their rights.

Participants in the session of the Central Committee of the World Congress of Churches, held in late July 1989 in Moscow, witnessed a demonstration of the Ukrainian Uniates calling for the legalization of their church. Speaking at a press conference that took place after those events, the general secretary of the World Congress of Churches, Dr. Emilio Castro, said that the problem of the Uniates was not a new one and was not a problem that affected the Soviet Union alone. It was a very sensitive issue for many other countries too and a cool head and calm approach were needed in order to find the right solution. He also voiced his conviction that the solution could be found only through serious dialogue. He called for maximum tact and warned against rash actions and any attempts to force a solution under any circumstances. One of the prominent hierarchs of the Syrian Orthodox Church, Metropolitan of Delhi Paulos Mar Gregorios, said that it was the same church that had been established several centuries earlier through violent measures. Uniates appeared not only in the Ukraine but also in India. He said that the future of the Uniate Church was a matter of principle, and he called for dialogue with the Christian Church.

TENSIONS BETWEEN UNIATES
AND ORTHODOX

Despite legal recognition of the Greek Catholic Church many acute problems remain unresolved. The tension between the Russian Orthodox Church and the Ukrainian Uniate Church has flared over division of existing cathedrals. Leaders of the Russian Orthodox and other Orthodox Churches have been concerned by Uniate attempts to seize cathedrals by force. On 6 January 1990 Patriarch Pimen received the following telegram from Cyprus:

"Now that we find ourselves in Nicosia as guests of our brotherly Church of Cyprus, we believe it is our duty to condemn the violation of religious rights and the events currently taking place in the Ukraine, which are aimed against the Russian Orthodox clergy, believers, and holy cathedrals. We also take this opportunity to express our full support and solidarity to your Beloved Holiness and the entire brotherly congregation of the Russian Orthodox Church on behalf of our churches. We will always be ready to use all available means to assist in the way Your Holiness might deem necessary. We pray to God to strengthen Your Lord-protected Holiness in his divine labors for the good of the Orthodox Church. With the love for Christ,

Signed   Patriarch Parfeny of Alexandia
             Patriarch Ignaty of Antioch
             Patriarch Diodor of Jerusalem
             Archbishop Chrysostom of Cyprus."

The Council of Hierarchs of the Russian Orthodox Church, held 30–31 January 1990 in St. Daniel's Monastery in Moscow, condemned what it described as "the activities of extremist groups of Catholics of eastern denomination." The statement issued by the council said:

"Despite [recent] agreements between the Russian Orthodox Church and the Roman Catholic Church, which provide for a mutually acceptable mechanism for resolving existing conflicts, Uniates continue with their violent actions aimed at seizing Orthodox cathedrals, even though these actions have been condemned through agreements. Very frequently their actions are condoned and in some instances even supported by local authorities. The most recent example of lawlessness on the part of the local authorities was the transfer of the cathedral in the city of Ivano-Frankovsk to Uniates, which was carried out in contravention of the law without the agreement or prior knowledge of the Russian Orthodox community, which used the cathedral in accordance with the rules established by law. Seizures of Russian Orthodox cathedrals pose a threat to the process of settling the situation in the western Ukraine as discussed during the official negotiations between our representatives and the delegation of the Vatican."

However, the prior meeting of the delegation of the Russian Orthodox Church and the Roman Catholic Uniate Church, held in Moscow, was constructive. What follows is the document adopted by both delegations:

RECOMMENDATIONS ON THE NORMALIZATION OF RELATIONS BETWEEN ORTHODOX BELIEVERS AND THE CATHOLICS OF EASTERN DENOMINATION IN THE WESTERN UKRAINE

As a result of an exchange of messages between His Holiness the Patriarch of Moscow and All Russia Pimen and His Holiness John Paul II, a meeting of the delegates of the Moscow patriarchate and the Holy See was held in Moscow 12–17 January 1990. Taking part in the meeting were:

On the Part of the Russian Orthodox Church:

1. Metropolitan Filaret of Kiev and Galitsia, the patriarch's exarch of the entire Ukraine, head of the delegations;
2. Metropolitan Juvenaly of Krutitsy and Kolomna;
3. Archbishop Kirill of Smolensk and Kaliningrad, chairman of the Department of External Church Relations of the Moscow patriarchate;
4. Archbishop Iriney of Lvov and Drogobych;
5. Hegumen Nestor (Zhilyayev), technical secretary.

On the part of the Roman Catholic Church:

1. Cardinal Ioann Villebrands, honorary chairman of the Papal Council for the Promotion of Christian Unity;
2. Archbishop Eduard Cassidi, president of the Papal Council for the Promotion of Christian Unity;
3. Archbishop Miroslav Marusin, secretary of the Congregation of Eastern Churches;

4. Bishop Pierre Duprey, secretary of the Papal Council for the Promotion of Christian Unity;

5. Monsignor Salvatore Scribano, technical secretary.

The meeting was marked by a spirit of brotherhood and mutual confidence, which made it possible to assess honestly the situation of Catholics of the eastern denomination in the western Ukraine and the sensitive consequences that arose in this connection for the Orthodox faithful. The participants gave thanks to God for leading them jointly to the following conclusions, which represented the first step in their joint efforts to resolve the existing problem.

1. Reaffirming the commitment of their churches to the principles of religious freedom; recognizing that under the conditions of a rule-of-law state these principles should be carried out equitably on the basis of law with regard to all without discrimination, both sides consider it necessary to rapidly normalize the situation in which the Catholics of eastern denomination in the western Ukraine find themselves.

2. This normalization should open a new page in the history of relations between the Catholics and the Orthodox faithful in this region. Past confrontation and mutual injustice should be overcome in the spirit of genuine forgiveness and reconciliation and give way to cooperation and the testimony of Jesus Christ whose gospel the church is called upon to preach.

3. This normalization carried out in the context of general democratic transformations in the country should guarantee to the Catholics of eastern denomination the right to engage in religious activities in accordance with the Constitution and the legislation of the USSR, which applies to everyone.

However, this right should not be implemented without taking into account the rights and legitimate interests of the Orthodox faithful and other religious communities. We believe that Christians in the USSR should make their contribution to the common effort aimed at the creation of a state based on the rule of law.

4. In this connection it is extremely important to avoid any illegal actions, particularly those that are coupled with violence. Such illegal actions are incompatible with the spirit of Christianity and must be condemned. Moreover, they represent an obstacle for the registration of the parishes of the Catholics of eastern denomination.

5. At the same time both sides believe that in the framework of existing legislation Catholic communities of eastern denomination have the right and the possibility to be registered in accordance with the rules established by law.

6. Catholic communities thus registered, on an equal basis with the communities of other denominations, have the right to receive from the state religious buildings free of charge and for an unlimited time. They also have the right to build new cathedrals, lease or buy real estate.

7. Having stated the fact that in several cases parish congregations have been divided, with both groups, Orthodox and Catholic, equally claiming exclusive rights to the use of cathedrals, we call on both side to overcome mutual prejudice without enmity, for the sake of achieving a brotherly agreement with due respect for the free choice of the people and without any pressure.

8. In order to resolve practical problems arising in the course of the normalization of relations between the Orthodox faithful and the Catholics of eastern denomination and on the basis of consensus it was deemed necessary to set up a joint commission with the participation of representatives of the Holy See, the Moscow patriarchate, and Orthodox faithful and Catholics from the western Ukraine. Every constituent part of the commission had to include one or two representatives at most. The commission should proceed with its activities on the basis of the present agreement and resolve contentious issues guided by the spirit of Christian love and brotherly cooperation. As a matter of particular urgency it was necessary to resolve the problem of the cathedrals occupied by the Catholics of eastern denomination without the consent of the communities.

9. The community of the Catholics of the eastern denomination in the western Ukraine emerged four hundred years ago in an attempt to overcome the division between the Orthodox and Catholic churches. This attempt did not lead to the desired objective. Over centuries the divisions persisted and served as a source of conflict and suffering for both the Orthodox faithful and the Catholics.

Remaining faithful to the commandment of Christ who said that all should be united, in their desire to implement this commandment in their relations, both churches have embarked on a new dialogue, profoundly convinced that it is not the method of union that was resorted to in the past, but a dialogue that will help them resolve jointly the problems that divide them. Such a dialogue has become possible thanks to new approaches to the question of Christian unity established by the Second Vatican Council and several All-Orthodox meetings.

The Eastern Catholic churches, which emerged as a result of a historical union, represent part of the Catholic Church and are guided in relation to the Orthodox faithful by the principles formulated by the Second Vatican Council, which make it possible for them to serve as a constructive element in Orthodox-Catholic relations.

Both sides are profoundly convinced that these relations both today and in the future should be free from any intent to proselytize and create mutual suspicion, because it is only in an atmosphere of trust and cooperation that both churches can successfully move ahead toward a dialogue.

10. Continuing and increasing efforts aimed at the achievement of unity, it is necessary to discuss the questions regarding the organization of the hierarchical structure of the Catholic Church of eastern denomination in the western Ukraine so as not to create the impression that one hierarchy is opposed to the other, and in order to make a joint effort to fulfill the mutual obligations that ensue from the

theological dialogue between our churches and establish the new kind of fraternal relationship that has begun to form between us.

11. Both delegations will immediately submit the above-mentioned recommendations, which were adopted with full agreement, to their respective church authorities. These recommendations will remain confidential until they are approved and will be published immediately following such approval. We hope that in the new spirit that was in evidence here both the Catholic and the Orthodox faithful in the western Ukraine will unite their efforts to normalize the process, which we hope will lead to the complete normalization of the situation and promote a dialogue between the Catholics and the Orthodox faithful for the glory of God.

Outside the Vilnius Cathedral, a statue commemorates an apparition of Mary.

The Roman Catholic Church

Statistics: The Roman Catholic Church has about 3 million followers. Lithuania has about 820 churches, 7 monasteries, and 690 priests; Latvia has more than 200 churches and 115 priests; Belorussia has about 300 churches with 97 priests; in the Ukraine there are over 200 churches with 63 priests; and the Russian Federation has 5 Catholic churches with 8 priests.

Organization: In Lithuania the Roman Catholic Church is headed by a Conference of Catholic Bishops led by Cardinal Vincentas Sladkevicius. It has two theological seminaries and a publishing department. In Latvia the Roman Catholic Church is headed by Apostolic Administrator Bishop Janis Cakuls, and it also has a seminary and a publishing department. In May 1991 Pope John Paul II ordained Bishop Tadeusz Kondrusiewicz as archbishop and appointed him Apostolic Administrator of the European Part of Russia with residence in Moscow.

Brief History: Catholicism began to spread in the territory of what are now Soviet republics in the 14th century, chiefly in regions controlled by the Polish-Lithuanian state. In 1987 Lithuania celebrated the 600th anniversary of its conversion to Catholicism. For many centuries its relations with the Russian Orthodox Church were tense. There was a particularly tense period during the time of the Stalin administration, which regarded Catholicism as its worse enemy. All relations with the state were severed at that time.

Perestroika initiated a fundamentally new stage of the USSR's relations with the Vatican. During visits to Italy, Mikhail Gorbachev met with Pope John Paul II in 1989 and 1991. Both agreed to normalize relations, exchange diplomatic representatives, and arrange a visit for the Pope to Moscow in 1992.

Current Situation and Problems: Roman Catholic churches and monasteries are being opened and the orders are resuming their activities. The shortage of clergy is a very acute problem, and consequently dozens of priests are being sent from Poland to the Soviet republics. Religious literature is also in short supply locally and a considerable share has to be brought from the Vatican and other countries.

Cardinal Vincentas Sladkevicius
Supports Lithuanian Independence

On Easter 1990, the Lithuanian Roman Catholic Church issued its strong support for Lithuanian Independence.

"The Lithuanian Catholic Church, expressing the sentiments of most of our people, has today joined in spirit all who rejoice at the restoration of Lithuanian statehood," said the Easter message from Cardinal Vincentas Sladkevicius and the Lithuanian Roman Catholic bishops. "It is our hope that in the very near future diplomatic relations with the Vatican shall be restored and that the Holy Father will be able to visit independent Lithuania as its first guest who loves our land ardently."

The cardinal noted in a separate address televised Easter eve that the rebirth of religious life was the result of national renewal and, thereby, of *perestroika* under way in the Soviet Union. "Of course, we understand better all those people who sincerely work for renewal, and they take a favorable attitude toward us. They look for the common elements that unite us, they try to find shared thoughts and are fair toward us. Many people admire the first steps of renewal in Lithuania because they see their own aspirations reflected in them. First of all, it is a yearning for the happiness of all mankind, freedom, the pursuit of truth, and liberation from violence. All this manifests itself more clearly in Lithuania than in other republics of the Soviet Union, although, in my opinion, there is no lack of like-minded people there too. However, they have lived under difficult circumstances and have been oppressed longer. In order to light a spark, we need freedom and air. If everything is airtight, even a spark will go out. Many nations were denied their rights even more than we were. We were able to find a breathing space, and many of our people have continued to keep their faith.

"The church has enabled us to maintain our links with the western world because the church itself and its activity are open to the world. The church cannot be walled off. The Catholic Church of Lithuania is part of the world Church. It has been able to make our people aware of all the sentiments in the world Church. Our nation's most precious values—freedom, a strong yearning for truth, faith in the future, and good—have been inherited from the church. Today the church also shows what we have to strive for and how we should grow.

"Faith has always helped preserve the basis of spirituality. Faith in God has always sustained believers. Even in exile, when there was absolutely no way out, people were not overpowered by hopelessness and despair. They hoped to return home. Every believer knew that if he did not return to Lithuania, he had the road to paradise open for him.

"Geographically, our nation is placed between great peoples. We have always felt the influence of the neighboring cultures and could not isolate ourselves from this influence. Interaction has evolved by itself. With the exception of Poland, the neighboring countries were not Catholic. On the one side, we had Old Believers [Russians], on the other, Protestants. However, we learned to live together with all of them.

"We, Catholics, do not find it difficult to interact with others because the basis for this is in our religion, in the Lord's commandment, 'Thou shalt love thy neighbor as thyself.' When we were still children living in the countryside, our parents taught us to share bread with a passerby, no matter what language he or she spoke. Today, we can assert that the Lithuanian people have acquired a high level of tolerance through education. We would like other people to reciprocate these sentiments.

"Today, we can say that the affairs of the Catholic Church in Lithuania have advanced positively in all principal questions. There is no question that the main thing for us was teaching the law of God and the religious instruction of the young. In the past, we confronted major obstacles along this path and suffered irreplaceable losses. For years it was alleged that man did not need faith and that it would only harm him. For some time we lost our influence and could make no impact. All that remained to the Catholic Church was the pulpit. We did not have our own publication. In many instances we were unable to take any steps without the blessing and agreement from an official responsible for religious affairs. Outsiders interfered in the appointment of clergymen or the selection of students for a religious seminary. Today, this is no longer the case. The leadership of the republic has radically changed its attitude toward believers and faith itself. For the second year in a row we have been publishing our own magazine, *Catalicu pasaulis*. Many Catholic churches have been returned to believers. But the most important thing is that we have the right to teach the law of God in schools. Of course, carrying out this important mission in full is a tough challenge for us. We need professionals. The number of Roman Catholic priests has dwindled so much that we do not have enough to work in churches. We also do not have teachers of the law of God. We have not yet trained lay people to become teachers of the catechism.

"We hope that in time everything will work out. All the conditions for this are in place: there is no limit on the number of people entering religious seminaries any more; we are accumulating strength for work with high school students. We are confident that the number of Catholic priests will continue to grow steadily. At the same time, we need not only a large quantity of people but also good quality specialists. It will, most likely, take five or six years for a new generation of Catholic priests to appear.

"The problem with Roman Catholic churches is also being addressed. Some of them have already been returned; others will be returned in the not too distant future. We do not have any major difficulties in constructing new churches. However, it will not be easy for us to solve this question on our own, because our financial resources are rather limited. That is why we try to practice economy and moderation and demand that Roman Catholic priests do the same. Generally speaking, we are convinced that moderation is the clearest sign of wisdom. It reflects God's kindness. The Almighty is generous and kind; however, he takes care of all our needs at the right time and in the right way. This is the sign of divine wisdom.

"Everything must happen in time and in an appropriate manner. When people are in no hurry to return something to us, we take it very calmly. However, will we be equal to this challenge when the return is made, and will we be able to put this something to a proper use? That is why we are not sad that not everything has been returned, that we have not yet received all. Yet the very fact that no obstacles are raised and that we are treated favorably shows that God is merciful to us and we have his blessing. This fills our hearts with joy. We shall wait and see what will happen next.

"Although Lithuania is small, our people are few and our land is not rich in natural resources that other nations enjoy and take pride in. We have folk simplicity and pride, sincerity and friendliness, that is, the spiritual values sustained by our faith. We are happy to see the church regain its treasures; however, it is even more significant that the church with all its spiritual wealth is returning to the people. It is coming back with its former influence.

"Easter's main theme is rebirth. It is the source of the greatest joy and a potent force stimulating all people to spiritual renewal and, in a broader context, to the national and spiritual rebirth of the nation. We, believers, are ready to travel Lithuania's road of renewal and to make our contribution toward its rebirth."

PERESTROIKA IN LITHUANIA

Perestroika marked a sharp change in the relations of the church and the state. Catholic festivals became regular events, a second seminary opened, it became possible for children to study the law of God, a Catholic magazine began its publication, the circulation of religious literature increased, and services were resumed in many churches that had previously been taken over by the authorities.

In February 1989, Vilnius Cathedral was solemnly consecrated. Forty years ago it had been taken from the church and turned into an arts gallery and a concert hall. Once again the relics of St. Casimir lie here; after the Vilnius church was closed down, they were moved to the Peter and Paul Church. A large procession accompanied the silver sarcophagus when it was returned to its former place—a chapel inside the cathedral. At the same time, authorities returned to the church St. Casimir Cathedral, where they had blasphemously located a museum of the history of religion and atheism.

Prince Casimir was the first Lithuanian saint. He lived in the second half of the fifteenth century and was renowned for his piety and religious devotion. He died young of tuberculosis in 1484. He was believed to be a miracle worker and was glorified as a saint. In 1602, on receiving a petition from the king of Poland, Sigismund III Vasa, Pope Clement VIII canonized Casimir, and thirty-four years later he was proclaimed the patron saint of Lithuania. In recent years, the cult of Casimir has noticeably increased.

Archbishop Khrisostom of Vilno and Lithuania (of the Russian Orthodox Church) also spoke his mind about what was happening. He said, "I cannot remain calm when representatives of the army participate in today's events in Lithuania. The army must not be used for what it is not intended; it must protect the borders and repel aggression. Restoring internal order is a task for other organs. The most regrettable thing, however, is that the inability to divide party property served as a pretext for the army's interference. I would like to recall that various churches of different confessions in the USSR are still used for purposes other than religious, which is an insult to believers. However, the church does not appeal for help, yet if we did, we would also find patrons."

Archbishop Khrisostom then went on to say that in Vilnius he notes different groups of people, different trends among the Russian population. "Of course, they do not share the same attitudes: some are unperturbed, others approve of and welcome the proclamation of Lithuanian independence, still others take a negative view. There are also people who are very aggressive, even toward me, a person representing Russian Orthodox believers here."

The archbishop then said, "I want to understand the Lithuanian nation since I live on its land. I take no offense at the criticism directed against me. I am only saddened by the shortsightedness of these people. No matter how arduous a road Lithuania will have to travel, it will be independent all the same. It is a different matter what means will be used to realize its independence and in what forms it will realize itself. However, this is something for politicians, economists, lawyers to discuss, who today shoulder a major responsibility.

"Lithuania wants to become an independent European state in the community of other civilized nations where human rights are at the top of the agenda. That is why I look with hope toward the future."

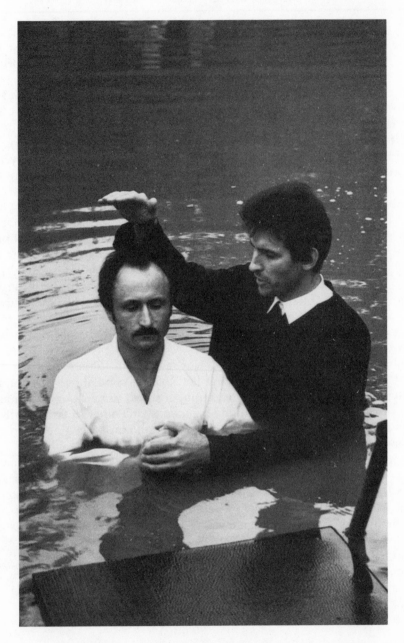

A Seventh-Day Adventist baptism.

Protestant Christians

Statistics: Protestant churches have more than 3 million followers, more than a thousand churches and prayer buildings, and 2,000 pastors (presbyters) and preachers.

Organization: Each Protestant religious group has its own church organization led by elected people. All Protestant communities are growing swiftly, opening new prayer buildings and theological seminaries, printing religious literature, and taking an active part in charity activities and in social life. The Baptist, Pentecostal, and Seventh-Day Adventist groups are perhaps the most dynamic.

Many of these Protestant groups have chosen to join together in the nationally recognized All-Union League of Evangelical Christian Baptists for fellowship and mutual aid in efforts of Christian mission. Others participate in the underground Council of Churches of Evangelical Christian Baptists. And others have chosen to remain independent.

Brief History: Protestant churches appeared in the territory of the present Soviet republics after Empress Catherine II issued her manifestos in the 18th century, encouraging the settlement of foreigners in Russia and guaranteeing them freedom of conscience. In the 19th and the early 20th century, nonetheless, Protestants were subjected to reprisals: many were evicted to Siberia and restricted in their rights.

During the first years of Soviet government, the new administration supported Protestant groups as a counterbalance to the Russian Orthodox Church, but in the 1930s launched a merciless offensive against "sectarians." Affiliation with some religious communities (for example, the Jehovah's Witnesses) was regarded as a crime. Many Protestant prayer houses have been restored or built anew in the *perestroika* years.

Current Situation and Problems: There are no longer any banned religious groups in Soviet society; religious groups are simply required to abide by the Soviet laws on religious cults, observe civic rights, and avoid actions harmful to people's health. Many evangelical and baptist groups, however, place strong emphasis on the need for separation of church and state. And difficulties arise in the relationship between government authorities and those religious groups which still prefer to act without legal sanction, refusing to recognize state institutions.

Charter of the All-Union League of Evangelical Christian Baptists

A wise man's heart discerneth
both time and judgment.

Eccles. 8:5

I. GENERAL PROVISIONS

1.1.   The All-Union League of Evangelical Christian Baptists (hereinafter referred to as "the league") consists of (inter) republican communities and associations of the Evangelical Baptist confession, united on a voluntary basis for fraternal Christian comradeship and joint work to the glory of the Lord. (Inter) republican associations with their own statutes shall be guided by them.

1.2.1.   The league consists of communities and associations of Evangelical Christian Baptists, Mennonites, and other evangelical confessions that profess the triunity of God—the Father, the Son, and the Holy Ghost—and Jesus Christ our Lord and Savior and whose members are baptized in faith after repentance and rebirth.

1.2.2.   Affiliation by other evangelical confessions to the league shall be decided upon by its All-Union Congress.

1.3.1.   The Holy Scripture (the canonical Old and New Testaments) shall be the basis of the doctrine, life, and activity of the league and local churches.

1.4.   All officials of the council of the league and its communities shall be elected with the approval of the churches of which they are members.

1.5.   The council of the league shall be located in Moscow.

1.6.   Only members of the Evangelical Baptist Church may be employed by the council of the league, associations, communities, departments, and offices of the league. All employment shall be on contract, which may be abrogated on the grounds of excommunication or unsuitability.

Tasks of the League

1.7.   The league and its (inter) republican, (inter) regional, and (inter) territorial associations and communities shall set themselves the following goals and tasks:

1.7.1.   They shall preach the gospel to all nations in the Soviet Union and the world, according to the commandment of God (Matt. 28:19–20; Mark 16:15), and assist churches in the preaching of the Evangelical Christian Baptist faith and the implementation of the principles thereof;

1.7.2. They shall assist the spiritual renaissance of Soviet nations and render charitable aid to all who need it (Gal. 6:10);

1.7.3. They shall promote unanimity and understanding in all local churches and communities within the league and retain the purity of the gospel teaching in all churches of the league (Titus 2:7).

II. THE LOCAL CHURCH

General Provisions

2.1. The local church shall be a voluntary community of believers of the Evangelical Baptist confession, who unite in fellowship for worship, spiritual advance, preaching of the gospel, and charitable works.

2.1.1. They who believe in Christ Jesus as their Savior, who have been spiritually reborn and received in faith the baptism of water by immersion shall be member of a local church.

2.1.2. Every member of a church shall participate in its life, serve God according to his or her gifts and abilities, be guided by this charter and the decisions of the church, and may be elected to the clergy according to vocation.

Tasks of the Local Church

2.2. A local church of the league shall set itself the following tasks:

2.2.1. Preaching the gospel (Mark 16:15; Acts 20:24);

2.2.2. Instruction of the faithful in sanctity, Christian piety, and the observation of all commandments of Jesus Christ (Matt. 28:20; 1 Tim. 2:1–4);

2.2.3. Instruction of children and young people in Sunday schools to raise them in the nurture and admonition of the Lord (Eph. 6:4);

2.2.4. The encouragement and promotion of unity among its members (John 17:21–23) and fraternal relations with other local churches of the league (Rom. 12:13; Gal. 6:2), and acts of charity.

Activities of the Local Church

2.3. To attain its goals, a local church of the league shall conduct:

2.3.1. Public worship with gospel sermons, Bible studies, prayer, singing (congregational, choir, group, and solo) accompanied by various musical instruments, recitals, baptisms of water, breaking of bread, weddings, prayers for children, ordinations, funerals, and other services;

2.3.2. Common prayers and biblical, edifying, evangelizing, and other gatherings.

2.3.3. A local church may establish Sunday schools and Bible classes to instruct children and adults in the teaching of Jesus Christ, as well as missions and charitable and educational groups.

2.3.4. To instruct the faithful and assist their spiritual progress and moral improvement, and to educate the clergy, a local church may establish circles for Bible studies, music and singing, needlework, and others, videoclubs, book and recording libraries, reading rooms, and other facilities.

2.4.1. Local churches of the league shall conduct liturgical gatherings on Sundays, also on workdays specified by the church, in particular, prayer and evangelization days, on Christmas, New Year's Eve, Epiphany, Candlemas, Annunciation, Easter, Ascension, Whitsunday, Transfiguration, Harvest Day, Unity Day, and other holidays.

2.4.2. The day of the breaking of bread shall be appointed at the discretion of the local church, usually the first Sunday of every month.

2.5.1. A local church shall hold public worship in its own buildings and those made available to it free of charge by the state or rented from the local secular authorities or from private persons. If necessary, such gatherings shall take place in the open.

2.5.2. At citizens' requests, public worship may be held in homes or—given an understanding with state and public bodies—at sports grounds, in public buildings, and in places of detention.

2.5.3. Funeral services and processions shall be held in the open, in houses of worship, private homes, and cemeteries.

2.5.4. If commissioned by the presbyter or the presbyter's deputy, members of other local churches of the league, children, and young people may take part in preaching, singing, recitals, and other forms of services on the instructions of a presbyter or a person acting in his place.

2.6.1. Every new believer wishing to be baptized by water according to the faith shall tell the presbyter and church, and after appropriate instruction (Matt. 28, 30), shall undergo a test.

2.6.2. Baptism shall be accomplished after the local church has passed a decision to admit the new believer to water baptism, which is done in natural bodies of water or in baptistries.

2.7. Admission to local church membership of those who arrive from other local churches shall be done after receiving a testimony of the church of which they were members.

2.8. Every local church shall retain its autonomy and shall decide at a meeting of members internal church affairs such as election and re-election of the presbyter and deacons, admission and excommunication, as well as economic, financial, and other matters submitted by the presbyter jointly with the church council.

Clergy of the Church and its Organs

2.9.1. The church shall elect a presbyter for daily services and conducting current affairs according to the Holy Writ. (1 Tim. 3, 11–12; Tit. 1, 5–9). If necessary, the church may have several presbyters, of whom one shall be the first, or chief, presbyter.

2.9.2. Election and re-election of the presbyter shall be done by the church with the participation of a representative from the Council of the ECB Association, by no less than two-thirds of the church members taking part in the voting.

2.9.3. A member of another ECB church may be elected the presbyter of the church, given the mutual agreement of the churches.

2.9.4. The one elected to serve as a presbyter shall have a period of probation lasting, as a rule, not more than a year.

　　　The ordination shall be carried out at a ceremonial divine service following an interview at the council of clergy and given the consent of the church.

2.9.5. Presbyters shall be accountable to the church and shall report to it not less than once a year.

2.9.6. As a rule, presbyters shall be supported by the church (1 Cor. 9:13–14; 1 Tim. 5:17–18).

2.9.7. Accusations against presbyters shall be examined by clergy in the presence of community council representatives (1 Tim. 5:19).

2.9.8. As the elder, the presbyter of a church is responsible for public worship and the spiritual instruction of the faithful. The presbyter shall administer baptisms by water, break bread, wed couples, pray for children, and perform other ministerial duties.

2.9.9. The presbyter shall be responsible for Sunday school activities and the organization of children's and youth choirs.

2.9.10. The presbyter shall conduct instructional meetings in the community and edifying talks with deacons, preachers, evangelists, precentors, young people and children, Sunday school teachers, and charity activists.

2.9.11. As spiritual leader, the presbyter shall defend the interests of the church and faithful before secular authorities and public organizations and shall draw up applications, contracts, and other official papers on behalf of the church.

2.10. Ministry shall be exercised by ordained clergy. On exceptional occasions, clergy-elect may exercise ministerial duties before ordination, should the church agree.

2.11.1. A local church shall elect deacons to assist the presbyter (1 Tim. 3:8–13; Acts 6:1–6) with a trial period not exceeding twelve months. They shall be ordained at ceremonial liturgies following an interview with the church council, should the church agree to their ordination.

2.11.2. Apart from presbyters and deacons, preachers that are members of the church and enjoy high spiritual repute shall take part in spiritual instruction, in which they shall be guided by the decisions of the church and its council.

2.11.3. A local church shall elect its council from among the clergy and the most experienced and authoritative laypeople to implement its decisions, draw

up suggestions and recommendations to the congregation, and coordinate the entire activity of the church. The presbyter shall perform the duties of the chair of the church council.

2.11.4. A church council may elect a youth officer to organize and supervise the activities of its young members and represent them on the council. Such work shall be directed by the Statute of the Youth Councils of the league's churches.

2.12. An auditing commission consisting of three persons shall be elected by a congregational meeting to verify the economic and financial activities of the church.

2.12.1. The auditing commission shall inspect the church's cash and noncash assets and material values at least once a year. The inspection results shall be reported to the general congregational meeting for its approval.

2.13. Choristers, precentors, and accompanying musicians shall belong to the Evangelical Christian Baptist confession.

2.13.1. The presbyter and the precentor shall effect the spiritual guidance of the choir.

The Economic and Financial Activity of the Church

2.14.1. The finances of a local church shall consist of donations, home and overseas legacies, and profits from publishing and other activities.

2.14.2. The finances of a local church shall be spent on the upkeep of the house of worship, salaries of clergy and managers, deductions to communities and the All-Union Council of the league, charitable donations, accommodations for clergy and their families, and other purposes.

2.14.3. Financial management shall be effected by the presbyter and the church council.

2.14.4. Every local church shall maintain a register of its members, protocols, and accounts of properties purchased by or donated to it or received from secular authorities on contract.

2.15.1. A church shall have the status of juridical person with the right of acquisition of movables and immovables.

2.15.2. Upon liquidation of a local church, its movables and immovables shall pass to an (inter) regional or (inter) territorial community of the league, after all debts have been paid.

2.15.3. A church shall possess a seal and stamp.

III. (INTER) REPUBLICAN AND (INTER) TERRITORIAL COMMUNITY OF EVANGELICAL CHRISTIAN BAPTISTS

Community Activities

3.1.1. An (inter) republican and (inter) territorial community is a voluntary association of league churches in a given region for fellowship and joint work in the name of the Lord.

3.1.2. An (inter) republican and (inter) territorial community may organize offices for evangelical missions, charity, theological education, Sunday schools, book publication, the press, youth affairs, and others. All these offices shall be part of the community under its direct management and the guidance of the community council, which shall determine the establishment of such offices, their staff, and budgets.

3.1.3. An (inter) republican and (inter) territorial community may organize missionary, charitable, religious instruction, and economic organizations and workshops producing objects necessary for community churches.

Activities of the Senior Presbyter and Community Offices

3.2.1. The senior presbyter (community elder) and the presbyter's deputies and assistants shall be elected at conferences of delegates of the regional churches by a majority of at least two-thirds. Republican elders of the league shall participate in the election of senior presbyters.

3.2.2. To pursue the goals specified in par. 1.7 of this charter, a conference shall elect an (inter) regional or (inter) territorial council of clergy with long records of ministry. A minimum two-thirds of the votes shall be required to be elected. The number of councillors (seven or more) shall depend on the number of churches in the given community. The council shall be presided over by the senior presbyter.

3.2.3. Should a senior presbyter, deputies, or assistants prove unsuited to their duties, their further ministry or dismissal shall be discussed by the regional council with the republican elders participating, for further consideration by a conference of the community clergy.

3.3. A community may elect an auditing commission with a minimum membership of three to inspect its financial and other economic activities.

3.4.1. The senior presbyter and the community council shall spiritually assist the local churches in the community in preaching the gospel and settling internal disputes.

3.4.2. When the senior presbyter and community councillors visit local churches, they shall take part in services by preaching the gospel and instructing the congregation and in conferences electing or dismissing presbyters or discussing other matters.

3.4.3. The senior presbyter shall discuss ordination applications from local churches with the community council and give approval after interviewing the candidates, mindful of a presbyter's responsibility for ordination (1 Tim. 5:22).

3.4.4. The senior presbyter and the community council shall jointly organize Bible classes, spiritual instruction conferences, and seminars for the clergy, young people, Sunday school teachers, precentors, musicians, and charity activists.

3.4.5. The senior presbyter shall maintain an account of the local churches, their staff, and congregations.

3.4.6. The senior presbyter shall conclude contracts and assume obligations and liabilities on behalf of the (inter) regional or (inter) territorial community as a local organization enjoying the rights of juridical person.

3.4.7. The senior presbyter shall represent the interests of the local churches and their individual members before secular authorities and public organizations.

Accountability of the Senior Presbyter; Community Conferences

3.5.1. The senior presbyter shall report on the presbyter's activities to conferences of the community and the (inter) regional and republican league council.

3.5.2. Conferences to endorse reports and elections shall be convened every four years and spiritual instruction conferences whenever necessary, but no rarer than once a year.

3.5.3. An extraordinary conference may be convened on the initiative of at least one-half of community councillors.

Community Legal Status and Finances

3.6.1. Community resources shall consist of deductions from local churches, donations from private persons at home and abroad, profits from publishing activities, and other moneys.

3.6.2. The community shall spend on the upkeep of its offices, remuneration of its staff, charity, evangelism, instruction of the clergy, book publication, deductions to the council and public foundations, and other purposes.

3.6.3. Estimate future outgoings of an (inter) regional or (inter) territorial council shall be discussed and approved by the senior presbyter of the republican community.

3.7. An (inter) regional or (inter) territorial council shall be entitled to a chancellery, library, archive, and recording and video studios.

3.8. As a juridical person, an (inter) regional or (inter) territorial community may acquire movable and immovable property.

3.8.1. Should an (inter) regional or (inter) territorial community be liquidated, its movables and immovables shall pass to the (inter) republican community after all debts have been paid.

3.9. The community elder shall possess a seal and stamp.

IV. (INTER) REPUBLICAN COMMUNITY OF EVANGELICAL CHRISTIAN BAPTIST CHURCHES

General Provisions

4.1. An (inter) republican community of Evangelical Christian Baptists shall be a voluntary association of league churches in a given region for fellowship and joint work.

4.2. The jurisdiction and competences of an (inter) republican community shall spread to all league churches, within the region and overseas, that have voluntarily joined it.

4.2.1. An (inter) republican community may have contacts with overseas churches and religious communities and organizations of related confessions by mail or by delegating its members to their congresses, conferences, and seminars, and by inviting foreign church activists to its congresses, conferences, and seminars to exchange spiritual experience and practice mutual aid.

4.3. The membership of local churches in an (inter) republican community shall be discussed at the request of the senior presbyter of an (inter) regional or (inter) territorial league community to be approved by the (inter) republican league council, which shall issue an appropriate certificate to every local member church.

Bodies of an (Inter) republican Community

4.4. The congress of church representatives elected at (inter) regional and (inter) territorial league conferences shall be the supreme governing body of an (inter) republican community.

4.4.1. As a rule, a republican congress shall be convened every four years. Representation quotas, election procedures, and the time and venue of the congress shall be determined by the republican league council.

4.4.2. The clergy shall gather for republican instruction conferences whenever necessary (no rarer than once a year).

4.4.3. An extraordinary republican congress may be convened on the initiative of at least one-half of republican councillors.

4.4.4. To pursue the goals specified in par. 1.7 of these rules, an (inter) republican league congress shall elect the senior presbyter (community elder), deputies, and republican councillors, who shall receive at least two-thirds of the votes. Senior presbyter elections shall be attended by a representative of the All-Union League Council Board.

4.4.5. The number of republican councillors (seven or more) shall depend on the number of local churches in the given community. They shall be elected from among the most authoritative clergy of the given churches.

4.4.6. Should a senior presbyter, the presbyter's deputies, or assistants prove unsuited to their duties, their further ministry or dismissal shall be discussed by the republican league council, with a representative of the All-Union League Council Board participating.

Activities of an (Inter) republican Community and the All-Union Council

4.5.1. Community life and activities shall be within the competences of the republican league congress.

4.5.2. The congress shall elaborate long-term programs for the evangelization and moral and spiritual instruction of the flock, determine community activities, and adopt resolutions.

4.5.3. An (inter) republican community may have departments for evangelism and charity; instruction of the clergy and Sunday school teachers; book publication and the press; youth affairs; economy and finances; external church relations; and others. The republican league council shall determine their establishment, staff, and budgets.

4.5.4. All departments shall be under community jurisdiction, and their activities shall be guided by the republican community elder.

4.5.5. Republican communities may publish the Bible, the New Testament, song collections, teaching aids, magazines, calendars, newspapers, and other printed matter necessary to the local population.

4.5.6. Republican communities may affiliate missions, charitable and educational societies, and economic bodies.

4.6. According to the procedure specified in par. 4.4.4, a regional congress may elect an auditing commission with a minimum membership of three to inspect the financial and other economic activities of an (inter) republican community.

4.7.1. The community elder and the republican council shall give spiritual assistance to local churches in the community in evangelism, disputable local matters, and the appointment of presbyters. They may give loans to local churches for the purchase or construction of houses of worship and dwellings for the clergy.

4.7.2. Republican communities shall assist local churches in the instruction and postgraduate education of clergy, choir precentors, orchestra conductors, and others in biblical classes and seminars at home and abroad.

4.7.3. The community elder, the elder's deputies and assistants, and republican councillors shall take part in public worship, preaching the gospel, and delivering sermons to the congregation. They may take part in community meetings when presbyters are elected or dismissed and when other issues are discussed.

4.7.4. Applications by local churches and elders of (inter) regional and (inter) territorial councils concerning presbyterial ordinations shall be offered for consideration to the republican community elder and the republican council, who shall issue presbyterial certificates.

4.7.5. The republican council shall register the local churches under its jurisdiction and their clergy and shall take stock of the congregations.

4.7.6. On behalf of the republican council, the community elder may conclude contracts and issue warrants and liabilities.

4.7.7. The community elder shall represent the interests of the local churches and their individual members before the secular authorities and public organizations.

4.7.8. The community elder's, activities shall be accounted by the elder to the regional church congress, the (inter) republican council, and the All-Union League Council Board.

Community Finances and Estimates

4.8.1. A community's resources shall consist of deductions from local churches and (inter) regional and (inter) territorial communities, donations and legacies from private persons at home and abroad, and profits from publishing, economic, and other activities.

4.8.2. An (inter) republican community shall have a pension fund. Pensions shall be paid as specified by pension regulations.

4.8.3. The community shall spend on the upkeep of its offices, remunerating its staff, traveling expenses, charity, evangelism, instruction of the clergy, loans to local churches to purchase, construction and reconstruction of houses of worship, deductions to the All-Union League Council Board, and other purposes.

4.8.4. The president of the All-Union League Council shall approve the republican council budget.

4.8.5. A community shall place its money in a state bank account.

4.9. A republican council may have a printing press, chancellery, library, archive, and recording and video studios.

4.10. As juridical person, a republican community may acquire movable and immovable property.

4.10.1. Should an (inter) republican Evangelical Christian Baptist community be liquidated, its movables and immovables shall be distributed among the local churches of the (inter) regional or (inter) territorial community, after all debts have been paid.

4.11. An (inter) republican community shall possess a seal and stamp.

V. ALL-UNION COUNCIL OF EVANGELICAL CHRISTIAN BAPTISTS

The All-Union Congress and Conference

5.1.1. The All-Union Congress shall be the supreme body of the All-Union League, headed by its council. Its delegates shall be elected by (inter) regional and (inter) territorial conferences and (inter) republican congresses.

5.1.2. All-Union congresses shall, as a rule, be convened every four years. Representation quotas, election procedure, and the time and venue of the congress shall be determined by the All-Union League Council.

5.1.3. The clergy shall gather for All-Union instruction conferences whenever necessary (no rarer than once a year).

5.1.4. An extraordinary congress may be convened on the initiative of at least one-half of the All-Union councillors.

5.2. The jurisdiction (competences) of the All-Union League is valid for all league churches, in the Soviet Union and abroad, that have voluntarily joined the council.

5.3.1. An All-Union Congress shall discuss and settle issues of the league's life and work;

5.3.2. elaborate long-term programs for the evangelization and moral and spiritual instruction of the flock, determine further activities, and adopt resolutions;

5.3.3. audit and approve All-Union League Council and auditing commission reports;

5.3.4. audit and discuss reports by department heads in conformity with par. 5.8 of these rules;

5.3.5. audit doctrinal proposals and adopt decisions on them;

5.3.6. amend these rules as proposed by the All-Union League Council Board on the decision of the council.

All-Union Council Bodies and Activities Thereof

5.4.1. To implement the decisions of All-Union League congresses, maintain the activities of the All-Union League according to the commandments of Jesus Christ our Lord in between congresses, and represent itself abroad, the league shall form its council out of its board, the elders and deputy elders of (inter) republican communities, senior presbyters of (inter) regional and (inter) territorial communities, and a coordinator for youth affairs.

5.4.2. The council shall convene whenever necessary (no rarer than once a year), and its board no rarer than once every three months.

5.5.1. The board—the council's executive body—shall consist of the president and the president's deputies, secretary-general, elders of (inter) republican communities and associations, and a Mennonite representative.

5.5.2. The league president, the president's deputies, secretary-general, and an auditing commission of seven shall be elected by the congress from among its delegates by a minimum majority of two-thirds. The election procedure shall be specified by the congress.

5.6. The league president shall head its council and board. As overall and spiritual leader, the president shall guide the council and board activities and, together with the league council board, determine the duties of the deputies and the secretary- general.

5.7. The All-Union League Council Board shall form an elders' council with one representative from every region to consider the suitability of clergy of all ranks and unclear doctrinal issues and to determine the Baptist stance on new trends in Christianity. The activities of the elders' council shall be determined by its regulations, approved by the league council board.

5.8. To implement the practical tasks of the league, its council may organize the following offices: evangelical mission and charity; instruction of clergy, Sunday school teachers, choir precentors, and orchestra conductors; publishing; youth affairs; external church relations; economics and finances; and others.

5.8.1. The league council shall determine the necessity, staff, and budgets of these offices.

5.9. The tasks of the league council board include:

5.9.1. The implementation of the tasks of the league council specified in par. 1.7 of these rules and implementation of All-Union Congress decisions.

5.9.2. Contacts with local churches through exchanges of letters, visits, and conferences in the center.

5.9.3. Aid to local churches and republican communities in ecclesiastical and economic matters concerning the design and construction of houses of worship; aid and consultations on legal matters to local theological schools.

5.9.4. Education and postgraduate instruction of the clergy, choir precentors, orchestra conductors, and others in biblical schools and seminaries, biblical and precentors' classes, and at educational and theological conferences and seminars at home and abroad.

5.9.5. The publication of the Bible, the New Testament, song collections, newspapers, magazines, and other necessary printed matter.

5.9.6. Organization of evangelism, missions, charity, and instruction by the league council through radio, television, and other mass media.

5.9.7. Contacts with overseas churches and religious communities of related confessions for an exchange of spiritual experience and mutual aid through exchanges of letters, delegation of representatives to their congresses, conferences, and seminars, and invitation of overseas church activists to Soviet congresses, conferences, and seminars.

5.9.8. Representation of the interests of republican councils and communities, local churches, and their individual members before the secular authorities, Soviet public organizations, and the international public.

5.9.9. Account of the local churches affiliated with the league, their presbyters, and congregations.

5.10. To implement these tasks, the league, as juridical person, may possess houses of worship, theological seminaries, biblical schools, charitable institutions, educational societies, missions, radio and television services, printing presses, enterprises, and housing accommodation for its functionaries.

5.11.1. An auditing commission of seven shall be elected by the congress from among its delegates by a majority of no less than two-thirds. The commission at its first session shall elect its chairman, who shall later take part in all sessions of the council board.

5.11.2. The auditing commission shall verify all economic and financial activities of the council board, offices, and regional communities and report the results to the nearest All-Union congress and to the council board.

All-Union League Finances

5.12.1. All-Union League finances shall consist of deductions from local churches and communities, donations and legacies from private persons at home and abroad, and profits from publishing, economic, and other activities.

5.12.2. The council shall have a pension fund. Pensions shall be paid as specified by pension regulations approved by the council.

5.12.3. The league council board shall spend on the upkeep of its offices, remuneration of its staff, traveling expenses, charity, evangelism, pensions, instruction of the clergy, loans to local churches, publishing, the purchasing, construction, and reconstruction of houses of worship, purchasing housing accommodation for the council staff, and other purposes.

5.12.4. The league shall place its money in a state bank account.

5.12.5. Local churches that fail to contribute to the league budget without valid reason shall not be entitled to money aid from its council.

5.13. The league council shall be entitled to a library, reading room, recording and video studios, record library, and archive.

5.14. As a juridical person, the league council may acquire movable and immovable property.

5.15. The council shall possess a seal and stamp.

Adopted by All-Union Congress
of Evangelical Christian Baptists
Moscow, 22 February 1990

Protestant Movements

In the eighteenth century, Russian Empress Catherine the Great issued a manifesto allowing all foreigners to settle in whatever Russian provinces they chose. Mass German settlement soon started in the Volga region and southern Russia, and the first group of Mennonites appeared in 1789. Their colonies in southern provinces became the cradle of Evangelical and Baptist confessions in Russia. The first water baptism was performed in Tbilisi in 1867.

Protestant preachers from Germany and Britain witnessed to the Word of God in St. Petersburg, then the Russian capital, and the first converts included aristocratic families—the Pashkovs, von Korfs, Bobrinskys, Gagarins, and von Liewens.

Two Baptist congresses convened in 1884 in the Crimea and in St. Petersburg. A League of Russian Baptists for South Russia and the Caucasus was established in Novo-Vasilievka (Taurida Province) and a League of Evangelical Christians in St. Petersburg. The southern league copied its community arrangements from Germany, while the northern league reflected England. There were no major confessional differences between them, though they disagreed on the position of the priest's hands while blessing the newly baptized.

The year 1905 brought a royal manifesto affirming freedom of conscience, speech, assembly, and league, but this liberty was short-lived. World War One created many problems for Russian Protestants. High officials chose to regard Baptists as potential German agents. Many chapels were closed and priests exiled.

The reprisals stopped after the monarchy fell in February 1917. Leaders of the Baptist League addressed the new Provisional Government with a list of political demands including the separation of the Church from the state; freedom of assembly, league and the press; freedom of public worship for all religions; abolition of criminal prosecution for crimes against religion; and guarantee of legal rights to religious communities. The practical activity of the Provisional Government supported freedom of conscience and removed obstacles to Protestantism, though it had no time to pass legislation regulating religious activities.

After the Bolsheviks seized power in the coup of October 1917, they initially treated Protestants mildly compared to the way they treated the Orthodox hierarchy, their bitter enemy. Evangelists were allowed to set up industrial and agricultural cooperatives and religious presses and hold prayer assemblies in prestigious halls. In 1928 the government allotted them a large land plot in the Far East to build a new town, Evangelsk. Protestants were active in the nationwide literacy effort and healthy-living campaign.

It became clear somewhat later that the secular authorities' tolerance was a mere tactical subterfuge. A Communist Party document of the 1920s said: "Sectarians have considerable economic and cultural forces now to be tactfully channelled to Soviet work." But the Bolsheviks' main goal was to undermine the influence of the Russian Orthodox Church, so the Bolsheviks supported not only Protestants, but also Old Believers and Orthodox Revivalists.

The year 1929 was a turning point. As the ruling party accepted the Stalinist course of rapid industrialization and coercive agricultural collectivization to strangle the New Economic Policy, which allowed private enterprise, it sharply changed its attitude to all religious confessions, Protestantism included. There was no room for religion under socialism. Communities were suppressed, houses of prayer closed, and priests arrested. The Baptist and Evangelical Christian leagues were banned in the early 1930s. Only a few tiny communities survived in the vast country, and these led a miserable existence under strict secular surveillance.

Protestants and other confessions became active again during World War Two. In 1944, Baptists and Evangelical Christians united in one league. Pentecostals joined a year later, Evangelical Christians of the Apostolic Spirit joined in 1947, and Mennonites in 1960.

That year was a grim one for the league. The secular authorities redoubled their militant atheist efforts. They closed houses of prayer en masse and cruelly persecuted recalcitrant clergy. They subjugated the league leaders and made them accept two documents running counter to the Gospel spirit: the Statute of the Evangelical Baptist League and an instruction to senior presbyters, which limited clerical activities and banned preaching to children and young people. In indignation, 30 percent of the League's members left it. Some of the breakaway communities united in the underground Council of Churches of Evangelical Christian Baptists. Others chose autonomy and were registered as independent religious organizations.

In 1963, the All-Union League of Evangelical Christian Baptists declared the adoption of both documents an error and annulled them. A new generation of ecclesiastical leaders took over, but they were linked with the secular authorities as closely as their predecessors. Whatever they said at conferences or stated in their documents followed official propaganda patterns.

In the meantime the underground council engaged for many years in successful work and gained authority among the believers. Pastor Gennadi Kryuchkov, council president, has refused to leave the underground despite Soviet democratic changes giving freedom to all religions and confessions. So the schism among Protestant confession remains.

Both centers have problems of another sort, too. The economic crisis and inter-ethnic strife now rampant in Soviet society caused mass emigration, especially now that the legislation and authorities no longer impede it. The Mennonite community shrank after ethnic Germans, many preachers among them, started massive emigration from Siberia, Kazakhstan and Kirghizia. Russian and Ukrainian Protestants are also emigrating en masse.

The 44th Congress of the All-Union League of Evangelical Christian Baptists (held in Moscow in February 1990) did much to consolidate the Protestant movement. The 714 delegates and 360 guests discussed structural reform of the league, the extension of theological education network, instruction of Sunday school teachers, the spiritual improvement of believers, the preservation of the Coopol doctrine in its purity and unity, mass evangelization, the publication and dissemination of edifying books and, last but not least, international contacts. The conferees sharply criticized the activities of several Council departments, among them the International Department, which is to undergo a radical reform.

The new statute adopted by the congress reflected current realities and new prospects for the Baptist and Evangelical movement. It chartered a new structure of the movement and elected a new president of the All-Union League of Evangelical Christian Baptists.

The new President is Grigori Komendant (b. 1946), a Ukrainian born into the family of a presbyter in the Khmelnitsky Region, Ukraine. His grandfather fell victim to Stalinist atrocities. Grigori Komendant was baptized by water at the age of eighteen. He was ordained deacon in 1971, and presbyter a year later. A graduate of the biblical correspondence courses in Moscow, he studied at the Baptist seminary in Hamburg from 1973 to 1975, was assistant to the senior presbyter of the Ukraine, and later senior presbyter of the Kiev Region. Early in 1981, Grigori Komendant was elected deputy senior presbyter of the Ukraine. He is married and has a son and a daughter.

Alexei Bychkov, Nikolai Kolesnikov and Alexander Firisyuk were elected his deputies in the League, and Vladimir Kunets chairman of the auditing commission.

The congress Appeal to the Churches of Evangelical Christian Baptists in the Soviet Union said, in part:

"We loved the people, yet we were rejected by the community. We did good in Christ's name, yet we were persecuted as violating socialist morals. We preached the Gospel to sinners, taught Christ's truths to children, and led them along the road of goodness and charity, yet we were fined and framed up. Now, thank God, things have changed for the better. Our community has the right to preach the Gospel overtly and take part in the works of charity and compassion. What will come next? God knows. We live at a time of hope.

"We are facing the last years of a century. The harvest is ripe in the vast field of our missionary activity. The Holy Ghost calls us all to diaconate, to service to our neighbors, to a pure and saintly life and permanent spiritual revival."

The latest events promise that these hopes will be realized. The last years of the twentieth century have seen new legislation on religion. Dozens of new houses of prayer have been consecrated; hundreds of thousands of copies of the Scriptures have been published; prayer assemblies are held in stadiums to attract many thousands; Sunday schools have opened here and there. The radio and television broadcast edifying programs. The best-known Soviet companies produce plays about Jesus Christ and perform them at charity evenings. These are only some features of the current spiritual revival.

Perestroika and the Baptists

Denton Lotz

"We have so many open doors we cannot use them all." "There are so many new opportunities we don't know what to do first." "We never dreamed five years ago that we would have the new freedoms of today." These are only some of the statements one hears frequently from Baptists in the USSR. There is no doubt that *perestroika* has brought new and radical life to all Christians in the USSR, including the Baptists.[1]

Changes in church life effected by new thinking in the USSR are discussed here only in broad terms. I hope, however, that readers glimpse the new realities emerging that give cause for thanks and praise to God.

MISSION AND EVANGELISM

The heart of Baptist life has always been its zeal to evangelize. Until now Baptist witness had been limited to the worship life of the church. Of course the holy life of the believer at home, work, and school was and is still a significant part of Baptist evangelism in the Soviet Union. But now public opportunities for witness are multiplying. Local Baptist churches are hiring public halls and openly inviting people to evangelistic meetings. For example, a small congregation of about twenty, mainly elderly, women rented a public hall for evangelistic services and invited a church choir and pastor from a neighboring town. To everyone's surprise, more than one thousand people showed up and one hundred made public confessions of faith in Jesus Christ as their Lord and Savior. The same story is repeated in city after city.

Such freedom brings new responsibilities and problems. How does the church nurture the new converts? What type of worship is appropriate? How can five times the number of new members be integrated into an old conservative church? Obviously, *perestroika* is forcing Baptists to learn how best to meet the spiritual needs of their Soviet neighbors with all the new openness that *glasnost* and the consequent new freedoms have brought. But one thing is sure: Baptists are eager to witness the saving power of Christ to a secular society. Although not a part of their tradition, Baptists in the Soviet Union are beginning to give an invitation to come forward at the conclusion of all their worship services. Many new converts have already joined the church by this method.

BIBLES AND CHRISTIAN LITERATURE

For years it was well known in the West that Christians in the Soviet Union suffered from a lack of Bibles and other Christian books. The Baptist World Alliance (BWA) was pleased when it used to receive permission to send ten thousand Bibles. Now the floodgate has been opened. Dr. Alexei Bychkov, a vice-chairman of the All-Union League of Evangelical Christians Baptists (AULECB), stated that in one recent year more than 1.2 million Bibles, concordances, commentaries, and hymnbooks were received. That in itself is indeed a miracle! In 1988 we thought one hundred thousand were a lot; that was the amount we asked the chairman of the Ministry of Religious Affairs for permission to send in recognition of the millennium of Christianity in Russia.

Recent news from the United Bible Societies (UBS) indicates that permission has been granted for the import or printing of 20 million Bibles! This has yet to be confirmed. However, such a large number would require some type of printing facility or Bible society. In fact, leaders of the UBS are recommending that such a Bible society be started in Moscow just as in Warsaw, Poland.

There is still a need for children's literature. Baptist leaders are painfully aware of this need and are working with churches abroad to receive appropriate material for the instruction of their children.

YOUTH WORK AND CONFERENCES

Although youth choirs had previously been allowed, the idea of youth leadership training or youth conferences was only a dream. Recently three hundred young Baptists held their first youth conference in Moscow. They rented a hotel and for a week prayed, studied, sang, and discussed with one another the joys and responsibilities of witnessing and living for Christ in a modern secular society.

In 1988 for the first time in seventy years a youth choir was allowed to attend a Baptist Youth World Conference. Forty-five young people traveled to Glasgow, Scotland, where they cheered the hearts of the ten thousand in attendance. Many young Soviet Baptists experienced culture shock when confronted with young Western

Christians and heard Christian rock groups for the first time. But by the end of the conference Baptists from the Soviet Union and youth from around the world were truly enjoying the international fellowship. Before and after the conference they traveled throughout Great Britain meeting with young people and singing in churches and public places.

Youth work is an essential ministry of the church, not only for the future but also now. In all of the churches a good number of young people have newly come searching for meaning in life. Many have confessed Christ and are seeking baptism.

THEOLOGICAL EDUCATION

For many years Baptists prayed for a seminary. They have offered a correspondence course in theology but have never run a seminary proper. Permission has now been granted for such a seminary to open.

A number of students have been sent abroad to further their theological education. Fifteen students recently returned from the Summer Institute of Theological Education (SITE) located at the Baptist Seminary in Rueschlikon, Switzerland. Baptist pastors and students from the Soviet Union have studied in Great Britain, Germany, Hungary, Sweden, and the United States.

Baptists in the Baltic republics of Latvia and Estonia already have opened their own seminaries. A new excitement can be felt there among young evangelicals who wish to enter the ministry with proper theological training.

TRAVEL ABROAD

Until recently Soviet citizens were not granted permission to travel abroad. But in the late 1980s travel restrictions began to be lifted, allowing religious delegations to attend conferences in other countries. In 1989 150 delegates from the USSR traveled to the European Baptist Federation congress. This was the largest religious delegation to travel outside of the USSR since the Revolution. Nowadays Slavic churches in many parts of the world are pleased to invite and receive many visitors from their related churches in the USSR.

Perhaps a negative aspect of this new freedom is that a number of visitors have applied for immigration and are receiving permission to leave the Soviet Union. From an evangelistic point of view it is regrettable that Soviet churches are losing these Christian witnesses.

CHARITABLE WORK

Heretofore in a socialist society the church was prevented from carrying out any type of social activity. Now Baptists in Moscow regularly visit children's hospitals and homes for the elderly. They help bathe and clothe the patients and comb the hair of the elderly. The leader of a hospital said when speaking recently to the Moscow Baptist Church, "If anyone had told me a year ago that I would be speaking in a church I would have said they were crazy. At first I did not want the believers in my hospital. But now I have seen how they love our patients and the positive response. It reminded me of what a French psychiatrist said: 'To have healing you need chemistry plus love!' We from the state hospital can only give chemistry, but you Baptists can give love, and that makes the difference!"

Baptists in the Soviet Union have established their own charitable organization. They helped the victims of the Armenian earthquake by taking care of two thousand children. Dr. Michael Zhidkov, chairman of the AULECB Charitable Committee, told how excited and eager to help were many Baptist members. This is a new avenue of ministry that *perestroika* has brought and one that caught the Baptists by surprise. They are now receiving help from Baptist World Aid and other relief agencies.

MASS MEDIA

For the first time a Baptist worship service was broadcast recently on national television. Frequent radio interviews with believers are broadcast, and Radio Moscow on Sundays has scheduled a ten-minute devotional, which occasionally is led by Baptist pastors.

Even such national newspapers as *Izvestia* and *Pravda* are now publishing interviews with Baptist leaders, who speak of their new freedom and ministries. The papers provide a historical background for these interviews, which helps interpret the various religious movements for a secular people. Newspapers cover church happenings with great frequency, and the hostility previously displayed toward religion is disappearing. The celebrated meeting of President Gorbachev with church leaders on the occasion of the church's millennial celebrations brought a new climate of openness within Soviet society toward the church. This has created an atmosphere where nonbelievers actually seek out the church and examine for themselves the gospel message.

TENSION BETWEEN FREEDOM
AND DISCIPLINE

The Reverend Vasile Logvinenko, of the AULECB, recently addressed the executive committee of the Baptist World Alliance. He said that the new freedom of *glasnost* also has brought its problems. Churches in various regions are becoming more independent. For example, the Baptist unions of Estonia and Latvia already have their own seminaries, as mentioned. Now they are questioning their membership in the All Union League. A number of Pentecostal churches have decided to withdraw from the AULECB and form their own union. All the Pentecostals of Moldavia, however, have decided to remain as members of the league.

Glasnost and *perestroika* mean that church leadership organizations must take more responsibility and be more accountable to their constituencies. Hard questions are asked of the union, and local churches expect answers.

The creative tension brought about by the new situation in the Soviet Union is very positive, because in that very tension brothers and sisters are able to confront problems honestly and openly. This new openness will have a profound effect on the work of local congregations.

In conclusion, new life is springing up among Baptist and evangelical Christians in the Soviet Union. New buildings are under construction, youth and adults are evangelizing, churches are growing, the Word is being preached, and Baptists are seizing the moment to witness for Christ in every way possible.

A Baptist leader explained *glasnost* by quoting Matthew 10:27: "What I tell you in the dark, utter in the light; and what you hear whispered, proclaim upon the housetops" (RSV). That is what Baptists in the USSR are doing today. And the response among the people has been one of thanksgiving. Therefore Baptists say with the apostle Paul, "Thanks be to God who gives us the victory through our Lord Jesus Christ!"

NOTES

1. Denton Lotz, General Secretary of the Baptist World Alliance, wrote this after a recent visit with Baptists in the Soviet Union.

Bright Prospects for
Seventh-Day Adventists

By Mikhail P. Kulakov,
President of the USSR Division

Glasnost and *perestroika*, which mean openness and restructuring, are constantly gaining momentum in the Soviet Union. The changes that the country is undergoing now are real and irreversible. The ideological monopoly has suddenly come to an end.

Many doors that had been closed for Seventh-Day Adventists are now opening. Christians are getting more and more opportunities to share their beliefs with others, although sometimes they still must overcome either the resistance of the local authorities or their own apprehensions.

Publishing houses usually belong to the state, and even though some of them are willing to print religious literature, because of the shortage of paper only a few of them can accept small orders from churches.

During the past few years the government not only abandoned all limitations on the construction of new church buildings, but also has been returning those buildings that were taken away in the past. In many cities local authorities are helping our pastors to rent music halls and theaters to conduct charity concerts of Christian music. Many of our pastors preach short Bible-based evangelistic sermons at such concerts. The general public and especially young people gladly attend such meetings. And those of our members who not so long ago suffered from oppression and persecution cannot help crying as they see these unbelievable changes.

PERSECUTION IN EARLIER YEARS

Are the long years of prohibition on religious activities really in the irreversible past?

My dear wife, Anna, does not like to speak about those things that she, the wife of a church leader and mother of six children, had to endure at those times. She is concerned about her friend, the wife of another minister, Mrs. Evdokiya Paratshuk, who is now confined to bed after a stroke. That dear sister, who like several others felt called to the ministry with her husband in the early 1960s, lived in constant expectation of that horrible night when her husband would be arrested. That night came, and Evdokiya was left alone to take care of not only three small children but also her elderly mother, who, having heard about the imprisonment of her son-in-law, became paralyzed.

I myself was arrested in 1948 in Latvia for my religious activities and spent five years in labor camps. Two years earlier my father was imprisoned for organizing a Seventh-Day Adventist church in Ivanovo. After spending those years in the labor camps, I was exiled to Siberia. I survived, but my brother, who also was exiled to Siberia, died there.

I was released after the death of Stalin in 1953, and I moved to Alma-Ata, the Kazakhstan's capital near the Chinese border, to continue my work for the church.

In the 1960s under Nikita Khrushchev the government again tried to abolish religion. We were not allowed to conduct worship openly. In the 1970s under Leonid Brezhnev the situation started to change. In 1977 Seventh-Day Adventist churches were established in the Russian republic and other republics throughout the Soviet Union.

The latter part of the seventies was marked by some changes in the attitude of the government to the church. Separated groups and communities of believers gradually began to receive government recognition, which meant registration and legitimacy. From there on the disparate groups began to develop a single unified structure. In some areas of the country Adventists were given opportunity to organize conferences and unions. Some contacts with the Adventist General Conference, an international body that gathers every five years to solve urgent problems and to elect new leaders, were established. Many Adventists of the older generation recall with gratitude the visits of such Adventist leaders as Theodore Carcich, Robert H. Pierson, and Alf Lohne, who visited the Soviet Union many times.

Elder Neal C. Wilson's visit to the Soviet Union in the summer of 1981, as well as his other successive visits, to a great extent effected the unification of all Adventists in the country and a greater recognition of our denomination by government authorities.

We believe God used Mikhail Gorbachev to introduce democracy into the country. My dream is that now with this freedom church membership will soon double in number.

The church survived. It could not be otherwise. In its ordeals it was comforted and sustained by the precious promises of the Lord: "And the gates of hell shall not prevail against it." "And this gospel of the kingdom shall be preached in all the world for a witness unto all nations; and then shall the end come" (Matt. 16:18; 24:14).

THEOLOGICAL EDUCATION

As far back as 1928, at the Adventist congress that turned out to be the last one before Stalin's era of total annihilation of religion and church life in the country, church leaders noted that they were praying for an opportunity to open a school in which ministers could receive theological training. All through these long years divine providence was preparing the country for the proclamation of the gospel. At last, after many earnest appeals and decades of prayers and persistent requests, in January 1987 the government finally gave permission to the church to open a four-year on-campus course for training young ministers.

At the same time in the village of Zaokski, seventy-five miles south of Moscow, the church received a hectare of land. After twenty-one months, at a site on which only three walls had been standing, a beautiful three-story building was erected to serve as the first Soviet Adventist theological seminary. It is also the first Protestant institution of higher theological education in the USSR.

From the first day of its operation in 1989 the seminary began to attract the attention of the national media. People, mostly intellectuals, want to get acquainted with the teachings of a church that is taking such practical, visible steps to promote Christian values. Many people want to use our library, meet with the teachers, and take part in our services. In the first year of its existence the seminary church baptized forty converts. Leading universities of the USSR are inviting our teachers to lecture on the teachings of the Bible. Many non-Adventist young men with university education are expressing their desire to study at our seminary.

In April 1989 on the campus of Zaokski Seminary a five-month intensive agriculture course was offered for the first time. The program was directed by Dr. Jacov Mittleider. Twenty students from almost every republic of the Soviet Union gained practical knowledge and received certificates from the Soviet National Academy of Agriculture and Home Study International. In 1990 forty students took the course.

The program is a great success. It caught the attention of the national media. Leading scientists and thousands of Soviet people have visited the seminary to observe its unique program. The first questions most of them asked were: How do your beliefs inspire you to become so involved in agriculture? Why is a theological seminary involved in an agricultural program, and with such incredible success? What does religion have to do with agriculture? These questions confirmed our belief that thorough theological training should be closely connected with practical missionary and welfare ministry. People should be able to see that theology is about what is happening now and not only about what has happened in the distant past.

In faraway Kazakhstan in the city of Dzhambul lives our sister Branislava Bullo. She heard about the construction of the first Adventist seminary in her country and wondered what she could do at age eighty-two. Her hands do not have the strength to carry and lay bricks, but she decided to earn money by sewing clothes. Before long she was able to give the church seven thousand rubles to help in the construction.

At the same time God impressed the hearts of Harold, Jr., and Rose Otis to dedicate their lives to the work of the Lord in the USSR. Harold is an elder and the former president of the Review and Herald Publishing Association, the Adventists' denominational house. Since 1988 Bud Otis, in the position of assistant to the General Conference president for Soviet affairs, and Rose have been involved in all the activities of our church in the USSR, becoming a living link between the believers here and our friends in the rest of the world. We wish we could mention all the names of the thousands of dear people in the West who have given their time and money for God's work in the Soviet Union. It would have been impossible to develop our agriculture program and to embark on the nationwide construction of 236 new church buildings without the help of such people as Garwin McNeilus, Thomas Zapara, Norman McDugal, and Norman Tarter from the U.S.

ADVENTIST PUBLISHING

The hour has come to evangelize the country with the largest territory in the world. Millions of people have great spiritual hunger. Fallen are the idols in whom people put their faith and whom they worshiped for decades. Many people feel that they have been deprived of the knowledge that is able to give them answers to the most painful questions of this world. The economic crisis that the country is suffering at the moment heightens the sense of spiritual emptiness. People are willing to spend a lot of money to buy a Bible and other religious literature. We can gather large crowds of people at theaters and cultural centers not only for musical concerts, but also for special programs where they can hear the gospel preached. At every such meeting hundreds of people present us with the same request: "Help us to buy a Bible."

In order to answer the spiritual needs of the people, with the help of the General Conference we have built a publishing house in the same place where we have our theological seminary. The equipment for a complete Bible book line was bought by the General Conference. By the end of this year we are planning not only to finish the construction of the building but also to start printing our first Bibles. It will be our own publishing house and will belong solely to the Seventh-Day Adventist Church.

We marvel at the changes that are taking place in the country, and with trepidation we realize how unprepared we are to use these suddenly opened opportunities. We ask the Lord to grant us a double portion of the Holy Spirit and his special blessings for our seminary, where 150 young men are receiving their ministerial training. We believe that our publishing ministry and newly begun radio broadcasting will greatly enhance the growth of the church. Members in every church are involved in the widening ministry through charity organizations. At public hospitals and prisons they are organizing Adventist Bible courses.

Our lay members and ministers believe that very soon thousands of those who are reaching for light in desperation and confusion will join our happy family.

Muslims in an Islamic temple.

Islam

Statistics: Muslim communities currently embrace over 20 million members; there are 2,300 functioning mosques with 7,200 clergy, 5 madrasahs, and 2 higher educational establishments. Muslims reside predominantly in Central Asia and Kazakhstan, in the Volga and the Ural Regions, as well as in the Caucasus.

Organization: The religious life of Muslims is guided by religious boards set up according to regional or republican principle. The largest of these are: the Muslim Board for the European Part of the USSR and Siberia headed by Mufti Talgat Tadzhutdin, the Muslim Board for Central Asia headed by Mufti Mukhammadsadyk Mammayusuf, and the Muslim Board for Transcaucasia with Sheikh-ul-Islam Allahshukur Pashazade at its head.

Brief History: Islam began spreading in Azerbaijan and Daghestan in the Caucasus in the middle of the 7th century A.D., and in the latter half of that century it reached Central Asia and became popular in such major cities as Samarkand, Bukhara, and Khoresm. In 921 a large group of Muslim preachers left Baghdad for the banks of the Volga River. The year 922 is considered the official date of the adoption of Islam in the Volga Region.

Empress Catherine II proclaimed freedom of religion in the 18th century enabling Muslims to set up their religious boards. But in subsequent years, the tsarist administration infringed on the rights of Muslims.

After the October Revolution of 1917 Muslims were subjected to even more pressure, and as a result most mosques and all educational establishments were closed down. A brief period of revival of religious activity in the years following World War II gave way to fresh reprisals in the 1960s. *Perestroika* opened up fresh opportunities for the Muslims.

Current Situation and Problems: Islamic fundamentalism is on the rise. The process is currently under way of the supplanting and replacement of clergymen who compromised themselves by having been in contact with government authorities. Soviet economic troubles are causing difficulties as well; the lack of hard currency makes it difficult for Muslims to perform the hajj, the required pilgrimage to Mecca. This difficulty gave rise to mass unrest in Daghestan in 1991. Thanks to assistance from abroad, about 10,000 pilgrims were nevertheless able to perform the hajj.

Muslim Revival

Stormy renewal is under way in the Soviet Muslim world after what seemed to be decades of total calm and rather sluggish discontent, not only with the arbitrary rule and control of the authorities, but also with the actions of certain officials-turned-bureaucrats and corrupt Moslem leaders.

A start was made in Uzbekistan.

In early 1989, after a Friday sermon in the Till-sheikh Mosque, hundreds of Muslims moved to the center of the Uzbek capital, Tashkent. They carried Islamic banners and slogans and demanded the resignation of the chairman of the Muslim Religious Board for Central Asia and Kazakhstan, Mufti Shamsuddinkhan ibn Ziyautdinkhan Babakhan. He was accused of arbitrary actions, dissipation, heavy drinking, and neglect of his immediate responsibilities.

As more and more people joined in along the way, the unprecedented procession reached the building of the Uzbek Republic Council of Ministers. Representatives of the crowd were taken to see the prime minister. After listening to their grievances, the head of the Uzbek government said that it was up to the Muslims themselves to elect the leader of the religious board and that the least he could do was not impede the convening of the presidium of the religious board and, later, of the congress (*kurultai*).

As soon as the presidium met, the mufti decided to submit his resignation. This brought to an end the career of a man who only recently had made reports at international conferences, headed and received delegations, and was elected member of the Jordanian Royal Academy of Muslim Civilization.

In his place was elected Mukhammadsadyk Mammayusuf, the rector of the Tashkent Imam al-Bukhari Islamic Institute. He was elected first to act as mufti, and at a subsequent *kurultai* he was confirmed as mufti and chairman of the Religious Board.

The new mufti expressed the hope that with the help of Allah, the merciful and the compassionate, many changes that people wanted would be made, including changes in the relations between religious organizations and the state. The mufti stated that the Religious Board was working to expand the publication of the Koran and other religious literature, open new mosques, increase the enrollment of students at the Bukhara Mir-Arab *madrasah* and the Imam al-Bukhari Islamic Institute and secure free exit from the country for the faithful going on the hajj (pilgrimage) to Mecca, in Saudi Arabia.

A momentous event happened later at the Tashkent *kurultai*. After many decades and much trouble, the Muslims received a holy relic that had been taken from them in 1869, the Koran of the caliph Osman. The book was presented by the deputy chairman of the Uzbek Council of Ministers, P. M. Abdurakhmanov.

Before central Asia was incorporated into Russia, Caliph Osman's Koran was kept at the Khodji Akhrar *madrasah* in Samarkand. It is believed that theologian Abu Bakr al-Kaffal brought it there from Baghdad. In 1869, the governor general of Turkestan, K. P. Kaufman, ordered that the Koran be sent to the minister of public instruction in St. Petersburg, where it was placed in the Imperial Public Library. All appeals by Muslims to return the Koran had no effect. Only after the 1917 revolution, on orders from the Soviet of People's Commissars, was the Osman Koran first taken to Ufa and, in 1923, to Turkestan. However, in 1926, the Osman Koran was taken from the Muslims once again and kept in a special safety deposit box at the History Museum of the Peoples of Uzbekistan.

At the 1989 *kurultai*, Mufti Mukhammadsadyk Mammayusuf welcomed the return of the Koran. He said, "There is already convincing proof that changes are real. The first piece of evidence is the return of the Osman Koran. We shall keep this ancient sacred book at the Muslim Religious Board in Tashkent and shall make every effort to create for it the conditions befitting this priceless treasure."

He is very active in charity work. He managed to open scores of new mosques, expand the publication of religious literature, launch a newspaper, *The Mirror of Islam*, increase the number of students at the Bukhara Mir-Arab *madrasah* and the Tashkent Imam al-Bukhari Islamic Institute.

As he had been elected amid controversy, so the young mufti also encountered major problems in the new job. It became clear that some mullahs, probably following the example of his predecessor, lived by no means ascetic lives. The council of *ulemas* (scholars) investigated one *qadi* (judge) and dismissed him.

The mufti was also pained by another unpleasant development: the news, unexpected for him and the people around him, that an independent Muslim religious board had been established in Kazakhstan, with *qadi* Ratbek Nisanbayev elected mufti. Tashkent condemned this move as a schism.

REFORM IN DAGESTAN

Just as in Tashkent, Muslims in the capital of Dagestan—Makhachkala, a city on the Caspian Sea—took advantage of new religious and political freedoms and made their wishes known to the religious leadership. In late April 1989, a few hundred people tried to storm the building of the Muslim Religious Board for the northern Caucasus. Their demands included the resignation of the chairman of the Religious

Board, Makhmud Gekkiyev, who had compromised himself by his constant subservience to the authorities, oblivious of the interests of the faithful, as well as the allocation of a site for the construction of a new mosque, because the old one was located in a shed. The demands were met. The mufti had to leave Makhachkala and flee to safety.

A month earlier, a group of believers in the small town of Nizhni Dzhengutai, Buynak region, seized a local club that was described grandiloquently as the Palace of Culture. The club was located in the requisitioned building of a local mosque. Believers demanded the return of the building to its rightful Muslim ownership. Negotiations continued for a few days, and after the local people placed their support behind the believers, the authorities had to give in.

As was reported by *Izvestia*, in the last thirty years, requests by believers in Dagestan to register religious communities were invariably turned down. The decades of government denial have taken their toll so that at present, out of the republic's forty regions, only thirteen have mosques. In order to practice their religion, every day thousands of elderly people must travel ten or twenty kilometers to the nearest mosque. One hundred and fifty-six houses of worship, many of them of architectural merit, are in a state of bad disrepair after decades of use as clubs and even warehouses. Recently, work has begun to convert thirty-three mosques to gyms. A congress of the Muslims of the northern Caucasus has not been convened for more than ten years.

All this has incited vast discontent among Muslims. As a result, the Muslim Religious Board for the northern Caucasus has been dissolved, and in its place, in each autonomous republic of the northern Caucasus, independent *qadiites* have begun to operate. The situation has begun to change rapidly. Scores of new mosques have opened in the northern Caucasus. Mullahs have become actively involved in social processes, having received for the first time mandates at elections for local councils at different levels.

EVENTS ELSEWHERE

Sheikh-ul-islam Allahshukur Pashazade, chairman of the Muslim Religious Board for Transcaucasia, was unanimously reelected to his high office in 1989. This energetic Muslim leader and theologian enjoys high reputation in the region. Many people view him as a spokesman for a new generation of imams and believers who are waging an all-out war on bureaucracy, corruption, ineffective management of the economy, and such social evils as crime, heavy drinking, prostitution, and drug addiction.

The chairman of the Muslim Religious Board for the European part of the USSR and Siberia, Mufti Talgat Tadzhutdin, who is the same age as the Transcaucasian sheikh-ul-islam, in 1989 successfully marked a double jubilee—the eleven hundredth anniversary of the adoption of Islam by the people on the Volga and in the Urals, and the two hundredth anniversary of the establishment of the Religious Board, initially known as the Orenburg Mahometan Assembly. To mark the occasions, fifty thousand copies of a new edition of the Holy Koran were printed; the book *Gibadat Islamia* and a collection of *hadiths* (traditions about the Prophet Muhammad), *Dhzau-migul-Kamil*, were published; *dastan Makhdi*—a musical theatrical show telling the history of the Volga Bulgars—premiered in the central stadium in Kazan, capital of the Tatar Republic; and a photography exhibition was organized in the art museum.

A moving moment for all the participants in the festivities was the solemn ceremony of putting a crescent on the minaret of a new mosque built in the Tatar Republic's major industrial city of Naberezhnye Chelny. Thirty thousand faithful gathered to attend. Built on a colorful bank of the Kama River, the mosque will be not only a place of worship, but also a major cultural center where meetings will take place and a library and Arab language courses will operate.

AN OVERVIEW

In the years of *perestroika,* the number of active mosques in the Soviet Union has increased sixfold. On 1 January 1985 their number was 395, while in 1991 the figure stood at 2,300.

In 1917, in the Tatar Republic alone there were 2,223 active mosques with 3,683 imams working in them. On the eve of World War II, the number of mosques dwindled to a handful, while thousands of imams were severely repressed. The Muslim community experienced a partial revival during the war, when the Soviet regime tried to consolidate society and reversed its policies on religion. Religious boards were set up in regions where Islam had been traditionally practiced. Some time later, Mir-Arab *madrasah* opened in Bukhara, in the Uzbek Republic, and later still the Imam al-Bukhari Islamic Institute in Tashkent. A new attack on Islam was mounted in the 1960s, when a few hundred mosques were closed down.

The current Muslim revival is accompanied not only by the construction of new mosques and the restoration of old ones, but also by more mullahs studying at religious schools. Schools have opened in Baku, in Azerbaijan, and Kazan, in the Tatar Republic. More young people are also going to study in Arab countries. The authorities have stopped creating obstacles for people who want to go on the traditional *hajj* to visit the holy places in Saudi Arabia, even though the number of pilgrims is still small because of the shortage of hard currency and the trip is difficult because of the absence of diplomatic relations between the Soviet Union and Saudi Arabia.

MUSLIM INTERNATIONAL RESPONSE

Despite its inconsistency and slow pace, *perestroika* has had a great impact on the life of Muslims, which has been noted by influential Islamic leaders.

After his visit to the Soviet Union, Dr. Inamulla Khan, secretary-general of the World Islamic Congress, stated, "We are happy that in a new age, the age of *perestroika*, the Muslims in the Soviet Union enjoy greater freedom of conscience. We support Gorbachev's call for new thinking in the society in the future. Participation in the festivities has brought us even closer to the Soviet Muslims. I hope that we have fulfilled Allah's commandment, 'Help each other in good and piety.' This, in turn, will promote mutual understanding, which we all need so much to secure lasting peace and preserve our civilization."

The dean of a faculty of the Al-Azkhar University in Cairo, Mokhammed Ibragim al-Diyushi, said, "While here, we felt that major changes are under way in your country. After seventy years of persecution and trials, believers now enjoy greater freedom of conscience and more rights. We support this process and would like to hope that changes will come in an abundant rain.

"Our university, which is a well-known center of Islamic scholarship, is prepared to provide the necessary number of grants for Muslim students from Bashkiria, the Tatar Republic, and other Soviet republics.

"We follow very closely the ongoing changes in the Soviet Union and hope that *glasnost* and *perestroika* will continue and gain momentum.

"We Muslims know well cities like Bukhara, Termez, Samarkand, which were renowned centers of the Islamic culture in their time. We hope that they will regain their former glory, and that new at-Termezi and new al-Bukhari will emerge here.

"The openness that we saw in the Soviet society will promote our relations with the Soviet Muslims and advance universal human principles and values."

The secretary-general of the World Islamic League, Dr. Abdulla Omar Nasyf, who took part in the festivities on the Volga, echoes these sentiments. "The impressions are symbolic; they show that people in the Soviet Union are very happy to have back their religious freedom and to be able to practice their faith, their Islamic culture, in a very democratic way. You can feel the happiness in their faces and their talks. It is a new era in the Soviet Union when people are given the constitution of rights in a proper way.

"It is very important that religion is given the ability to contribute toward changing the society, toward overcoming difficulties, problems, crimes, AIDS, drugs, and so on. We should not be enemies; we should live without any difficulties in spite of differences in religion and nationality. Religion is after all for the benefit of mankind, and it can improve the society of today, which is facing great difficulties."

He went on to make a profound statement that merits careful consideration: "The Muslims around the world are also facing their own difficulties, and unless they see cooperation and coordination and also help from certain directions, they can do nothing. They have lived with other religions for centuries; they have coexisted with all kind of religions and cooperated with them. But nowadays they are subjected to . . . attack from the West especially, so they are very much frustrated.

. . . We have to understand that we need each other; we cannot live in this world separately. We are human beings, and unless we coexist and cooperate these difficulties and problems will continue."

He suggested that the Soviet Union set the example for other countries by acknowledging the contributions of Muslims and giving them the status they deserve.

Islam and Other Religions

*Sheik-ul-Islam Allahshukur Pashazade
Chairman of the Muslim Religious Board
for Transcaucasia*

After the bloody clashes between people of different nationalities and denominations in 1989, as a Muslim theologian, I felt compelled to express my firm conviction that true Islam does not tolerate violence and preaches a respectful attitude to other religions. We, clergymen, are called upon to do all we can to bridle passions and quench the fire of ethnic conflicts, and make people understand the truth about Islam and the will of Allah.

According to the Islamic philosophy, the diversity of being in all its countless manifestations represents part of the divine essence and its expression. It is destined to be used for various aims in both nature and society, and it is known to only Allah's providence:

"And of His signs is the creation of the heavens and the earth, and the difference of your languages and colors. Lo! herein indeed are portents for men of knowledge" (Ar-Rum 22).[1]

This diversity is neither a sign of superiority nor a symbol of inferiority; it does not offer any advantages, but it does not constitute a flaw, either.

Looked at from this philosophical perspective, it is only logical that the diversity of the human intellect represents part of the above-mentioned diversity of being. This in its turn explains the pluralistic diversity of convictions and beliefs, which, however, does not represent an inevitable source of conflicts.

ISLAM REJECTS COERCION
IN MATTERS OF FAITH

It is clear that the truth always has only one face, while misconception has many faces. However, in such crucial matters as faith coercion is inadmissible. Man's consciousness is free by its nature, and it is part of the dignity and greatness, which the Creator granted to him. A man can be forced or persuaded to accept a doctrine, even publicly. But it is totally impossible to force him to *believe* it, because faith and beliefs are categories of consciousness, which cannot be coerced. This is explicitly stated in the Koran:

"There is no compulsion in religion. The right direction is henceforth distinct from error" (Al-Baqarah 256).

Therefore, the Koran leaves the fundamental question of human life—the question of faith—to man's conscience:

"Say: (It is) the truth is from the Lord of you (all). Then whosoever will, let him believe, and whosoever will, let him disbelieve" (Al-Kahf 30).

It is clear that he, who rejects the truth and the true word and turns his back on them, robs himself of something very precious without any hope of ever getting it back. But he does so voluntarily. Depriving himself of the only correct choice, he loses the possibility of a beneficent gain and becomes vulnerable to harm. But to coerce him in his choice would be wrong anyway. This is the first and most important freedom—to choose without restriction one's own symbol of faith, philosophical creed, and, in the final analysis, one's own destiny in life. In formulating its attitude to this freedom, the Koran goes even further and states that even God—He who has the power to do so—will not coerce anyone in the question of the freedom of conscience. No matter what a person does in this respect, he does it of his own free will:

"And if the Lord willed, all who are in the Earth would have believed. Wouldst thou (Muhammad) compel men until they are believers?" (Jonah 100).

On the other hand, it is man's responsibility to try and share with his brothers what he understands to be the truth, the more so since it is the truth that brings the greatest beneficence, and true fraternity demands that any beneficence be shared with your neighbor. However, even this noble desire should be fulfilled without violating the right to freedom, something that we mentioned above:

"Call unto the way of the Lord with wisdom and fair exhortation . . ." (An-Nahl 125).

"Revile not those unto whom they pray beside Allah lest they wrongfully revile Allah through ignorance. Thus unto every nation have we made our deed fair. Then unto their Lord is their return, and He will tell them what they used to do" (Al-An'am 109).

Therefore, the teaching of Islam categorically rejects ruthless and violent actions as a means of putting a person on the road of the truth. This conclusion is supported by concrete historical facts. All peace treaties concluded by Islamic warriors with the Transcaucasian tribes of Shirvana, Mugani, and so forth, contain special clauses that guarantee not only the preservation of their life and property, but also the *freedom of belief* and the inviolability of the right to perform their religious rites and ceremonies in their temples and houses of prayer. On the other hand, authentic *hadiths* of the Prophet—prayer and blessing for him!—and the reports about the acts and statements of early Islamic leaders (*al-amr al-avval*) testify that warfare itself was strictly regulated by humanitarian considerations. The Messenger—let Allah bless Him and greet Him!—told emirs and military leaders that it was inadmissible to commit crimes, kill children, women, the disabled, and old people, plunder fields and fruit gardens, and attack charitable and religious places. The following words belong to Abu Bakr as-Siddik: "Do not fight a wounded man, because he no longer has honor." He also told Islamic warriors, "Do not disfigure your enemies, do not kill either a small child or a man who reached old age, or women; do not destroy palm trees and do not burn them; do not cut fruit trees and do not kill either sheep, or cows, or camels for other purpose than food. You will leave in peace those people who devote themselves to piety in their cells: pass them by and do not bother them in the occupation they devoted themselves to."[2]

Allah reminded all those who have embarked on the road of *da'va* that they should be humane:

"For that cause We demand for the Children of Israel that whosoever killeth a human being for other than manslaughter or corruption in the earth, it shall be as if he had killed all mankind" (Al-Ma'idah 32).

It is true that we cannot ignore individual cases of repression and sad events entailing the loss of innocent lives. Such regrettable incidents have also been reported in reliable sources. Alas, war will always be war, and it is because of this that Allah's religion denounces its atrocities. However, we are trying to establish general regularities in history and not something that is fortuitous or atypical.

ISLAM AND OTHER FAITHS

It is from this angle that we should look at another important question that is relevant to our subject: What were the relations between Islam as a "religion of conquerors," if indeed it ever was such a religion, and other religious beliefs of Transcaucasian peoples, who became "oppressed," if indeed they became oppressed after Islamic warriors invaded their lands?

And again, we would do best by studying concrete facts, which are numerous and easily accessible. One of the most obvious facts is that the Christian religion and the churches in Georgia and Armenia have been preserved intact. This is something all can see with their own eyes. In Azerbaijan the Christian Albanian Church existed until the middle of the nineteenth century, when it was dissolved by the czarist government. A lot of other convincing facts could be cited, but we are running the risk of getting drowned in the sea of particulars without establishing generalities. A general principle is not constituted by accidental events even though they are numerous. A general principle, rather, reflects their inner logic. In our case it is the general attitude of Islam to other beliefs and their followers.

Islam has always treated other religions with profound respect because it is based on the truth, and it guarantees divine guidance as man's right for all times. It follows that all great religions are divine and should be treated with respect and deference. Islam stands for mutual understanding between all confessional communities on the basis of the recognition of the divine origin of all religions and reaffirmation of the belief in prophets and the founders of other religious teachings and Holy Scriptures. The Koran says, "We did reveal the Torah, wherein is the guidance and a light, by which the Prophets who surrendered (unto Allah) judged the Jews" (Al-Ma'idah 44).

"And We caused Jesus, son of Mary, to follow in their footsteps, confirming that which was (revealed) before him, and We bestowed on him the Gospel wherein is guidance and a light, confirming that which was (revealed) before it in the Torah— a guidance and an admonition unto those who ward off (evil)" (Al-Ma'idah 46).

"Say (O Muhammad): We believe in Allah and that which is revealed unto us and that which was revealed unto Abraham and Ishmael and Isaac and Jacob and the tribes, and that which was vouchsafed unto Moses and Jesus and the Prophets from their Lord. We make no distinction between any of them, and unto Him we have surrendered" (Ali-'Imran 84).

"Oh ye who believe! Believe in Allah and His messenger and the Scripture which He hath revealed unto His messenger, and the Scripture which He revealed afore time. Whoso disbelieveth in Allah and His angels and His scriptures and His messengers and the Last Day, he verily hath wandered far astray" (An-Nisa 136).

"And (We sent) messengers We have mentioned unto thee before and messengers We have not mentioned unto thee" (An-Nisa 164).

"And verily We have raised in every nation a messenger (proclaiming): Serve Allah and shun false gods" (An-Nahl 36).

"There is not a nation but a warner hath passed among them" (Al-Mala'ikah 24).

Thus, recognizing a divine origin of all religions and upholding the belief in all prophets and Holy Scriptures without distinction, Islam paves the way for good and peaceful relations among different groups of people that make up the human community. If other regions steered their followers to embrace the same principles, there would be no place for strife and wars on religious grounds. In this respect Islam is unique, because it recognizes an equal "right to vote," for all:

"Let not a folk deride a folk who may be better than they (are)" (Al-Hujurat 11).

Not only the word of our Lord, but historical precedents, which can be traced back to the Prophet Himself—let Allah bless Him and greet Him!—form the basis for Muslims' attitude to these matters. If it were right to assert that Islam considers it admissible to kill pagans and atheists simply because they are pagans and atheists, then the Prophet—let Allah bless Him and greet Him!—would have exterminated the pagans of Mecca after He had conquered it, and the pagans of the Havazin tribe after the battle in the Hunain Valley. However, the Prophet—prayer to Him and greeting!—formed a union with the Haza'a tribe, which was also pagan.

"Allah confirmeth those who believe by a firm saying in the life of the world and in the Hereafter, and Allah sendeth wrongdoers astray. And Allah doeth what He will" (Ibrahim 27).

Since time immemorial, this idea has been preached by all prophets of God, putting people on the road of the truth for which they sought. But again and again man has strayed from it. He has totally forgotten or perverted the code of conduct bequeathed by the Prophet. New prophets have been sent in order to restore the original idea and put man back on the road of the truth from which he wandered. The last of those messengers was Muhammad ibn 'Abdallah—let Him rest in peace!—who presented the teaching in its original and final form for all times and generations. It is this teaching that is known as Islam.

NOTES

1. Koran citations are from Mohammad Marmaduke Pickthall, *The Meaning of the Glorious Koran: An Explanatory Translation* (New York: Mentor Books, 1960), 464.

2. Ibn Al-Asir. Al-Kamil Fi-t-Tarih. II. Cairo, 1303, p. 310.

Buddhists at the Ivolginsky Datsan.

Buddhism

Statistics: There are about 300,000 people of Buddhist faith, 432 Buddhist communities, and 16 datsans (monasteries) with 70 lamas in Soviet republics. Most Buddhists are located in the Huryat, Kalmyk, and Tuva republics, in the Chita Region of the Russian Federation, and in Leningrad and other cities.

Organization: The highest authority for Soviet Buddhists is the Central Buddhist Board based in the Ivolginski Datsan in the Buryat Republic. (A permanent office in Moscow is concerned with external relations.) The congress of clergy and laity convenes once in four years and elects the members of the Board. Head of the Central Buddhist Board is Bandido Khambo-Lama Munko Tsybikov, 82.

Brief History: Mongolian and Tibetan lamas first appeared on the eastern shores of Lake Baikal in the middle of the 17th century and quickly spread Buddhism in the area. Later in that century Buddhism emerged as the dominant religion in Tuva. The Kalmyks who migrated from China to the lower reaches of the Volga in the later half of the 17th century also professed Buddhism.

Tzarist authorities were fairly tolerant with respect to Buddhists. In the 1930s the Buddhists suffered more than any other religious community in the Soviet Union. Prosperous monasteries and churches, many of which were architectural masterpieces, were closed. All Buddhist religious buildings in the Kalmyk Republics and Tuva were razed as were most Buddhist monasteries in the Buryat Republic. Not a single functioning temple and not a single lama remained. After the Second World War, two temples with a limited number of monks were built. Religious life was under rigid official control. The late 1980s saw a renaissance of Buddhism; monasteries were opened and the publication of spiritual literature and periodicals resumed. In early 1991 a Buddhist school opened at the Ivolginski Datsan.

Current Situation and Problems: There is a dire shortage of lamas, even though training is provided in Mongolia and Nepal. Contrary to the traditional view of their way of life, many of them are married and have children. Their families live in datsans. One new development is the nontraditional involvement of people in the west-European Soviet areas in Buddhist activities.

Rebirth of Buddhism

As the day of 15 January 1989 dawned, the people of the Kalmyk Republic capital, Elista, for the first time in fifty years heard the divine sound of a conch proclaiming the rebirth of a Buddhist community. People sitting in a praying posture expressed joy and had tears in their eyes when lamas who had arrived from the Ivolginsk *datsan*—a Buddhist monastery in Siberia—began the ritual of opening a Kalmyk holiday, the *khural*.

In 1991 the first Buddhist religious school opened in Buryatiya (Siberia) with sixty pupils not only from Buryatiya but also from the Kalmyk and Tuva republics.

The Kalmyk Autonomous Republic on the Caspian steppes of the lower Volga, the republics of Buryat and Tuva, and the Chita and Irkutsk regions in Siberia are the traditional areas of Buddhism in the Soviet Union. However, in the 1930s, at the height of Stalin's dictatorship, all Buddhist temples in the country were closed down, and thousands of lamas were persecuted. Buddhist monasteries were blown up, their priceless treasures thrown into the fire if attempts to hide them failed.

Only after World War II, when government policies toward religion softened somewhat, the Aginski *datsan* (monastery) in the Chita region reopened and the Ivolginsk *datsan* in the Buryat Republic was rebuilt. However, Buddhism remained a banned religion in the Kalmyk and Tuva republics.

The years of *perestroika* and *glasnost* have made it possible to correct this glaring injustice. A revival of Buddhism has begun both in Siberia and in the European Soviet republics. New temples are opening and the number of lamas is increasing. A Buddhist community is being established in Tuva, in south central Siberia.

SOVIET BUDDHIST HISTORY

Mongolian and Tibetan lamas first came to the area east of Lake Baikal, regions close to the Mongolian border, in the first half of the seventeenth century. Later, religious centers—Buddhist monasteries, or *datsans*—appeared in other areas of Buryatiya, too. Within a short time most of the Buryats living east of Lake Baikal were converted to Buddhism. In 1764, Damba Dorzhi Zayayev, the high priest of the Tsongolski *datsan*—the oldest in the Baikal region—became head of the entire Buddhist clergy with the title Bandido Hambo Lama.

In late sixteenth century the Kalmyks were converted to Buddhism by Mongolian lamas in Dzungaria (China). In the seventeenth century, they moved to the lower reaches of the Volga River, retaining their religion. At that time the Kalmyks gained access to the first works of Buddhist literature translated from the Tibetan language.

In Tuva Buddhism firmly established itself toward the end of the seventeenth century, having ousted shamanism, the traditional folk beliefs.

BUDDHISM IN THE USSR TODAY

Soviet Buddhism is representative of the Gelugpa school ("the School of Virtue"), which is a branch of Tibetan Buddhism in the Mahayana tradition, that is, "the broad path" of salvation from endless rebirth in the world of suffering.

Soviet Buddhism has a number of specific ritual peculiarities that have taken shape over the course of history.

Historically it is has been marked by the prevalence of rural lamas living outside *datsans* because of the nomadic way of life. To some extent, this tradition has survived to this day.

In keeping with tradition, six major holidays, *khurals,* are celebrated annually and are attended by a large number of people who bring various gifts to *datsans* as well as money and food for lamas.

Tsagaalgan is a holiday celebrated on the eve of the lunar new year, which usually falls in February. This *khural* is devoted to the twelve miracles of Buddha during his dispute with six preachers of heresy. Services and a series of religious rites are conducted to mark the occasion. Buddhists, dressed in their best clothes, come to pray together for well-being and more happiness. On the eve of the new year, a solemn evening ritual is performed during which food is served to the *doksheets,* the protectors of the faith. This involves the ritual burning of *Dugzhub,* a magic pyramid of paper and wood; according to a Buddhist belief, a ritual fire consumes all evil thoughts.

A long note from a big white conch proclaims the first day of the lunar new year. A traditional service is held to celebrate the Sagaan Sar ("white month") holiday.

In the main temple lamas, replacing one another, pray for fifteen days for peace and goodness.

The *khural* Duyn-khor, a second major holiday, lasts three days in April. It is dedicated to the preaching of the sacred teaching of Kalachakra.

The third major holiday is Gandan-Shunserme, devoted to the birth and enlightenment of Buddha and his attainment of nirvana. It is celebrated in early summer.

The fourth holiday Maidari is dedicated to Maidari, the Buddha of the future. It is always celebrated for two days in midsummer. People spend the first day in many hours of devout prayer. On the second day the gilded statue of Maidari is solemnly carried out of the temple and placed on a chariot twined with silk ribbons. It is surrounded by lamas in ceremonial dress. A green horse of plaster is harnessed to the chariot, and the procession sets off around the *datsan*. This ceremony symbolizes Maidari's tour of the universe and the spread of his grace throughout it. Several thousand people gather in the *datsan* for the procession. A kharang, a big copper shield, is struck with a mallet, and its sounds can be heard far away. There is a fanfare, the drums roll, and conchs are blown. The procession stops at every turn of the monastery walls for a reading of sacred Scriptures. Many Buddhists attending the procession try to approach the chariot, to hold onto its beam and harness, and to throw money at the feet of the statue of Maidari.

The last two *khurals* are celebrated with less splendor, but they also attract large crowds of believers. Lkhabab Duysen, marked in autumn, is devoted to the Buddha's return from the thirty-third heaven. The holiday Zula is dedicated to the passing away of the father of lamaism, Bogdo Tsongkhapa. A thousand candles are lit during the service.

During the *khurals* prayers are said in honor of the protectors of the faith and for well-being and peace on earth.

Lamas who live in monasteries observe the Dulva, a traditional moral and ethical code. Depending on the level of ordination, they participate in services and philosophical discussions and perform special religious rites at the people's request.

Recently, in addition to Buryats, Kalmyks, and Tuvinians, more and more Russians, Ukrainians, and people from the Baltic republics have been attending Buddhist services. Previously, they all went to pray at the Ivolginsk *datsan*, but today, with the 1991 reopening of the temple in Leningrad, followers of Buddhism from the European part of the country will travel there, too.

That temple was initially built from 1909–1915, but the social changes in Russia after 1917 forced its closure. In the first years of the Soviet regime, a military unit was stationed in the grounds of the Buddhist temple. The interior of the temple was seriously damaged, statues and manuscripts were destroyed, and soldiers used paper with ancient Tibetan texts to roll their cigarettes. Only after the famous Tibetan doctor Agvan Dordzhiev lodged a vigorous protest was the temple returned to the Buddhist community. In 1923 and 1924 the interior of the temple was partially restored. A 4.5 meter statue of the Buddha with colored porcelain eyes was brought in from Poland.

In 1938 the Buddhist temple was turned into a sports center, and during World War II grenades were manufactured in the building's basement. After the war, a radio station was located here, and in early 1960s the USSR Academy of Sciences took charge of the building and set up a zoological laboratory there. The building's outward appearance changed; certain parts disappeared. For example, copper hand-chased round cover plates that decorated three pairs of doors were scrapped, and their handles were substituted with iron handles typical of the period.

These days Buryat lamas are frequent visitors in Leningrad, just as in the Kalmyk Republic, where they are helping to revive spiritual life. Many of them have abandoned the traditional celibacy and now have families.

Hundreds of Muscovites also have applied for registration and permission to open a house of prayer.

SOVIET BUDDHIST SCHOLARSHIP

There is a growing interest in Buddhism among Russian scholars. The Russian buddhological school had won an international reputation already in the nineteenth century. Many books treating various Buddhist subjects were published in the Russian language during that time. For instance, the great Russian writer, Leo Tolstoy, outlined the biography of Buddha in a brochure issued by the Posrednik (Mediator) publishing house. He also used ideas borrowed from the Dhammapada, a code of Buddhist ethics, as a source for his moralizing works.

At present Buddhism is studied in research centers in Moscow, Leningrad, and Tartu, as well as in Central Asia, Ulan-Ude, Elista, and Kyzil. Together, scholars examine the Buddhist religious system, the social functions of Buddhism, and its influence on the culture and traditions of Oriental people.

The Moscow buddhologists concentrate on the role of Buddhist rituals as well as the place and role of Buddhism in the social and political structures of Asian countries. In Leningrad, scholars are engaged in deciphering ancient Indian inscriptions, textological research in the field of Buddhist terminology, the study of different aspects of Buddhist art, and old Uighur, Mongolian, Tibetan, and Chinese texts.

Buryat researchers focus on a broad range of social, ideological, and cultural phenomena linked with Buddhism. They analyze canonical literature, translate texts on Indo-Tibetan medicine, and carry out sociological research into the place of present-day Buddhism. The research covers all 108 volumes of the Kanjur, a collection of the most authoritative texts and sayings of Buddha Sakyamuni, that have canonical validity. The Kanjur of the Ivolginsk *datsan* library is one of the rarest. All of its volumes are handwritten in a highly artistic style using ink solutions of nine precious stones and metals.

The library also boasts a complete Tanjur ("collection of commentaries") in 225 volumes. It contains treatises on theology, philosophy, logic, medicine, philology, art, rituals, and architecture. The Tanjur includes all twenty-four existing Tantric systems, united into the four sections of the Tantra, and the most important writings of the "six decorations of India"—the teachers Nagarjuna, Aryadeva, Asanga, Vasubandhu, Dignaga, and Dharmakirti.

Among the library's other treasures are invaluable manuscripts in the Tibetan, Mongolian, Sanskrit, Buryat, and other languages. Alongside works devoted to the Buddhist history, mathematics, and folk medicine, the collection also includes *namtars,* the biographies of prominent Buddhist leaders and well-known lamas.

A group of scholars has prepared for publication a unique volume—a complete atlas of Tibetan medicine which has been used to teach many generations of Tibetan doctors. This unique book has been preserved in the Buryat Republic and will, of course, prove a priceless manual for modern physicians, too.

Buryat scholars believe that forgotten remedies of natural origin may be very effective in supplementing modern drugs, especially in treating diseases of the digestive organs. Buryat scientists have developed preparations that restore the functions of the liver in cases of hepatitis and are also effective in the treatment of chronic gastritis, ulcers, and enteritis. They also study many other ancient methods of Buddhist traditional medicine, such as massage, acupuncture, cauterization, phlebotomy or blood-letting, and hydrotherapy.

The chronopharmacological trend in Buryat medicine is also of considerable interest. What it entails is determining the best possible time for the action of drugs and medicines during the day, month, or year. This is to a great extent in line with the present-day concept of biorhythms.

A major research effort is the study of oncological diseases. Tibetan medicine has been accumulating clinical knowledge in this area. The Buddhists also have interesting methods of mental training, which can be extremely useful in conditions of stress.

Tuvinian lamas know a number of methods for brewing herbal teas or herbal lamb broth, which is herbs boiled with a shoulder of lamb. For some diseases lamas recommend eating half-raw meat, explaining that this meat preserves its healing properties better. Lamas treat measles with blood taken from a live female goat, wounds with the fat of a ram, and bear gall applied topically for fever, swellings, or contusions.

Only recently Buddhist physicians could not practice their art, because this was strictly prohibited. However, *perestroika* has made it possible for them to treat patients freely and to participate in scientific research.

Jews inside the Moscow Choral Synagogue.

The Jewish Community

Statistics: The Soviet republics have about 350,000 Jewish believers, 114 Jewish religious communities, 70 functioning synagogues, and 30 active rabbis.

Organization: Each Jewish religious community is autonomous. About half of them are to be part of the All-Union Jewish Religious Community. This organization has no administrative functions and its resolutions are not binding in the spiritual sphere.

Brief History: The first Jewish religious communities emerged on the northern coast of the Black Sea in the first century A.D. In the 8th century Judaism became the official religion of the Khazan tribe in the lower reaches of the Volga and Don rivers. Synagogues were built in a number of Russian cities, including Kiev.

In the late 14th and the early 15th century hundreds of thousands of Jews came from Germany. In the early half of the 18th century an influential Judaic reformist movement called hasidism (piety) developed in the Western Ukraine.

The 1917 revolution did not affect Judaism immediately. Even in 1924 about 2,000 synagogues were functioning. However, by the 1930s there remained only a few. Some synagogues reopened during the Second World War, but the 1960s saw a new spate of persecution. Under *perestroika*, synagogues now can be opened without restrictions, religious literature can be published, and children can be taught Yiddish and receive religious upbringing.

Current Situation and Problems: People of orthodox and Hasidic faith are increasingly in contact with each other, often saying prayers in the same synagogues. A great deal of religious literature comes from Israel, the United States, and Canada. Virtually every synagogue runs schools for small children and teenagers. Growth of Jewish communities is difficult because of the current Jewish exodus from Soviet republics. Other problems include a shortage of rabbis, the absence of one religious center, and rivalry between different Jewish groups.

Judaic Religious Life

The Stalin dictatorship carried out a hard-line policy of assimilating the Jewish population. Jewish schools, other educational establishments, and restaurants were closed down, publication of books and periodicals in Modern Hebrew and Hebrew were stopped, Jewish theater companies, cultural and sports societies were disbanded, and Jewish activists were harassed. Though a few score synagogues did exist, they suffered from a dire shortage of rabbis, cantors, reciters of the Torah, *soifers*, *shochetim*, and other clergy. The number of worshipers diminished all the time and some communities broke up. It was impossible to obtain kosher food and matzo. Few Jewish people observed the Sabbath or circumcised their sons and grandsons. Their dead were buried, and are still buried, in coffins.

The changes taking place in Soviet society under *perestroika* naturally brought about a Jewish revival and the restoration of Jewish religious life. New synagogues have opened and Jewish schools, clubs, newspapers, and magazines are now common in all Soviet republics. However, the process is proceeding with great difficulty. Russification has taken such firm root that even today Russian is spoken by most of the worshipers at the Moscow Choral Synagogue.

At present we are witnessing a mass emigration of Jews out of the Soviet Union due largely to increasing economic difficulties. No longer is there difficulty in getting permission to leave the USSR. More than half a million people have emigrated. As a result, the students of the newly opened religious schools prefer to leave the country at the first opportunity and go to Israel, the United States, or Canada.

Vladimir Fedorovsky, the present chairman of the community at the Moscow Choral Synagogue, gives a very good idea of the situation facing the Jewish religious communities in the USSR today. Before he was elected to the post, Fedorovsky worked at a research institute where he was engaged in applying mathematical methods to the economy. For many years he had considered himself a nonbeliever.

"I have a great deal of kindly feeling for those kinds of Jews," he said. "I understand their aspirations, I have gone through all that myself, and I do not think that people are frightened at the thought of communicating with the Almighty. I don't think it can frighten people. A person who has never had anything to do with the synagogue is shy of the ritual, strictness, and the need to give a considerable amount of attention to fulfilling his duty to God. If a person is not prepared to do so, he should not be forced into doing so. Coercion is intolerable under any circumstances, even in the name of a sacred goal. A person should be prepared for it so that the need to turn to God should be born in him, if the man has a need for it.

"I come from the great number of assimilated Jews who know neither their language nor their religion, who grew up in Russian-speaking families and were brought up on Russian culture. That is why my attitude toward religion is far from simple.

"I believe in a higher reason, as many people do who have lived sufficiently long. I believe in the higher predestination and try to live in accordance with the unchanging truths, and moral and ethical values," says Vladimir Fedorovsky.

"Any human community is viable only when it reproduces itself. Sad to say, human beings are not immortal; the old folk pass away, and if the younger generation does not come to replace them, the community dies away. Regrettably, little has been done over the years to inject young blood into the community. Today, we are trying to introduce among the assimilated Jews the knowledge that has been accumulated in the course of many centuries of Judaic religion, its moral and ethical values. We are trying to arouse a feeling of national awareness among the young," continues Vladimir Fedorovsky.

RELIGIOUS IDENTITY
AMONG JEWISH GROUPS

A sociological survey conducted back in the seventies by the Soviet Academy of Sciences showed that the level of religious consciousness among the Jewish population, which amounts to about 1.8 million, was lower than among other ethnic groups.

The survey in the Belorussian town of Bobruisk demonstrated that only 2 percent of the Jews there considered themselves religious. That figure, no matter how small it may seem, coincides rather accurately with attendance in the synagogue on the biggest Judaic feastdays such as New Year, Judgment Day, and Passover.

In Novosibirsk, where there are 11,000 Jews, some 100 to 200 persons (that is, 1 to 2 percent) attended feastday celebrations at the synagogue in the past several years; in Kuibyshev, where there are 16,000 Jews, synagogue attendance is from 150 to 450 persons (that is, 1 to 3 percent); in Leningrad, where the Jewish population amounts to 160,000 according to the 1970 census, attendance is at most from 2,000 to 2,500 persons (or about 1.5 percent).

Certainly, not all religious Jews go to the synagogue, but, on the other hand, not all the Jews who come to the synagogue are religious. Many of the latter do not even know how to turn the pages of the prayer book, and they come to the synagogue (as they themselves admit quite frankly) in remembrance of their deceased parents or to meet friends.

The sociological survey has shown that in the Soviet Union the level of religiousness among Jews is different depending on the ethnic group to which they belong. Religious feeling is stronger among Georgian, Bukharan (Central Asian), and mountaineer Jews.

Believers belonging to these ethnic groups, unlike other Jews, have a far greater devotion to traditional customs and ritual. There are from eight to ten times more worshipers in the Tbilisi, Georgia, synagogue on feastdays than in Samara on the Volga River,[1] where the size of the Jewish population is the same.

At present, synagogues have become centers of spiritual revival of the Jews. Religious schools, Hebrew language study groups, and libraries are being opened on their premises. Publication of religious literature has been renewed. *Menora*, a periodical issued by the Moscow Jewish religious community, is now available in newspaper kiosks. Jewish papers and magazines have started to come out in a number of cities, above all in the Ukraine and the Baltic republics. Numerous cultural and educational societies of a religious nature but with different orientation are being established in close contact with the synagogues.

The most active of these societies are the Hasidim of Lyubavichi (the Ukraine), the followers of Rabbi Menahem Mendl Schneyerson of New York. The movement is called HABAD, an acronym from *hahma* (wisdom), *bina* (perception), and *daat* (knowledge), which are the highest spiritual standards in Jewish mysticism. The Hasidim have had spiritual centers in Moscow, Leningrad, and other cities since the late seventies. In 1989 they opened a most prestigious yeshiva in Kuntsevo, one of the best districts in Moscow. Until recently the mansion in which it is housed was the official residence of the Moscow city council, where VIP's were received. Instruction is conducted in Hebrew and English by professors from the United States and Israel.

Also influential are groups that refer to the orthodox movement of Agudath Israel and are connected with the traditional Lithuanian yeshivas in Israel, the United States, and other countries. They are based on deep historical roots and a wealth of spiritual experience accumulated through many centuries by Lithuanian and Polish Jewry. Unfortunately, these rich seats of culture were completely destroyed by the Nazis during World War II when millions of Jews perished in ghettoes and concentration camps. Subsequent attempts to revive them under Soviet power were suppressed by the KGB and authorities.

A third group was born within the religious Jewry in the early eighties, called Mahanaim (two camps), meaning Moscow and Jerusalem. This group is under the strong influence of Rabbi Josef Dov Halevi Soloveitchik, and its supporters regard the state of Israel not only as a political but also a religious entity. They attach great significance to the harmonious combination of the Torah and modern science and regard the rights and dignity of the individual as the most important element of religious consciousness.

COOPERATION AMONG JEWISH GROUPS

These groups and trends, just like the synagogues that support them, try to cooperate with each other, but they do not always succeed. Different philosophical approaches to problems or traditions as well as strictly time-serving considerations contribute to isolating the various groups. Jewish religious communities are showing a distinct tendency toward uniting into a single organization, arranging reciprocal assistance in publishing, training of personnel, and acquiring articles of worship and international contacts. With that aim in view an All-Union Council of Jewish Religious Communities (ACJRC) was founded in January 1990 on the initiative of the rabbi of Moscow and Vladimir Fedorovsky, the chairman of the Moscow community.

This is what Vladimir Fedorovsky has to say about the new organization:

"You wish to know what our goal is? The Jews were never united either in pre-Revolution Russia or in Soviet times. We have more than a hundred communities, big and small. Many of them are declining, the prayer houses are falling into decay, and the ranks of worshipers are diminishing. There is a dire shortage of clergy. Can the thriving Moscow community watch the situation unmoved? Certainly not. Only reasonable centralization can help. The organization of the All-Union Council is the road to the restoration of our lives. We shall not interfere in the affairs of one or the other community; each will be guided by its own collective body, its own spiritual leader. But there are certain common issues like training personnel, supplying the communities with articles of worship and other things, that will become the concern of the ACJRC. The aid coming from abroad will be used more rationally. Very often today this aid is gauged not by the real need of the community but the energetic activity of some of its members."

However, at the initial stage of its activity the ACJRC has managed to unite no more than half of the synagogues. As a rule, it is the Hasidic communities that put up the greatest resistance against the new organization. The centrifugal tendencies now current in the USSR, which make the successful functioning of any organization acting on the all-union level difficult, also affect the situation. In this respect Vladimir Fedorovsky takes an integrative stand, which is often criticized by the religious communities connected with one or another separatist movement. He says, "Nowadays some people try to overhaul the notion of 'Soviet people.' Some feel it is an absolutely artificial category. Personally, I have respect for that notion. The Soviet people is a reality that has taken shape in our country, and it has to be reckoned with. Primarily, we all have to be decent and upright, and only after that can we be the supporters of one or another political or religious movement. That is the spirit of peace in which we try to educate our worshipers."

COOPERATION WITH JEWS IN
OTHER COUNTRIES

The most characteristic feature of the current religious life of the Jewish communities, which unites them far better than all their activities directed at creating their own organizations, is their growing cooperation with coreligionists in Israel, the United States, Canada, and the European countries. It takes various shapes: the Moscow synagogue, the Child Foundation, and the Foundation for the Promotion of the Cantorial Art of Gila and Chaim Vinner organized a festival in seven cities of the Soviet Union. Its participants were famous cantors from the United States, Canada, and Israel. Recently Shamir, the Israeli publishers, issued a Torah with commentaries in Russian, a dictionary of Modern Hebrew and Russian, an illustrated dictionary for children, a book of Jewish legends and tales, and other Jewish books. One can read these books in the special hall of the Library of Foreign Literature in Moscow. The Moscow magazine *Menora* is being published with the participation of Joint in Israel. Matzo and kosher food is being sent to the Soviet Union thanks to the activities of various Jewish organizations. Work has got under way to prepare this special food in the Soviet Union and to sell it not only in the synagogues, but also in kosher restaurants and canteens for the sick and aged.

As in previous years, large groups of rabbis and cantors arrived in scores of Soviet cities from the United States and Israel for the 1991 Passover celebrations and other feastdays. That is very important not only because of the shortage of clergy in this country (while Soviet youths are studying abroad to become rabbis and cantors), but also because it breathes life into religious communities and makes the people feel they are members of a large global family.

Is there any anti-Semitism in the Soviet Union today? In the context of other current interethnic conflicts, this subject has receded into the background. No serious manifestations of anti-Semitism have been observed recently at state, local, or public levels. In the press or at their own meeting, members of a group called the Pamyat society sometimes take up the subject of the "Jewish-Freemason conspiracy" designed to destroy Russia. However, the actions of this group have no support among the population.

NOTES

1. Samara, formerly Kuibyshev, is the pre-revolutionary name of this city. After *perestroika*, old names of Russian cities have been reestablished.

Officially Sanctioned Yeshiva in Moscow

Rabbi Gedaliah A. Rabinowtz (USA)

After seventy years of disintegration and diminution, organized Soviet Jewish communal life is experiencing a renaissance. One of the first signs of this reawakening is the establishment of the first officially sanctioned yeshiva in the Soviet Union. The yeshiva, officially known as the Judaic Section of the Academy of World Civilization, is the result of an agreement among Rabbi Adin Steinzaltz, world-renowned Talmud commentator, academician Evegeny Velikhov, vice-chairman of the Soviet Academy of Sciences and member of the Supreme Soviet, and other internationally prominent personalities. As a novel institution with unique historical significance the yeshiva was established with the purpose of developing native leadership for these budding communities.

Jewish religion and culture has flourished for thousands of years in the areas now making up the Soviet Union. The many great religious and cultural contributions that have been made by Jews living in this part of the world have become an integral part of Jewish history. Prominent among these achievements in recent history are the founding of the Hasidic movement in the Ukraine about two hundred years ago by the Baal Shem Tov, one of the greatest mystics in world history, and the establishment of the great yeshivot (academies of higher Jewish learning) in Lithuania around the same time at the initiative of the Gaon of Vilnius, who was considered the greatest Jewish scholar of the last few centuries. These two movements continued to flourish in eastern Europe for over a century, and their influence left an indelible mark upon world Jewry in particular and Western religion and culture in general. With the general decline of religious life in the Soviet Union these two movements came to a virtual standstill in these areas. However, we presently are witnessing a reversal of this trend. There is a resurgence of growing interest and involvement in Judaism, which is coupled with the desire to reestablish Jewish community institutions. The newly established yeshiva is at the forefront of this movement. The philosophy of the yeshiva is based upon a creative blend of the teachings of the aformentioned great Jewish movements.

Since 1989 the yeshiva has made great strides in firmly establishing itself as a significant academy of higher Jewish learning and as a catalyst for the reawakening of Jewish religious and cultural life in the Soviet Union. In addition to offering a full course of studies in Bible, Talmud, Jewish history, and culture, the yeshiva also serves as a nerve center for Jewish cultural life throughout the Soviet Union. Faculty members of the yeshiva are called upon to visit various Jewish communities and deliver public lectures there, and requests have been received to establish branches of the yeshiva in Leningrad, Tbilisi, Dushanbe, and Vilnius. While being gratified by this success, the directorate of the yeshiva faces difficulties in trying to meet the growing demand for help in developing Jewish cultural activities in so many communities that thirst for spiritual succor.

Soviet authorities are contributing a great deal to make this project a success. A magnificent dacha has been chosen to serve as the campus of the yeshiva, and full-time students receive stipends to allow them to free themselves from financial concerns so that they may pursue their studies without interruption. These factors have allowed the directorate of the yeshiva to pursue its goals without undue obstacles.

As Jewish communal life continues to grow and flourish in the Soviet Union, so the need for the continual growth of this yeshiva and many others in the future will serve as a beacon for all those seeking spiritual replenishment and intellectual challenge.

Directory of Religious Organizations

RUSSIAN ORTHODOX CHURCH

Head of the Church

Patriarch Alexis II of Moscow and All Russia (Ridiger), 5 Chisty Pereulok, Moscow. Tel. 201–34–16.

Members of the Holy Synod

Metropolitan Filaret (Denisenko) of Kiev and All Ukraine, head of the Ukrainian Orthodox Church.

Metropolitan Ioann (Snychev) of Leningrad and Ladoga.

Metropolitan Juvenaly (Poyarkov) of Krutitsy and Kolomna.

Metropolitan Filaret (Vakhromeyev) of Minsk and Grodno, Patriarchal Exarch for All Belorussia.

Metropolitan Vladimir (Sabadan) of Rostov and Novocherkassk, Chancellor of the Moscow Patriarchate.

Metropolitan Kirill (Gundyayev), Chairman of the Department for Foreign Church Relations.

Chancellery and the Patriarch's Secretariat

Chairman: Metropolitan Vladimir of Rostov and Novocherkassk, 5 Chisty Pereulok, Moscow. Tel. 201–23–40.

Department for Foreign Church Relations

Chairman: Metropolitan Kirill of Smolensk and Kaliningrad, 22 Danilovsky Val, Moscow. Tel. 235–07–08, fax 230–26–19.
Vice-Chairmen

Bishop Kliment (Kapelin). Tel. 230–24–31.

Hegumen Ioann (Ekonomtsev). Tel. 230–21–09.

Archpresbyter Vitaly Borovoi. Tel. 230–26–71.

Leningrad branch: 17 Obvodny Kanal. Tel. 277–83–29.

Economic Department

Chairman: Bishop Victor of Podolsk, 5 Chisty Pereulok, Moscow.
Sofrino Industrial Art Association: Yevgeny Alexeyevich Parkhayev, Director, Poselok Sofrino, Pushkin District, Moscow Region. Tel. 184–96–67.

Publishing Department

Chairman: Metropolitan Pitirim (Nechayev) of Volokolamsk and Yuryev, 20 Pogodinskaya, Moscow. Tel. 246–98–48, fax 230–27–35.

Academic Committee

Chairman: Archbishop Alexander (Timofeyev) of Dmitrov, 5 Chisty Pereulok, Moscow. Tel. 584–96–63.

Leading Religious Schools

The Moscow Theological Academy and Seminary,

Archbishop Alexander of Dmitrov, Rector, Zagorsk, Lavra, Moscow Region. Tel. 4–53–46.

The Leningrad Theological Academy and Seminary,

Archpriest Vladimir Sorokin, Rector, 17 Obvodny Kanal, Leningrad.

Publications

Journal of the Moscow Patriarchate, published monthly in Russian and English. Editor-in-chief, Metropolitan Pitirim of Volokolamsk and Yuryev, 20 Pogodinskaya, Moscow. Tel. 246–98–48, fax 230–27–35.

Moskovsky Tserkovny Vestnik, published weekly in Russian. 20 Pogodinskaya, Moscow. Tel. 201–24–62.

Informatsionny bulleten OVTsC, published monthly in Russian and English, 22 Danilovsky Val, Moscow. Tel. 234–00–06, fax 230–26–19.

Pravoslavny Vistnik, published monthly in Ukrainian. Editor, Archpriest Alexandr Kubelius, 36 Pushkinskaya, Kiev. Tel. 227–73–45.

Ukrainian Orthodox Church

Metropolitan Filaret of Kiev and All Ukraine, 36 Pushkinskaya, Kiev. Tel. 2–24–90–00.

Belorussian Exarchate

Metropolitan Filaret of Minsk and Grodno, Patriarchal Exarch of all Belorussia, 1 Osvobozhdeniya, Minsk. Tel. 23–44–95.

Diocesan Bishops

Archbishop Alexiy (Kutepov) of Alma-Ata and Kazakhstan, 10 Minina, Alma-Ata. Tel. 42–60–14.

Bishop Panteleimon (Dolganov) of Arkhangelsk and Murmansk, 80 Uchitelskaya, Arkhangelsk. Tel. 6–34–87.

Archbishop Khrisostom (Martyshkin) of Vilnius and Lithuania, 8 Ausros Vartu, Vilnius. Tel. 62–58–96.

Metropolitan Agafangel (Savvin) of Vinnitsa and Bratslavsk, 176 Ulitsa Pervogo Maya, Vinnitsa. Tel. 2–65–26.

Archbishop Valentin (Mishchuk) of Vladimir and Suzdal, 26 Vishnevaya, Vladimir. Tel. 2–40–54.

Archbishop Mikhail (Mudyugin) of Vologda and Veliky Ustiug, 62 Voroshilova, Vologda. Tel. 6–84–57.

Bishop Varfolomey (Vashchuk) of Volyn and Lutsk, 1 Plekhanova, Lutsk. Tel. 2–40–97.

Metropolitan Mefody of Voronezh and Lipetsk. 6 Osvobozhdeniya Truda St., Voronezh. Tel. 55–34–94.

Archbishop Nikolai (Kutepov) of Nizhni Novgorod and Arzamas, 58 Suzdalskaya, Nizhni Novgorod. Tel. 55–09–19.

Archbishop Varlaam (Ilyushchenko) of Dnepropetrovsk and Zaporozhye; 7 Krasnaya Pl., Dnepropetrovsk. Tel. 45–33–73.

Bishop Ioanniki (Kobzev) of Donetsk and Lugansk, 7 Tushinskaya, Donetsk. Tel. 66–01–48.

Archbishop Iov (Tyvoniuk) of Zhitomir and Ovruch, 19 Podolskaya, Zhitomir. Tel. 7–27–92.

Bishop Amvrosy (Shchurov) of Ivanovo and Kineshma, 24 Kolotilova, Ivanovo. Tel. 2–98–58.

Archbishop Feodosiy (Dikun) of Ivanovo-Frankovsk and Kolomyia, 15 Kovpaka St., Ivanovo-Frankovsk. Tel. 4–60–85.

Bishop Pallady (Shiman) of Izhevsk and Udmurtia, 116 Zhecheva St., Izhevsk. Tel. 77–11–87.

Bishop Vadim (Lazebny) of Irkutsk and Chita, 14 Angarnaya, Irkutsk. Tel. 24–53–68.

Bishop Anastasy (Metkin) of Kazan and Mari, 31-a Cheliuskina St., Kazan. Tel. 54–35–15.

Archbishop Kliment (Kapalin) of Kaluga and Borovsk, 44 Tulskaya, Kaluga. Tel. 7–27–00.

Bishop Vasily (Vasiltsev) of Kirovograd and Nikolayev, 50 Libknekhta St., Kirovograd. Tel. 2–48–48.

Archbishop Khrisanf (Chepil) of Kirov and Slobodskoi, 29 Gertsena, Kirov. Tel. 2–98–75.

Archbishop Vladimir (Kantaryan) of Kishenev and Moldavia, 3 Benderskaya, Kishenev. Tel. 26–44–76.

Bishop Alexandr (Mogilev) of Kostroma and Galich, 11-a Lvovskaya, Kostroma. Tel. 25–03–42.

Archbishop Isidor (Kirichenko) of Krasnodar and Kuban, 128 Br. Ignatovykh St., Krasnodar. Tel. 55–60–95.

Bishop Antony (Cheremisov) of Krasnoyarsk and Yeniseisk, the Cathedral, Krasnoyarsk.

Metropolitan Juvenaly (Poyarkov) of Krutitsy and Kolomna, 1 Novodevichy Proyezd, Moscow. Tel. 245–30–03.

Bishop Yevseviy (Savin) of Syzran, 86 Sadovaya, Syzran. Tel. 33–02–31.

Archbishop Juvenaly (Tarasov) of Kursk and Belgorod, 59 Volodarskogo, Kursk. Tel. 2–51–82.

Metropolitan Ioann (Snychev) of Leningrad and Ladoga, 1-aya Berezovaya Alleya, 18, Leningrad. Tel. 234–54–24.

Bishop Andrei (Gorak) of Lvov and Drogobych, 5 Khmelnitskogo, Lvov. Tel. 72–48–25.

Archbishop Maxim (Krokha) of Mogilev and Mstislavl, 16 Pereulok Krupskoi, Mogilev. Tel. 25–34–33.

Bishop Yevfimy (Shutak) of Mukachevo and Uzhgorod, Ul. 8 Marta, 12, Mukachevo. Tel. 14–61.

Bishop Lev (Tserpitsky) of Novgorod and Staraya Russa, 7 Gorodishchenskaya, Novgorod. Tel. 3–33–42.

Metropolitan Leonty (Gudimov) of Odessa and Kherson, 6 Mayachny Pereulok, Odessa. Tel. 44–55–80.

Archbishop Feodosy (Protsiuk) of Omsk and Tara, 26 Uspenskogo, Omsk. Tel. 22–37–00.

Archbishop Leontyi (Bondar) of Orenburg and Buzuluk, 10 Pugacheva, Orenburg.

Bishop Paisi (Samchuk) of Orel and Bryansk, 47 Normandiya-Neman St., Orel. Tel. 6–67–56.

Archbishop Serafim (Tikhonov) of Pensa and Saransk, 44 Proyezd Vodopyanova, Pensa. Tel. 33–14–83.

Bishop Afanasy (Kudiuk) of Perm and Solikamsk, 93 Ordzhonikidze, Perm. Tel. 33–74–71.

Bishop Manuil (Pavlov) of Petrozavodsk and Olonets, 43 Kotovskogo, Petrozavodsk. Tel. 5–00–01.

Bishop Stefan (Korzun) of Pinsk and Luninets, Slonimsk District, Zhirovichi, 59 Sovetskaya, Grodno Region.

Bishop Dmitry (Drozdov) of Polotsk and Vitebsk, 2 Pereulok Kosmonavtov, Polotsk. Tel. 4–15–33.

Archbishop Savva (Babinets) of Poltava and Kremenchug, 62-a Rozy Luxemburg St., Poltava. Tel. 2–05–98.

Archbishop Vladimir (Kotlyakov) of Pskov and Velikiye Luku, 83-a Pozemskogo, Pskov. Tel. 2–44–50.

Archbishop Iriney (Seredny) of Rovno and Ostrog, 39 Leninskaya, Rovno. Tel. 6–66–39.

Metropolitan Vladimir (Sabodan) of Rostov and Novocherkassk, 10 Odesskaya, Rostov on the Don. Tel. 22–49–28.

Archbishop Simon (Novikov) of Ryazan and Kasimov, 28 Frunze, Ryazan. Tel. 7–66–23.

Archbishop Pimen (Khmelevsky) of Saratov and Volgograd, 27 Pervomaiskaya, Saratov. Tel. 26–09–39.

Archbishop Melkhisedek (Lebedev) of Sverdlovsk and Kurgan, 56-a Vengerskikh Kommunarov St., Sverdlovsk. Tel. 72–46–62.

Bishop Gleb (Savvin) of Simferopol and the Crimea, 57 Yaltinskoye Shosse, Simferopol. Tel. 3–25–31.

Metropolitan Kirill (Gundyayev) of Smolensk and Kaliningrad, 5 Soborny Dvor, Smolensk. Tel. 3–25–46.

Metropolitan Gedeon (Dokunin) of Stavropol and Baku, 155 Dzerzhinskogo, Stavropol. Tel. 4–55–24.

Bishop Nikanor (Yukhimiuk) of Sumy and Akhtyr, 31 Lenina, Sumy. Tel. 2–24–53.

Bishop Yevgeny (Zhdan) of Tambov and Michurinsk, 133 Zheleznodorozhnaya, Tambov. Tel. 2–11–61.

Bishop Vladimir (Ikim) of Tashkent and Central Asia, 3-yi Tupik Zhukovskogo 22, Tashkent. Tel. 33–33–21.

Bishop Victor (Oleinik) of Tver and Kashin, 11 Perovskoi, Tver. Tel. 23–31–57.

Archbishop Lazar (Shvets) of Ternopol and Kremenets, 22 Lenina, Ternopol. Tel. 2–23–56.

Bishop Ilian (Vostryakov) of Tobolsk and Tiumen, Krasnaya Pl., Tobolsk. Tel. 2–34–22.

Metropolitan Serapion (Fadeyev) of Tula and Belev, 61 Zhukovskogo, Tula. Tel. 36–76–18.

Bishop Prokl (Khazov) of Ulyanovlsk and Melekess, 103 Parkhomenko, Ulyanovsk.

Bishop Nikon (Vasiukov) of Ufa and Sterlitamak, 35-a Mingazheva St., Ufa. Tel. 22–53–37.

Bishop Gavriil (Stebliuchenko) of Khabarovsk and Vladivostok, 65 Leningradskaya, Khabarovsk. Tel. 33–83–17.

Metropolitan Nikodim (Rusnak) of Kharkov and Bogodukhov, 98-a Minskaya, Kharkov. Tel. 72–50–76.

Bishop Nifont (Solodukha) of Khmelnitsky and Kamenets-Podolsk, 113 Kirova St., Khmelnitsky. Tel. 6–54–11.

Archbishop Varnava (Kedrov) of Cheboksary and Chuvashia, 89 Vodoprovodnaya, Cheboksary. Tel. 24–17–83.

Bishop Georgy (Gryaznov) of Chelyabinsk and Zlatoslovsky, 6 Sosnovskaya, Chelyabinsk. Tel. 34–96–41.

Archbishop Antony (Vakarik) of Chernigov and Nezhin, 92 Tolstogo, Chernigov. Tel. 4–84–78.

Bishop Antony (Moskalenko) of Chernovtsy and Bukovina, 33 Russkaya, Chernovtsy. Tel. 2–33–51.

Archbishop Platon (Udovenko) of Yaroslavl and Rostov, 72-a Yaroslavskogo St., Yaroslavl. Tel. 1–41–73.

Major Monasteries

The Trinity-St. Sergiy Lavra: Father Superior, Archimandrite Feognost (Guzikov), Zagorsk, Moscow Region. Tel. 4–53–47.

Danilov Monastery: Father Superior, Archimandrite Ippolit (Khilko), 22 Danilovsky Val, Moscow. Tel. 2–35–07–14.

The Kiev-Pechery Lavra of the Dormition: Father Superior, Archimandrite Elevferiy (Didenko), 25 Yanvarskogo Vossotaniya St., Kiev. Tel. 2–90–15–08.

The Pskov-Pechery Monastery: Father Superior, Hegumen Pavel (Ponomarev), Pechery, Pskov Region. Tel. 9–21–45.

Synodal Library

22 Danilovsky Val, Danilov Monastery, Moscow. Tel. 234–00–06.

THE ARMENIAN APOSTOLIC CHURCH

Head of the Church

Supreme Patriarch Vasken I, Catholicos of All Armenians, Echmiadzin Monastery, Echmiadzin, Armenia, Tel. 5–34–34, 5–28–40, 5–89–56; telex 243326 Krest, SU.

Educational Center

Seminary and Academy of Echmiadzin: Gework Bagdishyan, Rector. Tel. 5–31–41.

Publication

Journal: *Echmiadzin*. Editor-in-chief, Erwand Melkonyan. Tel. 5–59–72.

Dioceses

Ararat

Shirak

Gugar

Siumik (in Armenia)

Artsakh (in the Nagorno-Karabakh Region)

Georgia

Novonakhichivan Russian Diocese, Bishop Tiran Kyuregyan, 10 Sergeya Makeyeva St., Moscow D-22. Tel. 255–50–12.

GEORGIAN AUTOCEPHALOUS ORTHODOX CHURCH

Head of the Church

Catholicos Patriarch of All Georgia Ilya II (Erecle Shiolashvili)
4 Sioni, SU-380005, Tbilisi. Tel. 72–25–79, 72–10–59, 99–03–78.

Members of the Holy Synod

Metropolitan Grigoli Tsertsvadze, 3 Doashvili, Alaverdi, SU-Telavi. Tel. 33–151, 33–193.

Metropolitan David Chkadua of Sukhumi and Abkhazia, Head of External Relations Department, 75 Leselidze, SU-384900 Sukhumi, Georgia. Tel. 22–616, 22–971.

Metropolitan Kalistrate Margalitashvili of Kutaisi and Gaenati, 112 Djakhishvili, SU-384000, Kutaisi, Georgia. Tel. 60–105.

Bishop Zosima Srioshvili of Tsilkani, Head of the publishing department, 28 Diocese House, SU-384640, Khashuri, Georgia.

Archbishop Tadeozi Joramashvili of Manglisi, Katedral, SU-383112 Manglisi, Georgia. Tel. 445.

Metropolitan Konstantine Meliktsidze of Batumi Shemokmedi, 91 Telmann, SU 384500, Batumi, Georgia. Tel. 34–935.

Metropolitan Atanase Chakhvashvili of Bodbe, Monastir St. Nino, SU-383210 Bodbe, Georgia. Tel. 32–056.

THE GREEK CATHOLIC CHURCH

Head of the Church

Patriarch Mirnslav Ivan Cardinal Lubachivsky, Patriarch of Kiev and Galich, Metropolitan's Chambers at St. George Cathedral, Lvov, the Ukraine 290068. Tel. 79–86–93, 79–89–87.

Bishops

Archbishop Vladimir Sternyuk, Locum-Tenens of Cardinal Lubachivsky, St. George Cathedral, Lvov. Tel. 79–89–87.

Bishop Philimon Kurkhaba, Auxiliary of Lvov, 184 Kalinina St., Lvov 290068.

Bishop Julian Voronovksy, Auxiliary of Lvov, 66/50 Kiseleva, Lvov 290070.

Bishop Mikhailo Sabrykha, Auxiliary of Lvov, 3/30 Lesi Ukrainki St., Ternopol 282011.

Bishop Sophron (Stefan) Dmiterko, Ivano-Frankovsk Diocese, 36/1 Kolomiyska St., Ivano-Frankovsk 284006. Tel. 25201.

Bishop Paylo Vasilyk, Coadjutor of Ivano-Frankovsk, Nadvirnyansky District, Mikulishin Village.

Bishop Irinej Bilik, Auxiliary of Ivano-Frankovsk, 4 Barbiusa St., Ivano-Frankovsk 284006.

Bishop Ivan Semedi, Mukachevo Diocese, 21 Sandora Petefi, Uzhgorod 294015. Tel. 20512.

Bishop Ivan Marghitych, Auxiliary of Mukachevo, 4 Dobrovoltsev St., Borzharske Village, Zakarpatski Region.

Bishop Iosif Kholovach, Auxiliary of Mukachevo, 32 Lenina St., Onokokovshi Village, Uzhgorod District 295191. Tel. 79652.

Communication Representative

Father Valery Shkarubsky, 11 Gnata Yury, Apt. 52, Kiev 252148. Tel. 4778884.

THE ROMAN CATHOLIC CHURCH OF LITHUANIA

Chairman (President) of the Episcopal Conference

Cardinal Vincentas Sladkevicius, 4 Vilniaus St., Apt. 1, Kaunas. Tel. 22–61–32.

Archdioceses and Dioceses

Vilnius Archdiocese: Bishop Juozas Tunaitis.

Kaunas Archdiocese: Archbishop Vincentas Sladkevicius.

Kaisiadorys Diocese: Titular Bishop Juozas Matulaitis.

Panevezys Diocese: Titular Bishop Juozas Preiksas.

Telsiai Diocese: Ordinary Bishop Antanas Vaicius.

Vilkaviskis Diocese: Titular Bishop Juozas Zemaitis.

Seminaries

Kaunas Seminary: Bishop Vladislas Mihelevicius, Rector, 4 Vilniaus St., Kaunas. 162 seminary students.

Telsiai Seminary: Telsiai. 22 seminary students.

Publication

Journal: *Kataliku Pasaulis* (*Catholic World*). Fortnightly magazine, circulation 70,000 copies. Editor-in-chief, Father Vaclovas Aliulis, 16 Kretingos St., Vilnius-1, 232001. Tel. 62–70–98.

Episcopal Diocesan Curias

The Kaunas Archdiocese: Cardinal Sladkevicius, 4 Vilniaus St., Kaunas 233000. Tel. 22–61–32, 22–21–97.

The Kaisiadorys Diocese: Bishop Matulaitis, 30 R. Carno St., Kaisiadorys 234230. Tel. 52–208.

The Panevezys Diocese: Bishop Preiksas, 45 Pushkin Boulevard, Panevezys 235300. Tel. 35–156, 33–281.

The Telsiai Diocese: Bishop Vaicius, 4 Spaudos St., Telsiai 235610. Tel. 51–157.

The Vilkaviskis Diocese: Bishop Zemaitis, 4 Vilniaus St., Kaunas 233000. Tel. 22–20–07.

THE ROMAN CATHOLIC CHURCH OF LATVIA

Riga Archdiocese: Bishop Janis Cakuls, Riga Curia, 2a Maza Pils St., Riga 226050. Tel. 22–72–66, 22–43–14.

Riga Seminary: Bishop Vilgelms Njuks, Rector, 16 Kievas St., Riga 22603. Tel. 22–96041.

Journal: *Life of Catholics,* published monthly. Editor-in-Chief, Bishop Njuks; Editor, Andreas Agglonetis, 6 Kultur Square, Vilani, Rezekne District 228150. Tel. 62–372, 62–483.

THE ROMAN CATHOLIC CHURCH OF BELORUSSIA

Head of the Church: Titular Bishop Tadeusz Kondrusiewicz, Apostolic Administrator for the Catholics of Belorussia. (The address is not available, since the bishop's residence is currently under construction.)
Cathedral: St. Francis Xavier Church, 4 Sovetskaya Square, Grodno 230023.
Seminary: Father Stanislav Kuchinski, Rector, 11 Parizhskaya Kommuna St., Grodno 230023.

THE ROMAN CATHOLIC CHURCH OF THE UKRAINE

Major Catholic Churches

Dormition of Holy Mary, Father Vladimir Kernitsky, Dean, 1 Rosa Luxemburg Square, Lvov. Tel. 7–97–092.

St. John the Baptist Church, Father Kazimir Monchinsky, Dean, 6 Pushkin St., Sambur, Lvov Region.

St. John the Baptist Church, Father Iosif Legovich, Dean, 7 Kostiushko St., Mostiska, Lvov Region.

St. George's Church, Father A. A. Gorvat, Dean, 1 Oktyabrskaya St., Uzhgorod, Transcarpathian Region 294000.

St. Martin's Church, I. Chati, Dean, 4 Kommunisticheskaya St., Mukachevo, Transcarpathian Region. Tel. 2–39–24.

The Adoration of the Cross Church, Father Victor Antoniuk, Dean, 20 Lenin St., Chernovtsi 274000.

St. Anna's Church, Bronislav Bernadsky, Dean, 12 Vorovsky St., Bar, Vinnitsa Region. Tel. 20–09.

St. Florian Church, Zenon Turovsky, Dean, 100 Lenin St., Shargorod, Vinnitsa Region. Tel. 2–22–76.

Church of the Immaculate Conception, Stanislav Shulyak, Dean, Murafa Village, Vinnitsa Region, Shargorod District. Tel. 2–93–68.

St. Nicholas Church, Leonid Tkachuk, Dean, Chernevtsy Village, Mogilev-Podolsky District, Vinnitsa Region.

Holy Virgin of the Angels Church, Vladimir Khalupyak, Dean, 21 Lenin St., Vinnitsa. Tel. 5–65–26.

St. Trinity Church, Leonid Dubrovsky, Dean, 4 Shchors St., Khmelnik, Vinnitsa Region.

St. Anthony Church, Yan Purvinsky, Dean, Rylsky St., Zhitomir 262000. Tel. 37–50–47.

Church of the Exaltation of the Cross, Andrei Kasyanenko, Dean, 4 Krasnoarmeyskaya St., Fastov, Kiev Region 255530.

Sts. Peter and Paul Church, Iosif Budryavicius, Dean, 20 Karl Marx St., Kamenets-Podolsky, Khmelnitsky Region 281900.

THE ROMAN CATHOLIC CHURCH IN THE RUSSIAN FEDERATION

Functioning Churches

St. Louis Church, Father Francisk Raciunas, Dean, 12 Mal. Lubyanka, Moscow. Tel. 925–20–34.

Church of the Holy Virgin, Yazep Pavilonis, Dean, 7 Kovensky Per., Leningrad 191014. Tel. 272–04–42 (the dean's personal telephone).

Church of the Holy Virgin, Vytautas Saulius, Dean, 9 Second Mira Street, Novosibirsk. Tel. 47–88–88.

THE ALL-UNION LEAGUE OF EVANGELICAL CHRISTIAN BAPTISTS OF THE USSR (AULECB)

The All-Union League of Evangelical Christian Baptists of the USSR has 11 regional (republican) unions and associations of Evangelical Christian Baptist churches incorporating more than 2,500 communities with about 300,000 members. The League operates a seminary and offers correspondence Bible courses in Moscow and has branches in several other cities.

Address: 3 Maly Vuzovsky Per., Moscow 109028. Tel. 297–51–67, fax 227–39–90.

Chairman of the League

Grigori Komendant. Tel. 227–25–89.

Vice-Chairmen

Alexey Bychkov. Tel. 297–67–00.

Nikolai Kolesnikov. Tel. 297–85–02.

Alexander Firisyuk. Tel. 297–33–63.

Philanthropy and Charity Work

Mikhail Zhidkov. Tel. 297–02–07.

International Church Relations Department

Secretary: Nikolai Zverev. Tel. 227–89–47.

Publishing Department

Executive editor: Vitaly Kulikov. Tel. 297–96–26.

Training Ministers Department

Pavel Savchenko. Tel. 297–48–62.

Finances Department

Anatoly Voronin. Tel. 297–08–62.

Transport Department

Valentin Mokhov. Tel. 297–51–67.

Accounts Department

Svetlana Merkulova. Tel. 297–46–41.

Publications

Journal: *Bratsky Vestnik* (*Brotherly Herald*). Editor-in-chief, Alexander Firisiuk; executive editor, Vitaly Kulikov; 3 Maly Vuzovsky Per., Moscow 109028. Tel. 297–96–20, 297–98–46. Paper: *Khristianskoye Slovo* (*Christian Word*). Editor, Oleg Zhidulov. Office Tel. 297–20–07, 297–98–46.

Association of Evangelical Christian Baptist Churches of the Russian Federation

Address: P.O. Box 68, Moscow Zh-147, 197147. Tel. 297–55–98.
Association Chairman: Vasily Logvinenko.
Vice-Chairmen

Pyotr Shatrov.

Sergei Nikolayev.

Alexei Prokhorov.

Publishing House: Khristianin i Vremya (The Christian and Time) issues a paper and a journal of the same title. Editor-in-chief, Ivan Chekhunov.

Union of Evangelical Christian Baptist Churches of the Ukrainian SSR

Address: 3a Lev Tolstoi St., Kiev 252004. Tel. 224–82–41, fax 228–74–80.
Chairman: Yakov Dukhonchenko
Deputy Chairmen

Veniamin Goncharov, Kiev. Tel. 225–37–13.

Stepan Karpenko, P.O. Box 23, Donetsk 340066.

Vladimir Matveyev

International Relations: Victor Kulbich.
Publication: Paper *Khristianskaya Zhizn* (*Christian Life*)

Association of Evangelical Christian Baptist Churches of the Kazakh SSR

Address: P.O. Box 122, Alma-Ata 480001. Office Tel. 8–327–240–24–91.
Chairman: Victor Gorelov.
Vice-Chairmen, Senior Presbyters for the Regions

Alexei Burlakov (Northern Kazakhstan), 87 Proyezd Mikheyeva, Petropavlovsk 642019.

Vladimir Shokov (Southern Kazakhstan), 223 Nekrasov St., Chimkent 486032.

Franz Tissen (Central Kazakhstan), 16 Kievskaya St., Saran 472340.

Wilhelm Shults (Eastern Kazakhstan), 4 Tretiy Proyezd, Semipalatinsk 490016.

Franz Ens (Mennonites), 49a Residential Area Stepnoi I, Apt. 76, 47071.

Union of Evangelical Christian Baptist Churches of the Belorussian SSR

Address: P.O. Box 132, Minsk 220023. Tel. 8–0172–58–98–67.
Chairman: Ivan Bukaty.
Vice-Chairmen

Iosif Rachkovsky.

Konstantin Lomako.

Association of Evangelical Christian Baptist Churches for the Uzbek Republic, Tajikistan, and the Turkmen Republic

Address: P.O. Box 303, Tashkent 700055. Tel. 8–371–255–06–49.
Chairman: Boris Serin.
Vice-Chairman: Ivan Goncharov
59 T. Akbulatov St., Ferghana 713806

Union of Evangelical Christian Baptist Churches of Moldova

Address: 51 Severnaya St., Kishinev 277059. Tel. 49–89–72, 49–89–61, 49–89–82, code 8–042–2.
Chairman: Bishop Karl Sedletsky.
Vice-Chairmen

Leonid Agafonov.

Victor Loginov.

Publication: Newspaper *Svet Zhizny* (*The Light of Life*) in Russian and Moldavian.

Evangelical Christian Baptist Union of Estonia

Address: Pargi St., Tallinn 200016. Tel. 8–0142–51–30–05.
Chairman: Juno Meriloo.
Vice-Chairman: Ioosen Tammo.

Association of Evangelical Christian Baptist Churches for Georgia, Azerbaijan, and Armenia

Address: Tbilisi. Tel. 8–8832–23–29–10.
Chairman: Nodar Kvirikashvili.
Vice-Chairmen

Nikolai Grubich, 7a Seventh Residential Area, Apt. 57, Baku 370116.

Yuri Avanesyan, 90 Nardos St., Yerevan 375018.

Association of Evangelical Christian Baptist Churches for the Kirghiz Republic

Address: P.O. Box 189, Pishpek 720000. Tel. 8–331–225–19–50.
Chairman: Nikolai Sizov.

Evangelical Christian Baptist Union of Latvia

Address: 50b Revolution St., Apt. 1, Riga 226009. Tel. 8–0132–27–13–12.
Union Chairman: Janis Eisans.
Vice-Chairman: Andrejs Sterns.
Publication: Journal *Tree of Life*.

Evangelical Christian Baptist Union of Lithuania

Address: 56 Debretsenko St., Apt. 7, Klaipeda 235819.
Union Chairman: Albert Latuzys.

BROTHERLY COUNCIL OF INDEPENDENT CHURCHES OF THE SOUTHERN REGION OF EVANGELICAL CHRISTIAN BAPTISTS

Address: 18 Ladozhsky Per., Rostov-on-Don 344059. Tel. 54–02–97.

The Brotherly Council consists of more than 20 ECB communities with about 4,000 members not belonging to the ECB Union and situated in the Southern regions of the Russian Federation and the Ukraine.
Head of Brotherly Council: Mikhail Shaptala.
Secretary: Pavel Belenky.
Publishing House: Awakening, 64a Donetsky Per., Rostov-on-Don 56, 344056.
Journal: *Awakening*. Executive editor, Victor Zhovmiruk.
Mission: Awakening. Director, Victor Zhovmiruk; Deputy Director, Ivan Shvets, 64a Donetsky Per., Rostov-on-Don 56 344056.

PROTESTANT PUBLISHING HOUSE

Address: 1 Mukomolny proyezd, Kor. 2, Moscow 123290. Tel. 259-93-97, fax 7-095-292-65-11 BIBLESU, telex 411700 BIBLESU.
Editor-in-Chief: Alexander Semchenko.
Publishes newspaper *Protestant*. Editor, Pyotr Abrashkin.
Office Address: P.O. Box 83, Moscow 123290.

BIBLE SOCIETY

Address: P.O. Box 403, Pyatnitskaya Str. 51-14, Moscow 109017.
President: Sergei Averintsev.
Vice-President: Alexei Bychkov.
Executive Director: Anatoly Rudenko.

SOVIET DIVISION OF CHURCHES OF SEVENTH-DAY ADVENTISTS

Address: 43A Rudnev St., Pos. Zaoksky, Tula Region 301000. Tel. 2-22-69, fax 2-25-46.
Division President: Mikhail Kulakov. Tel. 2-28-90.
Division Secretary: Victor Krushenitsky.
Division Treasurer: Alexander Pankov.

Division Departments

Pastoral Serving: Mikhail Kulakov.
Church Serving: Ivan Gumeniuk.
Literary and Publishing: Uldis Liepins.
Education: Rostislav Volkoslavsky.

Theological Seminary

Rector: Mikhail Kulakov.

Association for Work with Prisoners

Chairman: Nikolai Libenko, 11 Klyuev St., Tula 300012. Tel. 25-76-72.

Radio and TV Center

Director: Pyotr Kulakov, 48 Stanislavsky St., Tula 300000. Tel. 25-49-64.

Adventist Assistance and Development Agency

Director: Pavel Kulakov, 9 Severodvinskaya St., Apt. 407, Moscow 129224. Tel./fax 476-53-48.

Russian Union of the Seventh-Day Adventist Church

Address: 43A Rudnev St., Pos. Zaoksky, Tula Region 301000. Tel. 2-21-99, fax 2-25-46.
Union Chairman: Mikhail Murga.

Ukrainian Union of the Seventh-Day Adventist Church

Address: 55 Botkin St., Lvov 290053. Tel. 63-53-10.
Union Chairman: Nikolai Zhukaliuk, Kiev. Tel. 293-44-72.

Baltic-Belorussian Union of the Seventh-Day Adventist Church

Address: 9 Yanka Kupala St., Riga, Latvian SSR 226000. Tel. 32-10-50.
Union Chairman: Valdis Zilgalvis.

Moldavian Union of the Seventh-Day Adventist Church

Address: 22 Bernardtsy St., Kishinev, SSR Moldova 277000. Tel. 26-51-48.
Union Chairman: Grigory Kochmar.

Southern Union of the Seventh-Day Adventist Church

Address: 83a Omskaya St., Alma-Ata, Kazakh SSR 480000. Tel. 34–23–58.
Union Chairman: Ilya Velgosha.

Moscow Community of the Seventh-Day Adventist Church

Address: 3 Maly Vuzovsky Per., Moscow 109028. Tel. 297–05–68.
Pastor: Pavel Kulakov.

PENTECOSTALS

No religious center. The registered and non-registered societies of various denominations operate both independently and as part of regional religious associations (the Union of Evangelical Christian Baptists included).

Russian Federation of Pentecostals

Address of Temporary Office: 178 Bolshaya Kosinskaya St., Moscow. Tel. 550–22–51.
Senior Presbyter for Russian Federation: Bronislav Bilas.

Ukrainian Pentecostals

Address of Temporary Office: 4 Karyernaya St., Kiev. Tel. 484–25–72.
Senior Presbyter for Ukrainian SSR: Nikolai Melnik.

Belorussian Pentecostals

Address of Temporary Office: 40 Sobinov St., Minsk. Tel. 62–63–73.
Senior Presbyter for Byelorussia: Nikolai Durilo.

Moldova Pentecostals

Address of Temporary Office: 83 Barbutse St., Beltsy.
Senior Presbyter for Moldova: Victor Pavlovsky.

CHRISTIANS OF THE EVANGELICAL FAITH IN THE SPIRIT OF THE APOSTLES

No single religious center. The registered and nonregistered societies operate both independently and as members of the regional center in the Russian Federation, actually carrying out the functions of the Union Society and one that unites several dozen societies, with over ten thousand members.
Address of Temporary Office: 3-e Pargolovo, 21 Polevaya St., Leningrad. Tel. 594–81–43.
Senior Presbyter for Russian Federation: Dmitry Shatrov.

RELIGIOUS ORGANIZATION OF JEHOVAH'S WITNESSES

About 400 societies, 40,000 members. Its Guiding Committee is its nonregistered religious center.
Temporary Address for Contacts: Dubno, Rovno Region, Ukrainian SSR. Tel. 4–16–18.
Committee Member: Anany Grogul.

ISLAM

Muslim Board for the European Part of the USSR and Siberia

Chairman: Sheikh-ul-Islam Mufti Talgat Tadzhutdin.
Address: 50-A Tukayev St., Ufa 45057. Tel. 22–74–46, 22–77–17; fax 23–16–65.

Muslim Board for Transcaucasia

Chairman: Sheikh-ul-Islam Allahshukur Pashazade
Address: 7 Mirza Fatali St., Baku 370001. Tel. 95–25–75, 92–39–21.

Muslim Board for Central Asia

Chairman: Mufti Mukhammadsadyk Mammayusuf.

Address: 103 Khamza St., Tashkent 700002. Tel. 44–24–60, 40–18–58.

Muslim Board for Kazakhstan

Chairman: Mufti Radbek Nasynbai-uly.
Address: 16 Pushkin St., Alma-Ata 480016. Tel. 30–63–65, 30–04–70.

Muslim Board for Dagestan

Chairman: Mufti Bagauddin Isayev.
Address: 2 Aziz Aliyev St., Makhachkala. Tel. 3–31–31.

Muslim Board for the Checheno-Ingush Republic

Chairman: Mufti Shakhid Khadzhi Gazabayev.
Address: 188 Lenin St., Grozny. Tel. 24–63–77.

Muslim Board for the Kabardin-Balkar Republic

Chairman: Mufti Chochayev Sharafuddin-Khadzhi.
Address: 43-A Sovetskaya St., Nalchik. Tel. 2–66–92.

Muslim Board for the North Ossetian Republic

Chairman: Mufti Khekilayev Zhankhot.
Address: The Mosque, Prigorodny District, Kurtat Village.

Muslim Board for Karachayevo-Cherkess and Stavropol

Chairman: Mufti Ismail Berdiyev.
Address: 5 Perevalnaya St., Pervomaiskoye Village, Malo-Karachayevsky District, Stavropol Territory 357185. Tel. 2–19–57.

Educational Centers

Mir-Arab Madrasah, 16 Kommunarov St., Bukhara.

Imam Al-Bukhari Islamic Institute, 69 Khamza St., Tupik 18, House No. 47, Tashkent. Tel. 48–03–58.

The Khadzhi Nasukh Madrasah, Kurchaloi Village, Shali District, Checheno-Ingush Autonomous Republic.

Publication

Journal: *Muslims of the Soviet East*, 103 Khamza St., Tashkent 700055.

THE CENTRAL BUDDHIST BOARD OF THE USSR

Head of the Central Buddhist Board: Bandido Khambo-Lama Munko Tsybikov, Ivolginski Datsan, Verkhnyaya Ivolga settlement, Buryat 671210.
Permanent Representative in Moscow: Lama Bazarsad Lamazhapov; Deputy Representative, Leonid Verkhovsky, 49 Ostozhenka St., Moscow 119034. Tel. 245–09–39, 245–09–39; telex 114670 Sovbud, fax 248–02–64.

Monasteries

Ivolginski Datsan, Lama Tsyren-Dondok Dorzhiyev. Tel. 21–231.

Aginski Datsan, Lama Zolto Zhigmatov, Aginsk, Chita Region 674460. Tel. 345–48.

Elista Datsan, Lama Tuvan Dorzhi Tsympilov, 83 Lermontova St., Elista, the Kalmyk Autonomous Republic 358000. Tel. 2–71–65.

Leningrad Datsan, Lama Chimit Dorzhi Dugarov, 91 Primorsky Bulvar, Leningrad. Tel. 351–71–65.

JEWISH RELIGIOUS COMMUNITIES

All-Union Council of Jewish Religious Communities

Head of the Council Presidium: Chief Rabbi Adolf Shayevich and Rabbi Vladimir Fedorovsky.

Chairman of the Council: Vladimir Fedorovsky.

Council Address: 10 Arkhipov St., Moscow 101000. Tel. 924–24–24 (Fedorovsky) and 925–42–80 (Shayevich).

Publication: Magazine *Menora*, Moscow Choral Synagogue, 10 Arkhipov St., Moscow 101000. Tel. 925–42–80, 924–24–24.

Largest Communities

Vladimir Fedorovsky, Chairman, Adolf Shayevich, Chief Rabbi, 10 Arkhipov St., Moscow 101000. Synagogue tel. 925–42–80.

Alexander Shentsis, Chairman, 5 Second Vysheslavtsev Per., Moscow 103055. Tel. 289–23–25.

Grigory Grossman, Chairman, Yefim Levitis, Rabbi, 2 Lermontovsky Pr., Leningrad 190121. Synagogue tel. 114–11–53.

Dmitry Levin, Chairman, 29 Shekovitskaya Kiev 252071. Synagogue tel. 416–13–83.

Zinovy Varnovitsky, Chairman, 8 Yakimovsky Per., Kishenev 277000. Synagogue tel. 22–12–15.

Lev Guldenberg, Chairman, 5 Odariya St., Odessa 270003. Synagogue tel. 270–370.

Andrei Levin, Chairman, 13 Kozhevenny tupik, Tbilisi 380005. Synagogue tel. 72–46–23.

Ashkenazi community: Israil Tsikanovsky, Chairman, 15 Second Sapernaya St., Tashkent 700015.

Bukhara community: Bension Nisamov, Chairman; Meir Bangiyev, Rabbi, 62 Gorbunov St., Tashkent 700000. Synagogue tel. 53–94–47.

INTERNATIONAL SOCIETY OF KRISHNAITES

About 100 societies with around 10,000 members.

The functions of the Union religious center are carried out by the Moscow Society of Krishnaites (MOSK).

Temporary Office: 2 Serafimovich St., Apt. 152, Moscow. Tel. 238–98–85.

Chairman of the MOSK Council: Aleksei Mikheyev.

MOLOKANS

More than 100 societies, over 8,000 members. No religious center; one is being set up at present.

Organizing Committee: c/o Ivan Alexandrov, P.O. Box 826, Moscow 113546.

Index

Abkhazians: conflict with Georgians, 120–21
Abovyan, Khachatur (*AAC*), 111
Adventist Church of the Russian Federation, Council of the, 56
Agafangel, Metropolitan (*ROC*), historical, 92
Aginski *datsan*, 178
Agudath Israel movement, 188
AIDS, 54
Alcohol abuse, 59, 168
Alexis, Metropolitan (*ROC*), historical, 80
Alexis II, Patriarch of Moscow and All Russia, xiv, 55, 65, 98; biography, 46; on the *ROC*, 72–81; visit to Kiev, 80
Alexiy, Metropolitan (*ROC*), historical, 92, 96
Allies: called for restoration of church, 96
An Analysis of Space and Time in Works of Art (Florensky), 101
Anticulture, 85
Anti-Semitism, 190
Antonin, Bishop, 12, 13. *See also* Renovation movement
Aphonite monasticism, 104
Armenian alphabet, 111
Armenian Apostolic Church, 55; current status of, 109, 112–13; history of, 109, 111, 112; Stalinist reprisals against, 112; statistics on the, 109, 112
Armenian earthquake of, 1988, 55, 113
Armenians, conflict with Azerbaijanis, 45
Atheism, xii, 88, 152; *Bezbozhnik*, 96; rights of atheist organizations, 32(Art.8)
At the Watershed of Thought (Florensky), 101

Autocephalists (Ukrainian), 80, 81
Azerbaijan, 165, 173
Azerbaijanis, conflict with Armenians, 45

Babakhan, Shamsuddinkhan ibn Ziyautdinkhan, Mufti (*I*), 166
Baptism, 138, 151; mass ceremonies of, 119
Baptists, 56, 57; the All-Union League of Evangelical Christian, 140–50, 151, 152, 153, 157; life of in USSR, 154–58
Baptists, League of Russian, 151
Bartholomew, St., 111
Belavin, V.I. *See* Tikhon, Patriarch
Benjamin, Metropolitan of Petrograd and Gdov, possible canonization of, 97, 98
Bezbozhnik, 96
Black Hundred clergy: 3, 4, 5, 10 n.8
Bogoslovski vestnik, 100
Bogoyavlensky. *See* Vladimir, Metropolitan of Kiev and Galicia
Brezhnev, Leonid, 159
Buburuz, Pyotr Archpriest: 49–50
Buddhism, 178; current status of, 177, 179–81; history of, 177, 178–79; statistics on, 177
Buddhists, persecution of, 177
Buddhology, 181
Bullo, Branislava (*PC*), 161
Bychkov, Dr. Alexei Vice Chairman (*PC*): 153, 155

Cakuls, Janis, Bishop (*RCC*), 133
Canonization Commission (*ROC*), 91, 97, 98
Carcich, Theodore (*PC*), 160
Caritas, 56
Casimir, Prince (St.), 137

Cassidi, Eduard Archbishop (*RCC*), 128
Castro, Emilio, Dr., 126
Catacombs, psychology of the, 75
Catalicu pasaulis, 135
Catechization, 62
Cathedral of the Dormition, 106
Cathedrals: at Tbilisi, 121; Cathedral of the Dormition, 106; Holy Trinity-St. Sergiy, 105; seizure of *ROC* churches by Uniates, 127–28; St. Casimir Cathedral, 137. *See also* Church property; Mosques
Catherine II, Empress ("The Great"), 139, 151, 165
Catholic Church. *See* Caritas; Greek Catholic Church; Roman Catholic Church
Charity: past prohibitions against, 54, 55; as a religious function, 49, 157; right of religious groups to perform, xiii, 28
Chesterton, Gilbert K., 74
Choirs, 155, 156
Christian rock groups, 156
Chrysostom, John, Archbishop of Constantinople, 117
Church: separation from state, 24(Art.8), 95
Church property: restoration and return of, 50, 64, 72, 83, 133; seizure and closure of, 3, 4, 82. *See also* Shuya, events in
Church-state relations: Archbishop Illarion challenges government, 93–96; during periods of repression, 74–75, 77; during World War, II, 96–97; normalization of, xii, 44, 61–62, 70, 77–78, 83–84; state authorities on, 29(Art.29), 29, 33(Art.12)

Clergy, 44, 122, 165, 179; collaboration of, 165, 166; role of, 142–43 (Provs.2.9.5–2.13.1), 144–45 (Provs.3.2.1–3.4.7); shortage of, xiii, 78, 133, 177, 186

Communist Party of the Soviet Union, 76, 77

Congress of People's Deputies. See Soviet Parliament

Conscience, freedom of. See Freedom of conscience

Conscientious objector status, 32(Art.7)

Constantine, Emperor (Byzantine), 117

Correctional facilities. See Prisons

Coup, of August 1991, xiv, 44

Crime and order, 84, 129, 168, 170

Cultural development, 85–87

Czars. See Russian monarchy

Daghestan, 165

Dastan Makhdi, 169

Data bank, on religious organizations, 29(Art.29)

Demonstrations: of Georgians resulting in deaths (1989), 119–20; of Muslims at Daghestan, 167–68; of Muslims at Tashkent, 166, 167; of Ukranian Uniates, 126

Denisenko. See Filet, Metropolitan (ROC) of Kiev and Galitsia

Dhzaumigul-Kamil, 169

Dordzhiev, Agvan, 180

Drug abuse, 59, 168

Dugzhub, 179

Duprey, Pierre, Bishop (RCC), 129

Duyn-khor, 179

Dzerzhinsky, F. E., 11n.16

Dzhvari vazisa (The Grapevine Cross), 119

Echmiadzin, the Holy, 111

Ecology and the environment, 49, 50, 53

Economic reform, 85

Education. See Schools; Theology, teaching of

Elderly, the, 55, 84

Emigration, 152, 156, 185

Equality, 84

Ethnic conflicts, 152, 171; in Georgia, 120–21

Ethnic relations, 53, 68

Evangelism, 154

Evangelsk, 152

Feasts. See Holidays

Fedorovsky, Vladimir, Rabbi (J), 186

Fedorov, Svyatoslav, Professor, 56

Filaret, Metropolitan (ROC) of Kiev and Galitsia, 128

Filaret, Metropolitan (ROC) of Minsk and Belorussia, 53, 54, 61

Firisyuk, Alexander (PC): 153

Florensky, Pavel: life and martyrdom of, 99–103; on the Optina Hermitage, 104

Florovsky, Georghy Father, 81

Freedom of conscience, 23(Art.2–3), 30(Art.30), 31–32(Art.4), 34(Art.15), 187; Islamic teachings on, 172–73; obstruction of penalized, 33–34(Art.13); pertaining to Uniates, 129

Freedom of worship. See Freedom of conscience: Religious rites and ceremonies

Gaaz, F. P., Dr., 57

Gandan-Shunserme, 179

Gaon of Vilnius (J), 191

Gekkiyev, Makhmud, Mufti (I), 168

Gelugpa school, 179

General Human Roots of Idealism, The (Florensky), 100

Genoa Conference, 4, 14, 15n.6

Georgian Autocephalous Orthodox Church: current status of, 115; history of, 115, 116–18; leadership of, 117–18; statistics on, 115

Georgians: persecution of by Islamic invaders, 118; recent persecution of, 119–20

Georgia, religious sites in, 116–17

Gibadat Islamia, 169

Glasnost, 60, 157–58, 178

Golden Horde, 80

Gorbachev, Mikhail, vii, 126, 160, 170; meets with Pope, 133; on rehabilitation of victims of religious reprisal, 90

Granovsky, A. A. See Antonin, Bishop

Grapevine Cross, The 116, 119

"Great Change, The", 100

Greek Catholic Church, xiii; current status of, 123, 126–27; history of, 123, 125, 126; statistics on, 123; tensions with Orthodox Christians, 123, 127–31. See also Lvov Council

Gregorious, Paulos Mar Metropolitan of Delhi (SOC), 127

Gregory the Illuminator, St., 111

Gundyayev. See Kirill, Metropolitan and Archbishop of Smolensk and Kaliningrad

HABAD movement, 188

Hasidim of Lyubavichi, 188

Hasidism, 185

Hesychasm, Byzantine asceticism, 104

Holidays, 21, 34(Art.14), 60–61, 141, 187; khurals, 178, 179–80

Holy Koran, 53, 166, 167, 169

Holy Synod, 65, 69, 90; Declaration of the (1990), 66–72; provisional, 93

Holy Trinity-St. Sergiy cathedral, 105

Holy Virgin: church of, 119; statue of, 133

Iconostasis, The (Florensky), 101

Ilia II, His Holiness and Beatitude Catholicos-Patriarch of All Georgia, Archbishop of Mtskheta and Tbilisi, 117, 119

Illarion, Archbishop (ROC), challenged state reprisals, 93–96

Imagery in Geometry (Florensky), 101, 102

Industrialization, 85

International contacts and relations, 28(Art.24), 30(Art.30), 36(Art.25), 149(Prov.5.9.7), 189–90

Inverse Perspective (Florensky), 101

Iriney, Archbishop of Lvov and Drogobych (ROC), 128

Islam: current status of, 53, 165, 166, 169; history of, 165; relations with other religions, 171, 172, 173–75; statistics on, 165

Islamic temple, 164

Israel, 188

Issaakyan, Avetik, poet, 111

Ivolginsky datsan, 176, 180

Izvestia, 14

Jews: international cooperation of, 189–90; orthodox, 188; persecution of by Nazis, 188; religious identification of, 187. *See also* Judaism

John Paul II, Pope, 123, 128

Judaic Section of the Academy of World Civilization, 191–92

Judaism, 184; current status of, 185; history of, 185; statistics on, 185

Juvenaly, Metropolitan (*ROC*) of Krutitsy and Kolomna, 128

Kalmyk Republic (*B*), 178, 179

Kanjur, 181

Kazanski. *See* Benjamin, Metropolitan of Petrograd and Gdov

Khan, Inamulla Dr., 170

Khrisostom, Archbishop of Vilnius and Lithuania (*ROC*): 137

Khurals, 178, 179–80

Kiev-Pechery Laura cathedral: 64, 103, 105

Kirill, Metropolitan (*ROC*) of Smolensk and Kaliningrad: on the church and *perestroika*, 82–90, 128

Kirill, Metropolitan (*ROC*): historical, 92

Kolesnikov, Nikolai (*PC*), 153

Komendant, Grigori, President (*PC*): 153

Komitas, Archimandrite (*AAC*), 111

Koran, Holy. See Holy Koran

Kovalev, Vadim, Pastor, presbyter of the Church of the Evangelist Christian Baptists, 56, 63

Kozha, Alexander Archpriest, 103–6; on Father Pavel Florensky, 99–103

Krushchev, Nikita, xii, 159

Krutitsky. *See* Pyotr, Metropolitan (*ROC*)

Kryuchkov, Gennadi, Pastor (*PC*), 152

Kulakov, Mikhail, Pastor, 56, 159

Kulikov, Vitaly, 60–61

Kuran, Holy. See Holy Koran

Lamas. *See* Clergy

Latvian Christian Mission, 56

Latvia, RCC in, 133

Law on Freedom of Conscience and Religious Organizations:

discussed, 19–22, 70–72; provisions of, 23–30

Law on Freedom of Worship: discussed, 19–22; provisions of, 31–37

Laymen (*ROC*), 79

Leadership training, 89–90, 155

League of Evangelical Christians, 151

League of Russian Baptists, 151

Lebedev, Lev, Archpriest (*ROC*), xiii

Legislation, 87. *See also* Law on Freedom of Conscience and Religious Organizations; Law on Freedom of Worship

Lenin, Vladimir Ilyich, 3–11

Likhanov, Albert, 56

Literature: Buddhist, 179, 181, 182; Christian and Bible, 155, 162; promoted and developed by GOAC, 118; religious, 28(Art.22), 36(Art.25), 149(Prov.5.9.5.). *See also by individual titles*; Holy Koran

Literaturnaya Gazeta, 72

Lithuania: independence of supported by church, 134–37; RCC in, 133

Liubachivsky, Miroslav Cardinal and Patriarch of the Ukraine, 123

Lkhabab Duysen, 180

Lohne, Alf (*PC*), 160

Lotz, Denton, 154–58

"Loyal clergy". *See* Renovation movement

Lutherans, 56

Lvov Council, 125

McDugal, Norman (*PC*), 161

McNeilus, Garwin (*PC*), 161

Mahanaim, 188

Mahayana tradition, 179

Maidari, 179

Makhdi, dastan, 169

Mammayusuf, Mukhammadsadyk, Mufti, 52–53, 166, 167

Marian, King of Georgia, historical: 115, 119

Martyrdom of St. Shushanika, The (Tsurtaveli), 118

Martyshkin. *See* Khrizostom, Archbishop of Vilnius and Lithuania

Marusin, Miroslav Archbishop (*GCC*), 128

Marxists. *See* Communist Party of the Soviet Union

Masteropulo, Alexey, Dr., 58

Maxim the Confessor, St., 117

Media, mass, religious programs on, 60–62, 149, 157

Memorial Society, 97

Mennonites, 151

Menora, 188, 190

Mesrop, Archimandrite (*AAC*), 111

Milyukovites, 5

Moldavia, revival of the church in, 50

Molotov, V. M., 6, 7

Monastaries, xi, 25(Art.10), 103–6, 176, 178. *See also* Church property

Monasticism, Aphonite, 104

Morality, 84–85

Moscow Baptist Church, 57

Moscow Choral Synagogue, 184, 186

Moscow Patriarchate: church bulletin of, 61; lost property of, xii

Mosques, 168, 169

Mother Teresa, 54–55

Multinationalism, 86

Muradbekyan, Khoren I, Catholicos (*AAC*), 112

Muslim Religious Board: for Central Asia and Kazakhstan, 166; dissolution of for northern Caucasus, 168; for the European Part of the USSR and Siberia, 56, 168; for Transcaucasia, 168; of Volga and the Urals, anniversary of, 168–69, 170

Muslims, 165, 167, 168, 169. *See also* Islam

Nazis, 188; collaboration with, 124–25

Nechayev, Konstantin. *See* Pitirim, Metropolitan of Volokolamsk and Yuryev

Nevsky, Alexander, 80

New Economic Policy, 152

Nikolai, Metropolitan (*ROC*), historical, 92, 96

Nina, St.: converted state of Georgia, 115, 116–17

Nonbelievers, 83, 186. *See also*
Atheism
Novodevichiy Monastery, 105
Nuns, 55

Obnovlenie. See Renovation
movement
October Revolution of 1917, xi,
100; and religious reprisals,
65, 67; Revolutionary Tri-
bunal, 6
Optina Hermitage, 104; plans to
restore, 105
Orthodox Christian Church, 58
Osman Koran, 167
Otis, Harold, Jr. (*PC*), 161
Otis, Rose (*PC*), 161

Parishes: life in, 88–89; rejected
declaration of loyalty, 93
Pashazade, Allahshukur,
Sheikh-ul-Islam (*I*), 51–52, 168
Pentecostals, 56, 158
People's Commissars, Council
of, 87–88
Perestroika, 51, 158, 178, 182; and
church-state relations, xi, 54,
82, 126, 133, 136, 154; and religious reawakening, 103, 113,
116, 169–70
Persecution, xi, 9, 67; against
the *ROC*, 65, 74–75, 152; of
Buddhists, 177; effects of in
Ukraine, 125; of Georgians recently (1989), 119–20; of Geor-
gians under Islam, 118; of
Jews by Nazis, 188; of Mus-
lims, 165, 167, 168, 169; of
Protestants, 152, 159–60; reli-
gious repression under Rus-
sian monarchy, 118, 151, 167;
response of *ROC* to, 76–77;
shooting squads, 76; Stalinist
reprisals against *AAC*, 112;
Stalinist reprisals against
ROC, 90–96, 98; statistics on,
91. *See also* Rehabilitation
Peter and Paul Church, 136
Pierson, Robert H. (*PC*), 160
*Pillar and the Affirmation of Truth,
The* (Florensky), 99
Pimen, Patriarch of Moscow and
All Russia, 46, 128
Pitirim, Metropolitan of Voloko-
lamsk and Yuryev, 47–48, 61
Poland, 76

Politburo: meeting of the Com-
munist Party, 7–8, 11n.15
Poyarkov. *See* Yuvenaly, Metro-
politan (*ROC*) of Krutitsk and
Kolomna
Pravda, 14
Preobrazhensky. *See* Agafangel,
Metropolitan
Presbyters. *See* Clergy
Priests. *See* Clergy
Prisons: religious activities, 38–
39, 59
Private, reinterpretation of term,
87
Profits, of religious organiza-
tions, 27(Art.19), 34(Art.18),
36–37(Art.28)
Protestant Christians: current
status of, 139; history of, 139,
151–52; persecution of, 152,
159–60; statistics on, 139. *See
also* Baptists; Pentecostals;
Seventh-Day Adventists
Pyotr, Metropolitan (*ROC*): his-
torical, 80, 92, 93

Qadiites, 168

Rabbis. *See* Clergy
Rabinowtz, Gedaliah A., Rabbi,
191
Radio. *See* Media, mass
Registration of religious organizations, 35(Art.20), 129; opposition to, 71–72
Rehabilitation, of victims of persecution, 91–91, 97–98, 98;
Gorbachev's announcement
regarding, 90
Religion: purposes of, 82, 140–
41 (Prov.1.7–1.7.3)
Religious Affairs, Council for,
xii, 124
Religious diversity, 171; teachings on, 110–11
Religious-Moral Education and
Charity, Commission on the
Revival of, 69
Religious organizations: closure
of, 26(Art.16), 35(Art.21),
144(Prov.2.15.2), 169, 180; defined, 21, 24–25(Art.7),
25(Art.8–9); as juridical persons, 26(Art.13), 34(Art.18),
144(Prov.2.15.1); profits and
enterprises of, 27(Art.19),

34(Art.18), 36–37(Art.28);
property and assets of, 26–
27(Art.17), 27(Art.18, Art.20),
36(Art.26–27), 37(Art.32). *See
also* Registration of religious
organizations, Taxation of religious organizations
Renovation movement: con-
vened ecclesiastical council,
93; participants of the, 14–
15n.2; supported by Trotsky,
13–14
Ridiger, Alexey. *See* Alexis II,
Patriarch of Moscow and All
Russia Rites and ceremonies,
27–28(Art.21), 34(Art.16)
Roads of Russian Theology, The
(Florovsky), 81
Roman Catholic Church, 76,
128–29; current status of, 133;
geographic areas of worship,
133; history of, 133; return of
church property to, 136; statistics on, 133. *See also* John
Paul II, Pope
Russia, baptismal millenium of, 83
Russian Communist Party, 7–8,
11n.15
Russian Federation Law. *See*
Law on Freedom of Worship
Russian monarchy, religious
repression under, 118, 151, 167
Russian Orthodox Church, xii,
xiii, 96; beliefs of the, 94; current status of, 65, 69–70, 77–
81; history of, 65, 67–68; rehabilitation and revival of, 50,
82, 90; restoration of cathedrals and monasteries, 64, 72,
83; schisms within, 65, 67, 80;
Stalinist reprisals against, 65,
74–75, 152; statistics on, 65;
tensions and dialogue with
GCC, 123; Trotsky on, 13. *See
also by individual church leaders;*
Alexis II, Patriarch of Moscow
and All Russia; Church property; Church-state relations;
Florensky, Pavel; Holy Synod;
Moscow Patriarchate; Renovation movement
Russian Patriarchate: four hundredth anniversary of, 58; revived, 65
Russian Revolution. *See* October
Revolution of 1917

Sagaan Sar, 179
Sakyamuni, Buddha, 181
Sapronov-Unshlikht commission, 8
Scherbitsky, Vladimir, 126
Schneyerson, Menahem Mendl, Rabbi, 188
Scholarship, Buddhist, 181–82
Schools: religious, 20, 79, 87–88, 170, 178; separation of (public) from church, 24(Art.6), 32–33(Art.9); yeshivot, 191–92
Sergius, Metropolitan, historical position on church-state relations, 74–75
Sergiy, Metropolitan (ROC): historical, 92, 93, 96
Sergiy of Rodonezh, St., 104
Seventh-Day Adventists, 57, 138, 158–63
Shuya, events in, 3, 5, 7n.4, 8, 10n.14, 10–11n.15
Simansky. See Alexiy, Metropolitan
Sladkevicius, Vincentas, Cardinal (RCC), 133; supports Lithuanan independence, 134–37
Slipyi, Iosof Metropolitan (GCC), historical, 123
Smenovekhovstvo, 13, 15n.4
Sobornost, conciliarity principle, 68
Social insurance, 29(Art.28)
Social issues, 77–78; church's role in addressing, 83–85
Social Revolutionaries, 4
Social security, 84
Soldiers, right to public worship of, 21, 28(Art.21)
Soloveitchik, Josef Dov Halevi, Rabbi, 188
Soviet Mercy and Health Fund, 55, 56
Soviet Parliament, clergy in the, 43–53
Soviet Peace Committee, 54
Stalin Constitution of the USSR, 88
Stalin era, 152, 160; attempts to assimilate Jews during, 186; GCC ties with Rome dissolved during, 123; reprisals against AAC during, 112; reprisals against ROC during, 90–96, 98
Stalin, Joseph: death of, 97, 159; relations with the church during WW, II, xii, 96–97

"Stance of the Church on Martyrdom, The", 97
Starchestvo, form of monasticism, 104
St. Casimir Cathedral, 137
St. Daniel's Monastery, xiii, 65
Supreme Court, 98
Synagogues, 188; attendance at, 187
Syrian Orthodox Church, 127

"Table Calendar, 1941", vii
Tadzhutdin, Talgat, Mufti, Sheikh-ul-Islam, 56, 168
Tanjur, 181
Tarter, Norman (PC), 161
Taxation, of religious organizations, 20–21, 27(Art.19), 71
Tbilisi: plans for cathedral at, 121; site of demonstration and government reprisal, 1989, 119–20
Television. See Media, mass
Temples, 178
Teresa, Mother, 54–55
Tertullian, Quintas Septimius, 75
Thaddaeus, St., 111
Theater, 169
Theological Academy in Tbilisi, 119
"Theological Works," 119
Theology, teaching of, 25, 156, 160–62
Tibetan Buddhism. See Buddhism
Tibetan medicine, 181–82
Tikhon, Patriarch (ROC), 3, 5, 10n.9; led during period of repression, 14, 73
Tiridates III, King, 111
Tolga Convent Varvara, 61
Torah, 186
Triunity, principle of, 99
Troitsky. See Illarion, Archbishop (ROC)
Trotsky, Leon, 5, 6, 12–14
Troyanovsky, Igor, xi–xiv
Tsagaalgan, Yakov, 118, 179
"Tsvetskhoveli" ("the life-giving pillar"), 119

Ukrainian Autocephalous Orthodox Church, xiii, 65
Ukrainian Catholic Church. See Greek Catholic Church
Uniates. See Greek Catholic Church

Union law. See Law on Freedom of Conscience and Religious Organizations
Urbanization, 85

Vakhromeyev, Kirill. See Filaret, Metropolitan of Minsk and Belorussia
Valaam Monastery, 106
Vasken I, Supreme Patriarch and Catholicos of All Armenians, 44–45, 110–13
Velikhov, Evegeny (J), 191
Villebrands, Ioann, Cardinal (RCC), 128
Vilnius Cathedral, 132, 136
Vladimir, Metropolitan (GCC): 124
Vladimir, Metropolitan of Kiev and Galicia, possible canonization of, 97, 98
Vladimir, Metropolitan of Rostov and Novocherkassk, Head of the Chancellery of the Moscow Patriarchate, 90
Vladimir, St. Grand Prince, 65
Volokolamsk cathedral, 61
Voskresenski. See Sergiy, Archbishop (ROC)
Voskresenski, Sergiy Archbishop (ROC), historical, 92

"White month", 179
Wilson, Neal C., Elder (PC), 160
Women's organizations. See Caritas
World Congress of Churches, 126
World War I, 151
World War II, xii, 65, 169; relations between ROC and state during, 96–97, 152
Worship, freedom of. See Freedom of conscience
Writing: GAOC promoted and developed, 118

Yarushevich. See Nikolai, Metropolitan
Yiddish, 185

Zaokski Seminary, 160
Zapara, Thomas (PC), 161
Zhidkov, Mikhail, presbyter (PC), 57
Zula holiday, 180